Ethics and Foreign Intervention

This book is a collection of original essays by some of the leading moral and political thinkers of our time on the ethical and legal implications of humanitarian military intervention. As the rules for the 'new world order' are worked out in the aftermath of the Cold War, this issue is likely to arise more and more frequently, and the moral implications of such interventions will become a major focus for international law, the United Nations, regional organizations such as NATO, and the foreign policies of nations. The essays collected here present a variety of normative perspectives on topics such as the just-war theory and its limits, secession and international law, and new approaches toward the moral legitimacy of intervention. They form a challenging and timely volume that will interest political philosophers, political theorists, readers in law and international relations, and anyone interested in the moral dimensions of international affairs.

DEEN K. CHATTERJEE is Associate Professor of Philosophy at the University of Utah.

DON E. SCHEID is Professor of Philosophy at Winona State University.

Cambridge Studies in Philosophy and Public Policy

General editor: Douglas MacLean, *University of North Carolina, Chapel Hill*

Other books in series

Ethics and Foreign Intervention

Edited by

DEEN K. CHATTERJEE
University of Utah

DON E. SCHEID
Winona State University

PUBLISHED BY THE PRESS SYNDICATE OF THE UNIVERSITY OF CAMBRIDGE
The Pitt Building, Trumpington Street, Cambridge CB2 1RP, United Kingdom

CAMBRIDGE UNIVERSITY PRESS
The Edinburgh Building, Cambridge, CB2 2RU, UK
40 West 20th Street, New York, NY 10011–4211, USA
477 Williamstown Road, Port Melbourne, VIC 3207, Australia
Ruiz de Alarcón 13, 28014 Madrid, Spain
Dock House, The Waterfront, Cape Town 8001, South Africa

http://www.cambridge.org

© Cambridge University Press 2003

First published 2003
Third printing 2006

Printed in the United Kingdom at the University Press, Cambridge

Typeface Palatino 10/13 pt.   *System* LATEX 2$_\varepsilon$ [TB]

A catalogue record for this book is available from the British Library

ISBN 0 521 81074 4 hardback
ISBN 0 521 00904 9 paperback

Contents

vii

Contents

Notes on contributors

MICHAEL BLAKE is Assistant Professor of Public Policy and Philosophy at the Kennedy School of Government at Harvard University. His research focuses on social and political philosophy, with an emphasis on the relationship between social justice and group membership. He is currently writing a book on multi-cultural politics titled *The Politics of Survival: Liberalism, Tolerance, and Multiculturalism*. He has also published work on international distributive justice, international criminal adjudication, and immigration. From 1998 to 2002, he was an Assistant Professor in the Department of Philosophy at Harvard. In 2001–02 he was a Laurance S. Rockefeller Fellow at the Center for Human Values at Princeton University.

CHRIS BROWN is Professor of International Relations at the London School of Economics. He writes on international political theory, human rights, and issues of global justice and is the author of *International Relations Theory: New Normative Approaches* (1992), *Understanding International Relations* (1997; 2nd edn. 2001), *Sovereignty, Rights and Justice* (2002) and editor of *Political Restructuring In Europe: Ethical Perspectives* (1994) and (with Terry Nardin and N. J. Rengger) *International Relations In Political Thought: Texts from the Greeks to the First World War* (2002) as well as numerous journal articles.

ALLEN BUCHANAN is Professor of Public Policy and of Philosophy at Duke University. His research is mainly in two areas: bioethics and political philosophy, especially ethics in international relations and the ethical foundations of international law. His latest books are *From Chance to Choice: Genetics and Justice*, with Brock, Daniels, and Wikler (2000) and

Justice, Legitimacy, and Self-Determination: Moral Foundations for International Law (forthcoming from Oxford University Press).

DEEN K. CHATTERJEE is Associate Professor of Philosophy at the University of Utah. His areas of interest are political philosophy, applied ethics – especially international development ethics – and philosophy of religion and culture. He is editor of *The Ethics of Assistance: Morality and the Distant Needy* (2003) and, with Michael Krausz, co-editor of *Globalization, Development and Democracy: Philosophical Perspectives* (2003). He is Advisory Editor of *The Monist* 86:3 and Managing Director of Beas Foundation (a project of Tides Corporation in Washington DC). He is currently completing a book manuscript on human rights and development assistance.

CHRISTINE CHWASZCZA is a Professor in the Department of Philosophy at Christian-Albrechts University in Kiel. Her publications include *Zwischenstaatliche Kooperation: Perspektiven einer normativen Theorie der Internationalen Politik* [*International Cooperation: Perspectives on a Normative Theory of International Politics*] (1995), *Politische Philosophie der Internationalen Beziehungen* [*Political Philosophy of International Relations*], co-edited with Wolfgang Kersting (1998), and *Praktische Gründe: Vorarbeiten zu einer ethischen Anthropologie* [*Practical Reasons: Prolegomena for an ethical anthropology*] (2003). Currently she is writing a book for DeGruyter Publisher on international justice. She is also the author of many journal articles on international justice and secession.

C. A. J. (TONY) COADY is Deputy Director and Head of the University of Melbourne division of the Centre for Applied Philosophy and Public Ethics. He was Boyce Gibson Professor of Philosophy at the University of Melbourne from 1990 to 1998. His publications include *Testimony: A Philosophical Inquiry* (1992) and *Terrorism and Justice: Moral Argument in a Threatened World*, co-edited with Michael O'Keefe (2002). He is writing a book for Cambridge University Press on morality and political violence.

TOM J. FARER is Dean of the Graduate School of International Studies at the University of Denver. He is a former President of the University of New Mexico and of the Inter-American Commission on Human Rights of the Organization of the American States. A former Fellow of the Council on Foreign Relations, the Carnegie Endowment and the Smithsonian's Woodrow Wilson Center, he has been an official in the

US State and Defense Department and served as the UN's legal consultant for the 1993 intervention in Somalia. He has published eleven books and monographs and his many shorter pieces have appeared in such journals as the *New York* and *London Review of Books, Foreign Affairs, Foreign Policy, World Politics, the Human Rights Quarterly,* the *Harvard* and *Columbia Law Reviews* and *the American Journal of International Law.*

STANLEY HOFFMANN is the Paul and Catherine Buttenwieser University Professor at Harvard University and is the former chairman of the Minda de Gunzburg Center for European Studies (1969–95) at Harvard. He has published many books and articles, including *Gulliver's Troubles, or the Setting of American Foreign Policy* (1968), *Primacy or World Order* (1978), *Duties Beyond Borders* (1980), *Dead Ends* (1983), *Janus and Minerva* (1986), *The European Sisyphus: Essays on Europe, 1964–1994* (1995), *The Ethics and Politics of Humanitarian Intervention* (1996), and *World Disorders: Troubled Peace in the Post-Cold War Era* (1998). He is also one of the authors of *In Search of France* (1963) and *Living with Nuclear Weapons* (1983), and is co-editor of *After the Cold War* (1992). He is working on a book on ethics and international politics and another on French nationalism.

ERIN KELLY is Associate Professor of Philosophy at Tufts University. Her main research interests are in moral and political philosophy. Her recent papers include, "Personal Concern," published in the *Canadian Journal of Philosophy,* and "Doing without Desert," published in *Pacific Philosophical Quarterly.* She is editor of *John Rawls, Justice as Fairness: A Restatement* (2001).

GEORGE R. LUCAS, Jr. is Professor of Philosophy and Associate Chair of the Department of Leadership, Ethics and Law at the US Naval Academy. He is author of *Perspectives on Humanitarian Intervention* (2001) and several articles on justifiable uses of military force for the purposes of international law enforcement. He has taught at Georgetown University, the Catholic University in Leuven, and Santa Clara University.

RICHARD W. MILLER is Professor of Philosophy at Cornell University. His writings, in social and political philosophy, ethics, epistemology, the philosophy of science and aesthetics, include many articles and three books, *Analyzing Marx* (1984), *Fact and Method* (1987), and *Moral Differences* (1992). He is writing a book on the norms appropriate to current international interactions and relationships, including the circumstance of American hegemony.

DON E. SCHEID is Professor of Philosophy at Winona State University. He has taught previously in the philosophy departments at Bowdoin College, University of Illinois-Urbana, and the University of Utah. His main interests are in moral and political philosophy and the philosophy of criminal law. He has published journal articles in the areas of moral theory and philosophy of law.

HENRY SHUE is Senior Research Fellow in Philosophy, Merton College, and Visiting Professor of Politics and International Relations, University of Oxford. He was a Founding Member of the Institute for Philosophy and Public Policy at the University of Maryland and the first Director of the Program on Ethics and Public Life at Cornell University. Best known for *Basic Rights* (1980, 2nd edn. 1996), his article, "Limiting Attacks on Dual-Use Facilities Performing Indispensable Civilian Functions," appears in *Cornell International Law Journal*, vol. 35 (2002).

IRIS MARION YOUNG is Professor of Political Science at the University of Chicago, and is affiliated with the Human Rights Program, the Center for Comparative Constitutionalism and the Center for Gender Studies. She is author of several books and numerous articles on theories of justice, feminist theory, group difference, and democracy. Her most recent book is *Inclusion and Democracy* (2000).

Preface

At the bitter end of the twentieth century, the crisis in Kosovo threw into high relief certain issues of morality and international law. The issues raised have to do with the use of foreign military forces in sovereign states for humanitarian purposes. Taking as the reference point the 1999 NATO intervention in Yugoslavia, the articles in this anthology address the normative dimensions of such interventions. The main issues cluster around the limits of state sovereignty and the conditions under which military intervention by foreign forces for humanitarian purposes are morally justified.

All essays in this volume are original contributions, written specifically for this collection. They reflect the latest ideas of the authors on this complex and timely international issue, which will become increasingly important in the coming years. The articles represent a blend of younger and more established scholars, a mix of authors from the United States, Europe, and Australia, and a variety of perspectives and styles.

Special thanks are due to Richard Miller, not only for his own contribution, but also for valuable suggestions at every step in the development of this anthology. Particular thanks also go to Michael Doyle of Princeton University, Joel Rosenthal of the Carnegie Council on Ethics and International Affairs, and Rebecca Bruschek of the University of Utah for their valuable help in the preparation of the volume. Finally, special gratitude goes to Hilary Gaskin of Cambridge University Press for her patience and for the unfailing support which made this volume possible.

Chapter 1

Introduction

DEEN K. CHATTERJEE AND DON E. SCHEID

Foreign interventions have occurred throughout history, but interventions for humanitarian purposes would seem to be a relatively new phenomenon on the world stage. The category of interventions this volume sets out to address is commonly referred to as "humanitarian military intervention." Such interventions are military ones with a humanitarian purpose. They are intended to rescue and protect people in a foreign territory from gross violations of their basic human rights. Thus, they are in contrast to those interventions that are in defense of people in the home territory of the intervenor, which are usually regarded as acts of self defense. Also, humanitarian military interventions are "humanitarian" in the sense that they are undertaken out of a concern to help, rather than out of any interest in political domination, territorial acquisition, or the like.

THE CONCEPTUAL TERRAIN

"Humanitarian aid" usually has meant non-military aid, such as food and medical supplies, given to a country in crisis – whether because of natural disasters like famine, flood, or earthquake, or because of disasters like war, tyrannical oppression, or revolution. "Intervention," in the context of international affairs, usually means a coercive action of some kind by an outside party (or parties) that takes place within a sovereign state. To be an intervention, the action must be coercive; it normally does not include actions that are desired or requested by the host country. Many types of actions, besides military ones, can be coercive and may count as "interventions," including: espionage; discriminatory economic policies such as trade sanctions and embargoes; selective foreign aid (that is, granting or denying foreign aid); financial aid to subversive

1

movements within a foreign country; the arming, supplying and training of rebel forces; and so on. "Military intervention," of course, means outside coercion brought to bear upon a state by military means. The intervenors may actually engage in hostilities, but they need not, so long as the presence of their military forces plays a coercive role. Of the many forms of intervention, military intervention is the paradigm, the most controversial and the subject of the essays in this volume.

Putting "military intervention" together with the previous example of food and medical supplies as "humanitarian aid," one might conclude that "humanitarian military intervention" means a military intervention used to deliver and protect foreign aid like food and medical supplies. This, indeed, was the initial purpose of the US military intervention (under United Nations auspices) in Somalia in 1993 – to secure the delivery of food to a starving population suffering from famine and the anarchism of civil war among local warlords. Nevertheless, most writers understand "humanitarian military intervention" to include more than the delivery of food and medicines.

States undertaking humanitarian military interventions typically do so in pursuit of a mixture of both humanitarian goals and goals of national self-interest. Some have suggested, therefore, that to be a truly humanitarian military intervention, the overriding reason for the intervention must be humanitarian. Thus, the US-led war against the Taliban and Al Qaeda forces in Afghanistan or the US-led invasion of Iraq would not be considered a case of humanitarian military intervention, even though humanitarian concerns may have played some role. A true "humanitarian military intervention," the suggestion goes, should be understood to mean a military intervention that has humanitarian goals as its central and predominate purpose.

This is helpful, but it seems to be too broad. For example, some have maintained that no vital US interests were at stake in the Vietnam conflict and that whatever US interests may have been at stake were of only indirect, secondary importance. On this view, the main goal was to make South Vietnam safe from communism, thus securing liberty and human rights for its people. Indeed, President Lyndon Johnson presented the war in this light in 1965:

To any in Southeast Asia who ask our help in defending their freedom, we shall give it.

In that region there is nothing we covet, nothing we seek – no territory, no military position, no political ambition. Our one desire – our one determination – is that the people of Southeast Asia be left in peace to work out their own destinies in their own way.[1]

If this sort of view is taken of the US goals in Vietnam, then the US military involvement could be regarded as a "humanitarian military intervention" in a civil war. Yet most commentators and scholars would not put that label on that conflict.

The need for a more precise definition of "humanitarian military intervention" is obvious. It cannot simply mean "morally justified," as in the expression, "a morally justified military intervention." Although most would agree that the United States' involvement in World War II was morally justified and, perhaps, a moral duty, few would characterize it as a "humanitarian military intervention." Furthermore, it cannot literally mean the same thing as "morally justified," as there is always the logical possibility that some humanitarian interventions may *not* be morally justified, all things considered, even if motivated by purely humanitarian purposes. In practice, "humanitarian," in the context of military interventions, usually refers to only certain kinds of moral concerns, such as protecting the welfare of some group of people, where this involves preventing widespread human-rights violations, preventing genocide, or preventing mass expulsions.

Usually, "humanitarian military intervention" has been used to refer to discrete events of limited duration. It is a response to an emergency situation; once the emergency has passed, the intervenors pack up and move out. One objection to this understanding is that this "fire-fighting approach" is ill conceived for handling more structurally entrenched crises. The concept of humanitarian intervention needs to be expanded, according to this objection, to include long-term commitments of resources and sustained campaigns, rather than the more limited crisis-focused efforts that are usually labeled "interventions."

It is not obvious, however, that any clarity of thought is gained by expanding the definition of "humanitarian military intervention" in this way. Nevertheless, the objection does indicate an important issue, which is that the justification of a case of humanitarian military intervention must inevitably depend to a very great extent on what comes next. Will there be follow up? Stopping the evil should lead to making the peace, which should lead to peacekeeping, which, in many cases, should lead to nation building or rebuilding. Obviously, a military intervention that merely stops the current violence, without more, may simply postpone further violence to a later date. It may even make things worse by giving warring parties time to regroup and rearm. Hit-and-run interventions may be worse than no intervention at all.

RECENT DEVELOPMENTS

On March 24, 1999, the North American Treaty Alliance (NATO) began a bombing campaign against Yugoslavia that continued without interruption for over two months. The express purpose was to halt the "ethnic cleansing" of ethnic Albanian citizens, which Yugoslav forces were then undertaking in Serbia's southern province of Kosovo. The NATO campaign to stop the killings and mass expulsions was deemed a humanitarian military intervention.

NATO's intervention to halt ethnic cleansing in Kosovo was not the first military campaign to be called a "humanitarian intervention," but it is regarded by many observers as a crucial point that marks a sea change in the normative context of international relations. Accordingly, it is this particular intervention which serves as the focal example for many of the articles in the present collection. Whether Kosovo indeed represents a major precedent ushering in a new era of military interventionism or merely an incidental aberration in the course of global affairs remains to be seen. How influential a precedent it really becomes, however, may depend, in part, on current assessments and evaluations of humanitarian military intervention – the subject of this anthology.

Worldwide, there has been a significant increase in the number of intrastate conflicts since the end of the Cold War. In some cases, the violence has arisen in the clash of ethnic, religious, or nationalistic allegiances. In other cases, it has been the result of battles among warlords within malfunctioning states or "failed states," states that have degenerated into anarchy. In the Balkans, old ethnic and nationalistic animosities and passions seemed to be released from a kind of suspended animation in the deep freeze of the Cold War. The nationalism that had been suppressed in Tito's Yugoslavia sprang forth with full force and fury.

At the same time, the influence of the idea of human rights has gradually spread and strengthened since World War II. The idea that universal rights attach directly to individuals has become a compelling counterweight to the notion of state sovereignty both within the structure of international law and within moral perspectives on international relations more generally. In recent years, the spread and promotion of human rights has owed as much to international non-governmental organizations (NGOs), like Amnesty International and Human Rights Watch, and to local human-rights groups as it has to state governments or the United Nations itself.

One consequence of these developments has been an increase in the number of military interventions conducted for humanitarian purposes. The occasions for interventions has increased at the same time that the humanitarian justification for such actions has become more acceptable. The importance of this appearance of humanitarian military interventions is difficult to overestimate. The traditional model of an international system based on equal and sovereign states has begun to break down over the past few decades. As the presumption of non-interference in the internal affairs of a sovereign state has weakened, a presumption in favor of the legitimacy of humanitarian military intervention has strengthened.

NORMATIVE ISSUES

In Rwanda in 1994, a Hutu majority went on a killing rampage against the Tutsi minority, with the support and encouragement of the Hutu government. Neither the United States nor any of the other major powers undertook military intervention, and most of the international UN peacekeepers on the scene at the time were recalled. As a result, a full-fledged genocide erupted, bringing about the deaths of some 800,000 Tutsis. Millions more became refugees.

For most observers, Rwanda stands as a horrific moral failure and marks a huge inadequacy in the world order of international law. After Rwanda, something of a consensus developed, namely, that a state's sovereignty should not shield it from outside military intervention when it brutalizes its own people, certainly not when a genocide is taking place.

When the NATO bombing occurred in Yugoslavia in 1999, therefore, it raised in a dramatic way a host of pressing and difficult normative questions (both moral and legal) about humanitarian military intervention. Granted that a state's sovereignty should not provide complete immunity from foreign military intervention in extreme cases like Rwanda, what exactly should be the conditions under which such interventions may and may not be undertaken against a sovereign state? Who may undertake them? Who should authorize them? What adjustments are required in the concept of state sovereignty, and what should be the rights and duties of states that are in a position to undertake interventions?

The NATO bombing over Kosovo became the catalyst for an effort, now on-going, to work out the moral and legal contours of humanitarian military intervention – an effort that is joined by the contributors to this volume. In the opening article, in Part I, Stanley Hoffmann notes certain important changes in the international system, including the phenomenon of state disintegration; and he recognizes the shift in human consciousness away from the idea of unfettered sovereignty. He then takes up neo-realist arguments against humanitarian military intervention and shows that the neo-realist position can be refuted on both empirical and moral grounds. Turning to the effort to develop appropriate guidelines for humanitarian military interventions, Hoffmann elaborates the enormous obstacles to successful and ethical interventions with armed forces. He implies that the task is hopeless. Yet, with a nod to Samuel Beckett, he urges that, while we can't go on, we must go on. We must work out the conditions for humanitarian military interventions as best we can if we are to be saved from future Rwandas and if we ever hope to arrive at a new, more humane, world order.

In the view of many commentators at the time, NATO's action against the Federal Republic of Yugoslavia (FRY) was a clear violation of international law, as well as being contrary to NATO's own charter. However, in public statements, the US Administration skirted the legal issue entirely, and, instead, emphasized the moral need to stop the ethnic cleansing. The Administration was careful to pitch US and NATO action as being justified in terms of "moral imperatives" and not in terms of standards of international law. As the bombing began, President Clinton stated the goals of the NATO campaign in a TV speech (March 24, 1999), saying in part:

We act to protect thousands of innocent people in Kosovo from a mounting military offensive ... We act to prevent a wider war, to defuse a power keg at the heart of Europe, that has exploded twice before in this century with catastrophic results. By acting now, we are upholding our values. Ending this tragedy is a *moral imperative*. [emphasis added]

Later, during the NATO bombing, on May 23, President Clinton published a letter in the *New York Times*, entitled "A Just and Necessary War," in which he again defended the NATO operation for moral and strategic reasons. European leaders made similar statements but stressed even more strongly that NATO's intervention was necessary to prevent a humanitarian catastrophe. The British Prime Minister, Tony Blair, for instance, published an article in *Newsweek* in which he stated:

We need to enter a new millennium where dictators know that they cannot get away with ethnic cleansing or repress their peoples with impunity. In this conflict we are fighting not for territory but for values. For a new internationalism where the brutal repression of whole ethnic groups will no longer be tolerated. For a world where those responsible for such crimes have nowhere to hide.[2]

Accordingly, the legal issue was set aside and the central issue became the moral rightness of the bombing. Regardless of whether the bombing was consistent with international law, was it right as a moral matter? In seeking to answer this moral question, one is led to other, more general questions. For example, how are decisions about humanitarian military interventions to be made? What moral factors should be considered? Are such interventions morally obligatory, and if so, what are the limits of such obligations? If they are supererogatory, then should anything at all be done; and if so, by whom? If Kosovo was a legitimate intervention, why not interventions in other crisis spots around the world?

One of the complaints, widely expressed at the time of the Kosovo crisis, was that exercises in humanitarian military intervention appeared to be inconsistent. If Kosovo, why not Rwanda? If East Timor, why not Tibet or Kurdistan? Chris Brown, in Part I, addresses this charge of inconsistency. He argues that the charge often arises from a misunderstanding of moral reasoning as merely involving a mechanical application of moral rules. For example, critics Noam Chomsky and Edward Luttwak both make this mistake, according to Brown – though Brown believes Chomsky's real point, behind his rhetoric about selectivity, is that none of the interventions made by the West are actually humanitarian in motivation.

Beginning with a sympathetic consideration of criteria laid out in a speech by Tony Blair, Brown suggests that the development of practical judgment is crucial to moral reasoning. Brown takes his lead from Aristotle and maintains that what is needed is an agent-centered morality that emphasizes cultivating one's facility for making moral judgments. A naive, rule-based model of moral reasoning is inadequate. Brown considers an interesting set of triage rules for deciding the sorts of interventions that should be undertaken but claims it is not sufficiently subtle for adequate moral decisions. He also points out that while rule-based moral theories like Kantianism and utilitarianism provide general principles and summaries of past experience, they are only starting points for moral reasoning. This is so because they require subtle judgment for their application to specific cases that always involve a complex of morally relevant details.

The starting point for deciding the morality of a particular military intervention might well be the criteria of the Just War tradition. Even here, however, many subtle and sophisticated judgments must be made in applying and evaluating the criteria. In particular, Brown emphasizes that different *kinds* of judgments must be called into play, including mental, legal, diplomatic, strategic, and military, as well as more straightforwardly moral judgments.

Humanitarian military intervention also raises normative issues at a number of levels, from practical and operational issues to broad questions of political philosophy. The authors of Part II take up some of these issues by referring to the just-war tradition from a broadly liberal perspective. Beginning with *A Theory of Justice* (1971), the work of John Rawls has been tremendously influential in Anglo-American political philosophy; and in his *The Law of Peoples* (1999), Rawls develops principles he believes should govern the international relationships among different peoples worldwide. Hence, Rawls is a natural starting point for a consideration of humanitarian military intervention from the point of view of political liberalism. Michael Blake's contribution to the present volume is critical of Rawls' contractarian political theory, a theory that involves a hypothetical contract among peoples (or states) instead of among individual persons. Blake believes Rawls' misconceived approach leads to a misguided toleration of illiberal states and to an overly rigid commitment to respect for state sovereignty. Some forms of toleration are fine, but a liberal theory cannot be neutral towards all forms of toleration without becoming neutral towards its own validity. Accordingly, we need not be so respectful of the sovereignty of illiberal states as the Rawlsian approach implies. Nevertheless, according to Blake, even from a more acceptable (non-Rawlsian) liberal viewpoint, humanitarian military interventions should be undertaken, and state sovereignty violated, only very rarely. Blake goes on to spell out a series of prudential and just-war types of considerations for avoiding interventions in all but the most egregious cases.

Many writers and commentators, besides Blake, have drawn on the just-war tradition as a framework for thinking about the moral evaluation of humanitarian military intervention. In the present collection, George Lucas takes up a careful consideration of the just-war doctrine itself. He points out that humanitarian interventions are very different sorts of military operations from those called for in traditional wars.

Thus, the standard application of just-war doctrine fails, according to Lucas, because the use of force in humanitarian cases is much closer to the use of force in domestic law enforcement and thus subject to more stringent restrictions than *jus in bello* conditions normally require. Consequently, one needs to rework the criteria of the just-war doctrine to develop a just-war sort of theory that applies specifically to humanitarian military interventions. This is precisely what Lucas does. Building on suggestions of Stanley Hoffmann, he develops criteria for what he calls *jus ad interventionem*.

The development of guided missiles, high-altitude precision bombing, unmanned combat aircraft, and other modern weaponry has created the possibility of engaging in "immaculate war-making," or what has also been termed "riskless war." But is this a blessing or a curse in connection with humanitarian military interventions? On one hand, it seems a blessing. If a country can undertake a military operation without any significant risk to its own personnel, then the operation is similar to sending food and medical relief to earthquake victims somewhere in the world. There is the financial expense, but little risk of lives being lost. Under these conditions, it must be much easier politically for a government to convince its citizenry that the country should do the right thing. On the other hand, riskless war may be a curse. For one thing, if the risks are minimal, a country may all-too-readily jump into a military intervention that is not really justified. For another, by choosing a form of military action that insures maximum protection for one's own forces, one almost inevitably introduces greater costs to civilians on the other side; but this hardly seems like taking the moral high road. Implicit in this latter worry is the just-war principle of discrimination, which makes a moral distinction between combatants and non-combatants. The principle requires that non-combatants never be directly targeted but that if non-combatant casualties are unavoidable, then a certain proportionality must be maintained.

Addressing a closely related issue in his article, Henry Shue applies the just-war principle of discrimination to criticize the practice of attacking "dual-purpose" installations and infrastructure, targets that serve both military and civilian needs. The NATO bombing within Serbia was mostly aimed at such dual-purpose targets. The problem is that while bombings of dual-purpose infrastructure attack facilities that contribute to the enemy's military effectiveness, they also wreak hardship and death on the civilian population. Dual-purpose targets seem to be a hybrid or cross between traditional military targets of "denial" bombing and civilian targets of "punishment" or "strategic" bombing. Under the principle of discrimination, military targets are legitimate, while civilian targets are not. So-called strategic bombing, in fact, has rarely, if ever, effectively contributed to military victory, Shue argues. But how should dual-purpose targets be regarded morally and legally?

Although dual-purpose targets are legal under current international law, Shue believes the relevant laws of war should be changed on moral grounds, because the present legal understanding undermines the purpose of the combatant/non-combatant distinction. Accordingly, he proposes an important modification to the rules.

Somewhat surprisingly, Shue believes the practice of attacking dual-purpose targets can be defended by appeal to double-effect analysis. Nevertheless, he argues, dual-purpose targets that serve predominantly civilian functions crucial for civilian life are morally illegitimate and should be made illegal. Shue also addresses the worry that, if international law is changed as he proposes, the possibility of bluffing an opponent into surrender by threatening civilian devastation is seriously reduced. Yet, some have argued, this was exactly how Milosevic was brought to terms. In the end, Shue maintains that the NATO bombing was immoral partly because the attack included vital dual-purpose targets and partly because one of the avowed intentions of the bombing campaign was to inflict misery on the Serbian civilian population – as a means of provoking political opposition to coerce the Milosevic regime to surrender.

One challenge to the just-war distinction between combatants and non-combatants is the theory of collective liability developed by Erin Kelly. Applying her theory to interventions, a military attack on non-combatant (as well as combatant) members of a group or society can be justified so long as all the members in question are "collectively liable." Essentially, Kelly's theory implies that non-combatant members are liable to life-threatening attack because of serious and wide-spread human-rights abuses when:

(i) The group or some of its members are causally responsible for horrendous human rights abuses (via the political and social arrangements they impose or administer).

(ii) The passive, non-combatant members of the group receive benefits from these political and social arrangements.

(iii) The non-combatant members of the group have had an opportunity, weakly construed, to refuse the benefits that accrue to them as the result of human-rights abuses or to take action to combat the violations of human rights.

If these conditions obtain, Kelly argues, then intervention is morally permissible, provided the other just-war sorts of requirements, such as last resort, the likelihood of success, and proportionality also obtain.

Just-war perspectives on humanitarian military intervention inevitably raise the question of the appropriate international legal framework. As noted above, certain interventions could be hailed as morally right and yet be illegal under prevailing international legal standards. Such standards are now in flux in view of two competing claims: (i) the right of self-determination of peoples and (ii) the respect for the integrity of state borders. Deference to state sovereignty has become weaker in recent years because of the impact of globalization in communication and economic activity, but especially because of increased support for human rights, which is often connected to the emergence of various ethnic, religious, and nationalistic uprisings with the post-Cold War thaw. On the other hand, support for the self-determination of peoples and their secession from existing states is ambiguous, at best. First, under international law, the right of self-determination vests with "peoples," a concept open to a wide variety of interpretations. Second, while there are only 191 member states to the United Nations, there are some 5,000 ethnic groups in the world. If each grouping of "peoples" followed the example of the Kosovo Liberation Army, there would be no end to wars of independence. Finally, and most importantly, the ideal of self-determination simply conflicts with the concept of sovereignty.

Secession from a sovereign state can, of course, sometimes be legitimate; and foreign military intervention to aid a secessionist movement is perfectly conceivable. Indeed, from one perspective, the NATO intervention was in aid of the Kosovars in their legitimate quest to re-establish autonomous rule and to eventually achieve full independence. Hence, one important aspect of the general issue concerning the legitimacy of humanitarian military intervention is whether, or under what conditions, such interventions are justified when in support of secession. This raises the question of the moral and legal significance of political borders and that of the need for reform in the international law of secession. These issues are addressed by the contributors in Part III.

Tom Farer explores the moral basis of military intervention in cases of secessionist movements of self-determination. He first sketches an interesting brief history of "humanitarian intervention" as that concept has been used and as its meaning has evolved, and he recounts the recent evolution of the concept of "self-determination" in international relations. Farer then takes up a critical review of Michael Walzer's theory on military intervention in cases of self-determination movements. Among other things, Farer introduces a distinction between (i) a secession movement in response to oppression by the established government and (ii) a secession movement within a liberal state (for example, Basque movement within Spain). As he argues, the right of self-determination does not automatically entail a right to secede. On Farer's view, only secessionist initiatives of the first kind justify humanitarian military interventions in their support, and then only in exceptional cases of mass killings or other egregious violations of personal security rights.

Farer also distinguishes (i) a blood community from (ii) a constitutional community. The first is constituted of people who typically share culture, language, and ancestors. A constitutional community is a grouping of people based on political and legal norms and perceived as a community of choice. The members of a constitutional community may differ in race, religion, and even language; but they share a common political culture. Both kinds of community have a sense of collective political identity. Blood communities, by their nature, aspire to autonomy; and Farer takes up the question of secession movements by blood communities. He considers a thought experiment: what if the world were cut up into sovereign blood communities? Would this be a good thing from a liberal point of view? Although blood communities do have their merits, as Farer elaborates, their essential exclusionist impulses run against liberal values. Consequently, Farer is skeptical that armed struggles to transform blood communities into sovereign states will often yield net humanitarian benefits.

Setting aside cases of de-colonization and treaty-based secessions, Christine Chwaszcza asks whether there is a right to secede in other cases. On her view, libertarian and communitarian arguments based on personal liberty or some right of political membership fail. On the other hand, secession may sometimes be justified when it is a response to massively unjust rule. In such cases, secession may be thought of as a special instance of the right of resistance. A number of important qualifications and practical considerations must be taken into account, however, before secession can be fully justified even in these circumstances. According to Chwaszcza, once a given secession is justified, the question arises whether there is a duty of humanitarian military intervention on behalf of the secession. Since such a secession is a form of resistance to massive human-rights violations, and since the subject of human rights is humankind, their protection is a common duty. Armed interventions require members of the intervening forces to risk their lives, however; so Chwaszcza maintains that such an intervention cannot be regarded as a perfect duty, but only as an imperfect one. She suggests that to avoid abuses and assure that humanitarian military interventions are really undertaken for the protection of human rights, it seems appropriate to restrict their authorization to the United Nations. Procedures within the United Nations can provide mechanisms both for identifying human-rights violations and for designating those who are to take on the duty of intervention.

In his contribution to this collection, Allen Buchanan provides an analysis and then a reformist interpretation of two principles associated with the governance of secession under international law (*uti possidetis* and effectivity). He notes an inadequacy in current international law, pointing out that although the Kosovar Albanians had a strong case for secession, their case did not fit existing categories of legitimate secession. In Buchanan's view, international law has two, related inadequacies. First, it does not provide a coherent and morally defensible account of when secession is justified. Second, the legal constraints on military intervention are so stringent as to make humane responses to secessionist conflicts nearly always illegal. Thus, as a first step in developing a theory of military intervention in secessionist conflicts, Buchanan's goal is to reform the law of secession so that members of the international community will know when support for a secessionist movement is permissible. Buchanan sets out to rehabilitate the principles involved by establishing their proper interpretation and application. Once these principles are rightly understood, a more extensive right to secede will have been forged. In turn, this will broaden the scope of justified military interventions in support of secessions. Like Chwaszcza, Buchanan believes that unilateral secession is justified only as a remedy to massive injustice. Besides allowing that a group may have a right to secede as a means of escaping from tyrannical rule, Buchanan also allows that his "remedial-right-only theory" might be extended to include cases in which a group seeks to form a new state in the territory of a failed or failing state. He points to the secession of Slovenia and Croatia as examples. In those cases, the constitutional order of Yugoslavia was breaking down, creating serious insecurity of basic rights for people. Hence, the secessions by Slovenia and Croatia could be seen as acts of self-defense.

The kinds of normative issues about intervention raised above indicate a delicate balance of various moral and legal considerations which incline toward making the practice of intervention a rare occurrence – more an exception than a common phenomenon. Yet contemporary global events indicate the prospect of a steady rise of such operations worldwide. In fact, humanitarian military interventions seem to be an emerging global trend, which may increasingly dominate international events in the years to come. At present, the label is even being applied to those military operations whose stated goal is to "flush out terrorism" or to "destroy weapons of mass destruction" in a foreign country. This may indicate a possible gap between the normative theories and the imperfect realities or a defect in the theories themselves. Thus, one may either question the adequacy of the prevailing theories or suggest how a new approach toward the moral adequacy of intervention may be worked out, given the complex and fluid realities of the world situation.

Others may wonder whether violence is an inevitable means and whether it is ever really legitimate, even while recognizing the need for intervention in exceptional cases. Perhaps, if governments and other organizations worked together to create a more equitable and just world, then the need to resort to violence to remedy egregious wrongs could be eliminated. Thus, critics of military intervention who may not be against the idea of intervention in principle may, nevertheless, raise serious doubts about the advisability of a country's launching into a policy of military intervention or the advisability of the system of international law allowing such a practice. These views are expressed in various ways by the three authors of Part IV.

Richard Miller maintains that leading moral theories about humanitarian military intervention are out of touch with social realities and rely on overly idealized conceptions of political conduct. He finds the "law of peoples" developed by Rawls to be of severely restricted use because Rawls' norms for a society of well-ordered peoples are of little relevance to the real world where nearly all peoples are "ill-ordered," including potential intervenors as well as plausible targets of intervention. Miller finds Michael Walzer's communitarian approach lacking for similar reasons. Walzer's argument for a strong presumption against intervention relies on a seriously inaccurate and over-valued assessment of communal autonomy.

As we have already noted, much recent thinking (reflected in some of the articles in this volume) holds that sovereignty should be subject to strict conditions: when a state engages in grave human-rights violations of its own people, it loses its legitimacy and, thus, its right to non-intervention. A state may enjoy its sovereign immunity to foreign intervention only on condition that it treat its own citizens decently. Miller, however, believes that the hope for world improvement based on this broader license to intervene is unrealistic. He warns that advocates of this license underestimate the harms of armed interventions and their aftermath, and overestimate the attentiveness of governments to restraints on intervention accompanying the restrictive view of sovereignty. In particular, he warns against naivete in assessing the impact of geopolitical interests on decisions to intervene. Military interventions by great powers tend to expand their geopolitical reach, leading to harms of hegemony while creating dangerous antagonisms.

Miller begins his constructive proposals by distinguishing (i) what the terms of justification should be among governments in the global forum, and (ii) what the terms of assessment ought to be for a morally conscientious person evaluating a state's decision to intervene. The terms of debate by governments are codified in the UN Charter and other sources of international law. Miller points out that the various pronouncements about sovereignty, self-determination, and intervention approach mutual inconsistency. Yet, interestingly, Miller believes these tangled foundations of intergovernmental discourse are, from a humanitarian standpoint, a nearly optimal source of incentives for actual governments. They allow for different yet plausible interpretations so that a strong argument for intervention can be presented against an oppressive state and a strong argument can also be presented against an aggressive would-be intervenor. Miller believes the resulting overall balance is about right, and that the introduction of a substantially broader license for intervention would upset this balance. As for the individual's moral assessment of interventions, it must be guided by diverse and conflicting considerations embodied in concrete situations. Miller surveys typical constellations of considerations, beginning with two contrasting situations, the "pretty good" politics of actual liberal democracies and the "utterly appalling" situations of widespread massacre, as in Rwanda. The survey leads him to conclude that considerations such as respect for communal autonomy, the inevitable carnage of military action, and the risks of regional instability nearly always exclude military intervention. Nevertheless, he maintains that military intervention was justified in Rwanda, East Timor, and East Pakistan.

In other cases, in which Miller admits that an intervention may have been justified at the time it was imposed, he thinks that the process leading up to the intervention should, nonetheless, be subjected to searching moral scrutiny. He treats NATO's military offensive against Serbia as a case in point. In his view, the decision-making that culminated in the ultimatum at Rambouillet should be condemned because of a failure to engage in a sustained, good-faith exploration of less violent options. As a practical outcome of his view of harsh international realities, Miller emphasizes the need to combat American self-righteousness in order to improve the practice of intervention.

Iris Young begins her article with an analysis of two sets of distinctions made by Hannah Arendt: a distinction between violence and power and another between legitimacy and justification. Applying these distinctions to the question of humanitarian military interventions, Young argues that violence or the use of force, as such, can never be legitimate in the sense that its use can be thought to follow from principles of law. Young agrees that outsiders have a moral right to do what they can to prevent or halt egregious violations of human rights, and that this right overrides sovereignty rights. She warns, however, that a right of intervention does not entail a right to use force. There are many means short of military action for pressuring a state to change its behavior when it violates human rights. There should be a strong presumption in favor of the principle of state sovereignty.

According to Young, we must develop a framework (set of international institutions) of cosmopolitan authorization for interventionist war; the UN is not enough. In principle, such a cosmopolitan legal assembly could authorize a state, alliance of states, or other organizations to undertake military interventions, thus "legitimating" this use of force. But while a right of intervention requires authorization to be legitimate, this is only a necessary moral condition for military action; a military intervention also requires "justification." Somewhat like the use of force by police within domestic law, a given act of violence requires justification in terms of the consequences of the proposed action. Here, Young sets out the kinds of conditions typical of just-war doctrine.

Young finds that the NATO war against Yugoslavia was not justified, partly because not all alternatives had been exhausted, but mainly because the NATO violence ended up causing more destruction than it prevented. The fact that NATO's air war was said to be "as good as an air war can be" (that is, minimal number of civilian deaths) only underscores for Young the need to resist the use of force in all but the most desperate situations. Young counsels against moving too quickly from the right to override state sovereignty for the sake of defending human rights to the position that the means of intervention should be war. Since war nearly always does more harm than good, alternative mechanisms and new international institutions with global regulatory and enforcement powers need to be created to manage the world's problems.

In the final offering of this collection, C. A. J. Coady presents something close to a pacifist position, warning against the pitfalls of high-minded, humanitarian motivations and unwarranted enthusiasms for military intervention. He first sets out certain definitional aspects of the concept of humanitarian military intervention, noting that the primary motive for the intervention must be the humanitarian one of rescuing people from harm. He then points to the problem of determining mixed motives and the attendant conceptual issue of distinguishing "humanitarian motives" from "national interest."

Coady recognizes the intuitive moral appeal of altruistic wars to rescue people from genocide or other extreme oppression, and he admits the contemporary notion of conditional sovereignty has something to it. He notes, however, that the older, more absolute notion of sovereignty is based on two important insights, namely, the right of self-determination and the need to limit resort to war. Coady cautions that these crucial insights are in danger of being forgotten in the renewed enthusiasm for humanitarian interventions.

Ultimately, Coady admits that altruistic wars may theoretically satisfy the just-war criterion of just cause, even though this is a departure from the more conventional view that only self-defense can be a just cause. Nevertheless, there are many further problems and ambiguities to be faced in satisfying other of the just-war criteria, including right authority, proportionality, last resort, and prospect for success. Detailed and insightful considerations of these criteria lead Coady to conclude that there must be an extremely strong presumption against humanitarian military interventions.

A great many issues are addressed, or at least touched upon, by the authors of this collection of essays. But the work has only begun. Certainly, many other issues will also need to be explored and brought together, as the philosophical dimensions of the relatively new subject of humanitarian military intervention are mapped out. The present collection, therefore, is but a first step in what, it is hoped, will eventually become a well-developed area of normative understanding in international relations.

NOTES

1 President Lyndon B. Johnson, news conference, March 13, 1956. Quoted in Henry Kissinger, *Does America Need a Foreign Policy?* (New York: Simon and Schuster, 2001), p. 247.
2 Tony Blair, "A New Generation Draws the Line," *Newsweek*, April 19, 1999, p. 40.

PART I

The conceptual and normative terrain

Chapter 2

Intervention: should it go on, can it go on?

STANLEY HOFFMANN

This essay tries to be a reasonably comprehensive survey of issues and viewpoints about intervention. What I will address here is not "humanitarian" intervention in the sense of an intervention to deliver food and medicine to relieve human suffering, but what might be called "humanitarian military intervention," that is, outside interventions entailing a resort to force, or to forces, in the domestic affairs of a country, in order to protect people from extreme violence.[1]

THE IMPORTANCE OF THE ISSUE

There have been many such examples in recent years: in Africa, in Asia, in Central America. This corresponds to two series of factors. The first is an important evolution of the international system: the phenomenon of internal disintegration or malfunction of many states, resulting from a multiplicity of causes. Many states are devoid of national consciousness or effective integration: Somalia, Rwanda, the Sudan, former Zaire, Sierra Leone, Angola, and Liberia. Other states are under attack from rebellious minorities: Indonesia as the occupier of East Timor, Sri Lanka, Ethiopia, Iraq, Turkey, and Russia. Several multi-ethnic states have disintegrated; Yugoslavia and the USSR are the best examples. Transnational terrorism is a major contributing factor to the weakening of the units that constitute the foundations of the international system. Finally, there are many murderous states: Iraq, the Haiti of the military, Rwanda under Hutu rule, and the Khmer Rouge regime.

This is not a purely contemporary trend but it has been masked for a long time by the bipolar context. It corresponds both to the release from forced Communist cohesiveness imposed by and during the Cold

War (on the late Soviet Union and on Tito's Yugoslavia), and to the unexpected dividends from decolonization, which left behind a large number of purely formal, or pseudo-states, many of which had been established by nationalists but were in fact not nations. The importance of this trend lies, of course, in the role of the state and of state sovereignty, as the cornerstones of international law and of the international system.

The second set of factors is subjective: the evolution of human consciousness. An international law predominantly rooted in the concept of state sovereignty is now challenged by an accelerating, if not yet universal, revolution against unfettered sovereignty. It began with the restrictions put on the state's right to go to war, especially after 1918 and 1945, and it continued with the emergence of human rights as an international concern. The information revolution has played a major role in this. This has amounted to a double innovation of enormous significance: the scope of international law now extends to a domain that has been the core of "domestic jurisdiction," and states are no longer the predominant subjects of the rights and duties conferred by international law; it now gives rights to and imposes obligations on individuals directly.

The effects of these developments are enormous. Just as there are different kinds of wars, there are different types of internal crises. They range from crises provoked by the absence of a genuine government (as in Somalia), to crises resulting from a struggle for the control of central power (as in Rwanda or the Congo), to crises provoked by the desire of minorities for self-determination and the creation of new states, as in East Timor, Yugoslavia, or Chechnya, and finally to crises created by the central government itself in its attempts at crushing secessionists or religious and political dissenters.

This complex scene forces a bewildering number of choices on outsiders. They can opt for non-intervention in the name of sovereignty, and limit themselves to humanitarian aid for victims of internal strife (this has been the prevalent reaction to the civil war in Sudan). They can resort to traditional peacekeeping: the dispatch of observers or of lightly armed forces whose duty is to be politically neutral among the contending factions and to deal evenly with them, without using force (except if they come under attack). This has been the case in post-Dayton Bosnia and in Kosovo. There is also the option of what might be called mild coercion, diplomatic or economic: it worked against Indonesia in East Timor, and was followed by the peacekeeping force led by Australia. Finally, there is strong coercion, that is, peacemaking, which targets one of the parties, as in Bosnia before Dayton, in Kosovo before Milosevic caved in, in Haiti, and so on...

SHOULD SOMETHING BE DONE AT ALL?

A neo-realist view has been sharply critical of the interventionist trend. In this conception, what matters in world affairs has not changed: the relations between the great and potentially great powers – today, the United States, Russia and China, and the fate of strategically and economically important areas: the Middle East, Korea, Taiwan. Anything that threatens the security of the major actors is important. Thus, the destruction of terrorist cells and the punishment of states that support them is a priority. But many of the internal crises that rack states and pseudo-states are in backwaters of no strategic significance and little importance for the internal and external security of the major players. If these crises occur in one of those players (China v Tibet, Russia v Chechnya) an external forcible intrusion is far too risky to be undertaken. This creates a conundrum of (in-) consistency: why intervene to protect Iraq's Kurds, and not the victims of Russian repression in Chechnya? The neo-realists also point to the dangers of intervention in secondary areas from the viewpoint of conserving one's forces and concentrating one's attention on the major flash points. Finally, they denounce the restraints imposed by such interventions, if they are undertaken under international auspices or by coalitions of the willing, on a great power such as the United States: multi-lateralism for a "real" national security operation, yes if necessary, for a "trivial" cause, no.

This thesis is ultimately unconvincing. The legal argument on which critics of intervention often rely – the importance of respecting internal sovereignty – has been badly frayed both by frequent violations during the years of the Cold War (remember US subversive intervention in Guatemala or Santo Domingo, for instance) and, more recently, under the rubric of "self-defense" by war against the Taliban. The old distinction between "possession" and "milieu" goals also argues against an excessive priority to strategic and economic possession goals: a major power needs a milieu that will support world order (or its conception of it) and the benign neglect of domestic upheaval abroad risks producing epidemics of regional disorders, with massive flights of refugees, inter-state tensions among neighbors (as around the Congo), and risks of escalatory intervention by states or by mercenaries. Also, when is a "backwater" trivial, when is it not? After all, Zbigniew Brzezinski,

Carter's national security adviser, once predicted that Ogaden was of vital importance for victory in the Cold War because of Soviet involvement. Also, the rising costs of chaos left unattended provide fine opportunities for tyranny. At this point, the problem of moral duty cannot be avoided. Economic assistance has been advocated for a combination of ethical (that is, non-selfish) and self-interested arguments. Intervention to protect victims of tyranny or repression can be defended for exactly the same mix of reasons: all states have an interest in order, and order without a modicum of (internal and global) justice can only lead to disaster (surely this is also one of the lessons of 9/11/2001).

WHAT IS TO BE DONE?

This is the toughest issue. A criterion of "humanitarianism" is both elusive and unsatisfactory. The kind of humanitarianism offered by an organization such as Doctors without Borders both advocates a "duty of interference" in case of humanitarian disasters, and yet distrusts the self-interested states that may want to intervene; they trust disinterested agencies like themselves, for the relief of human suffering. They particularly dislike state military interference because it tends to create more victims – which is indeed frequently the case. However, "pure" humanitarian action is often insufficient: if the causes of the humanitarian crisis are not addressed, such action risks being no more than a temporary Band-Aid: important, to be sure, but limited in time and scope. Moreover, even pure humanitarians cannot avoid taking political decisions at every turn. For instance, in cases of ethnic cleansing, does humanitarianism dictate a refusal to contribute to it, by trying to encourage its potential victims to stay in their homes and hereditary provinces, or does it mean accepting such cleansing and relocating its victims in order to save their lives? Another example: what to do when the humanitarian aid provided to refugees in camps is confiscated by armed guards, and when the camps become places for the forcible recruitment by such guards, eager to enlist more fighters for guerrilla actions? This was a dilemma faced by, and divisive of, humanitarian organizations both in Sudan and in Rwanda. Indeed, pure humanitarianism can even be counterproductive: in Bosnia, these organizations were often at the mercy of Serbia; their lack of means of self-defense often led to the pilfering of aid by the Serbs and thus to a prolongation of the war. One doesn't need to be a realist or a neo-realist to understand that wars, internal and interstate, are about politics, whereas humanitarianism, insofar

as it wants to be non-political, is insufficient at best, and counterproductive at worst. The evolution of Bernard Kouchner, the founder of
Doctors without Borders – from a doctor's approach to the choice for
political action as a cabinet minister and international civil servant – is
instructive.

This of course does not mean that intervening with armed force is
easy. Let us begin with traditional peacekeeping. It presupposes, by
definition, an agreement of the fighting parties to call in the peacekeepers. If one party resists, or delays, or violates such an agreement, the
peacekeeping mission is in a quandary (in East Timor, it took strong
pressure on Indonesia to get it to accept one, and during that time many
people died). Moreover, the duty of such forces to remain neutral and to
use weapons only for self-defense places them at the mercy of the "bad
guys": the most frightening example was what happened at Srebenica;
the observers – sent with Serb consent – to Kosovo at the end of 1998
were powerless to stop Milosevic's attempt at subjugating the Kosovars.
Often, these peacekeepers are the victims of events too big and murderous for their size and their means: the withdrawal of UN peacekeepers
from Rwanda before the massacres began, the fate of General Dallaire's
mission and pleas, are a tragic reminder of this frequent impotence.
Attempts to mix peacekeeping and peacemaking, entrusted to forces
established only for the former task, have turned out disastrous, as in
Somalia, when the change of mission – from protecting to feeding of
the people to disarming those who were preventing it – led to the collapse of the attempt, and as in Bosnia where, in 1992–95, peacekeeping,
favored by Britain and France, became an obstacle to coercive peacemaking, which would have put the peacekeepers in peril (in Somalia,
peacemaking "sank" peacekeeping; in Bosnia, peacekeeping prevented
peacemaking).

Let us move from "peace after war" and its problems, to "war for
peace" in internal crises, and its obstacles, that is, to the difficulties of
military intervention for peacemaking. A first issue is a double question
of when? On the one hand, what is the right threshold for intervention?
Too low, it sacrifices completely the legitimate claims of sovereignty
in order to protect human rights. Too high, it limits intervention to the
most extreme cases of human rights violations, which means, in practice,
that by then it is already much too late and that genuine (although
perhaps not genocidal) atrocities may end up being tolerated. On the
other hand, at what moment in an internal crisis is it right to intervene?
The argument of "last resort," derived from (inter-state) just war theory,

is doubly troublesome: opponents of military force will rarely concede that all possibilities of peace have been exhausted, and proponents of intervention will tend to argue that an early one will save lives (think of Rwanda), whereas a late one will allow for abominations to occur (like the expulsion of Kosovo's Albanians).

A second issue is that of authority to intervene: who, not when. Here also there are two questions: on the one hand, who has the right to intervene or to authorize external intervention? The Charter gives this authority to the UN Security Council. But here we face a paradox. Under international law (which includes the Charter), the use of force is justified only for self-defense against armed attack, or for collective security in conformity with the Charter; all other uses of force violate the principle of domestic jurisdiction. As a consequence interventions because of human-rights violations have to be presented to the Security Council as violations of global or regional security. An intervention provoked by a massacre committed in an island far from any neighbor would be challenged by many states as incompatible with the Charter. Let us assume that the "threat to regional or global security" case can be made. What happens if serious violations of human rights are committed by both sides, as is presently the case of Israel"s repression of Palestinian resistance and of Palestinian terrorism? What happens if the Security Council is paralyzed? In Kosovo, the United States and its allies anticipated paralysis and acted under their own (or rather NATO's) authority – a deviation that was, so to speak, semi-legitimized by the Security Council's failure to protest, but also a potentially dangerous precedent. What about regional organizations, if the Security Council is paralyzed? Unfortunately, as we saw in Rwanda, they are often not up to the task, and as divided as the UN, or (as in the Middle East) missing. Coalitions of the willing, even when they act in good faith, take time and preparation to be able to exercise authority. On the other hand, the question of external authorization is not the only one. Intervention also needs domestic support, which is often lukewarm (as in Kosovo: would it have lasted if Milosevic had not given up?) or missing (as in the United States after the killing of American soldiers in Somalia). This issue may become particularly troublesome in the US, needed for many interventions that require advanced weapons or sophisticated technology. It may well be – in a country where a sizable part of the public and of the politicians are or have become highly susceptible to the neo-realist arguments, and suspicious of international organizations not controlled by the US – that support will exist only for interventions *à la* Afghanistan, that is, against attacks perpetrated on US civilians by foreign states and terrorists, but not for the interventions that try to protect peoples from their regimes or from civil wars.

A third issue is the necessity for effective intervention. Multi-lateral action is never easy. Often, the partners are divided, and the results risk being catastrophic: as in Bosnia, until the spring of 1995, or in Somalia, when the US and the UN had rival strategies. Even when, as in Kosovo, there is a firmer unity, each member may have its preferred strategy and targets. This is not only caused by divergent preferences among allies; it is also because the strategy most likely to succeed is not always obvious. In Kosovo, the ends – preventing or stopping ethnic cleansing – may not have been reachable with the means available (and with the targets selected), and it was the concern with minimizing US losses which both limited and dictated the targets.

The fourth issue concerns not effectiveness but ethics: the necessity for intervention to be just. The categories that have been invoked have been those of traditional just-war theory. They are not fully adequate either for internal conflict, or for the international relations of the twentieth and twenty-first centuries. I have already questioned the "last resort" criterion. Proportionality of means to ends is a notoriously elastic concept: it all depends on the importance the actors attribute to the ends. Reasonable chance of success is a highly iffy and subjective condition (in Kosovo – as later in Afghanistan – observers within a few weeks went from deep pessimism to eating their hats). As for non-combatant immunity, however careful the targeting, "collateral damage" (a hideous euphemism) has turned out inevitable and sometimes horrendous.

From the points of view of both effectiveness and ethics, there is the difficult problem of unintended consequences. In Kosovo, the foreign intervention contributed to the speedy ethnic cleansing of the Albanians; later, the coalition's victory made possible the ethnic cleansing of the Serbs (as in Croatia in 1995).

After the headaches of action come those of the aftermath of war. If the crisis ends by agreement, there are likely to be vast unresolved issues. Is there really a future for a multi-ethnic Bosnia or Kosovo? What will the final status of Kosovo be (independence? partition? autonomy within a new Yugoslavia?)? Will peacekeeping survive the post-war tensions? The record in places like Angola or Cambodia has been mixed. Next come the long-term issues of reconstruction. What will be the fate of the refugees? Many are still in camps (Rwanda) or incapable of returning (East Timor, exiled Serbs from Kosovo). Who will pay for economic reconstruction? Can outsiders really engage in "nation-building," especially when there had never been a genuine nation? In Haiti and in much of Africa the "rescuers" have tacitly abandoned that goal. When they have not, as in Kosovo, there is the risk of crossing the border between helping the local factions set up a new state, and establishing a kind of protectorate, thus creating tensions with one's protégés. Lastly, there is the familiar dilemma of criminal justice. One option has been purely judicial: international criminal justice for war crimes, crimes against humanity, and genocide, as well as domestic judicial punishment. It has been a slow and rocky road, both in the case of Yugoslavia and in that of Rwanda; the question of bringing the accused and the suspect to trial has not been resolved. The other side of the dilemma is that of "reconciliation" rather than trials. Truth commissions have the merit of dampening polarization and facilitating a return to a kind of normalcy, but they upset human-rights defenders, and it is far from clear that there can be "closure" and firm reconciliation without a modicum of criminal justice.

"I CAN'T GO ON, I MUST GO ON..."

This long and sketchy list of difficulties is not aimed at a negative conclusion about the wisdom of interventions. It is meant to goad their champions into a realistic assessment of the magnitude of their task. In my view, some interventions may be unwise, but the principle itself is not; ultimately, what is involved is a choice of values and goals. There should be no retreat. We owe it to the victims of internal crises and crimes. We saw what happened when opportunities were missed, as in Yugoslavia in 1991; when Rwanda turned into a bloodbath with the flight of the UN and the inaction of the great powers. The coddling of Indonesia, especially by the US, the abdication of the "world community" confronted by Tibet and Chechnya (and also, until September 2001, by Taliban atrocities) are enough to induce nausea. Also, it is in the direction of a far more energetic priority for human rights that lie the signs of a new kind of world order, in which states would be at the service of their inhabitants, rather than the other way around; in which statecraft would be guided by an enlarged definition of what is in the national interest, by a greater commitment to multi-lateral cooperation and action; in which non-governmental organizations and "world public opinion" (that is, the opinions of foreign publics) would play a greater role. In this new world order, the norms restricting sovereignty would clearly extend to serious violations of human rights (including those that terrorism, public and private, entails). Norms and institutions that extend to individuals directly would constitute revolutionary progress in international law (which is why America's hostility to the International Criminal Court is absurd).

The problem will be managing the coexistence and interpenetration of two very different types of international relations. The traditional competition of states for resources, prestige, and power, motivated by ambitions and fear, licensed by the paucity and weakness of supranational institutions, will continue. But there will also be a global politics, with more actors – individuals and groups both constructive and destructive, in addition to states and public international agencies – with greater centralization, although no world government yet, more of a role both for public international organizations and for an incipient (if flawed) global civil society, and above all more of a concern for individuals, both the victims and the guilty. *Raison d'état* and *raison des individus* will compete and partly blend.

The new global politics will also have to deal with conflicts among its own concerns – for instance, between stopping "internal aggression against people" (if necessary by force), and defending the environment against the ravages of war; between priority to economic development and priority to human rights and democracy; between capitalist growth and social justice; between self-determination and the need to limit fragmentation and parochial nationalisms; between sanctions on criminal leaders and punishing their populations. Such tensions, and the major one between the world of Machiavelli and that of the idealists, will not be easy to resolve. The agenda of the new global polity will require action on multiple fronts: an effective network of international criminal justice, with sanctions if the criminals are not delivered; far greater coordination among the NGOs and between them and public international organizations; measures making it possible for the latter to act preventively and quickly, which means having forces in readiness; reviving a non-post-colonial form of trusteeship for the restoration of collapsed states; encouraging adequate forms of democracy in a highly heterogeneous world, etc. These are just examples.

Obviously the responsibility of the "lone superpower," the United States, is enormous. The present mix of "sovereignism," neo-realism and unilateralism, enhanced by American power and by the new challenge of terrorism (even though no part of that mix is well adapted to it) is both dangerous and paradoxical. Let us hope that it does not prevail.

The questions for American statecraft are: leading for what? And with whom? The reality, in world affairs, is the colossal erosion of the differences between what is domestic and what is global. It occurs both through globalization and through violence. Insofar as intervention is concerned, to borrow and adapt a line from Samuel Beckett, some say it can't go on but it must go on, if we want the progressive components of the new global politics to prevail both over the traditional "state of war" and over the destructive aspects (such as global terrorism) of the emergent world society.

NOTE

1 For my own previous writing on the subject, see *World Disorders* (Rowman and Littlefield, 1998), chs. 10–11; *The Ethics and Politics of Humanitarian Intervention* (University of Notre Dame Press, 1996); and "The Debate about Intervention," in Chester A. Crocker, Fen Osler Hampson, and Pamela Aall, eds., *Turbulent Peace: The Challenges of Managing International Conflict* (US Institute of Peace Press, 2001), pp. 273–84.

Chapter 3

Selective humanitarianism: in defense of inconsistency

CHRIS BROWN

The circumstances under which it can be morally right for one state to intervene forcibly into the "internal" affairs of another are the subject of considerable controversy. States have always attempted to influence each other's behavior in international relations, and, as Stephen Krasner has recently demonstrated, have quite often done so on matters that could be regarded as the subject of domestic jurisdiction.[1] Still, the number of occasions in the last decade when states have actually used force against each other, not simply in pursuit of the usual goals of diplomacy, but, at least partly, in response to human-rights violations of one kind of another, has been far greater than usual.[2] There are, of course, other forms of intervention which continue to occur more frequently – trade boycotts or sanctions, investment strikes, the ending of cultural or sporting contacts and so on; but the greater willingness to use force in pursuit of humanitarian goals represents an escalation from such actions and, as such, may be seen as particularly morally problematic. The "non-intervention" norm of the old, so-called "Westphalian" system may have been superseded by the norms associated with the post-1945 international human-rights regime, but there is still a great deal of uneasiness with the notion of military humanitarianism.[3] Partly this unease reflects an understandable concern that too ready a willingness to legitimate the employment of force in pursuit of humanitarian goals could lead to more suffering and instability than it is intended to remedy, but another serious set of concerns revolve around the issues of "selectivity" and "consistency" in humanitarian interventions.

This is so because, even setting aside the vexed question of how exactly to define "humanitarian", as opposed to other kinds of intervention, it is clear that the number of actual interventions there have been in the past decade or so is only a small subset of the number of cases where it might plausibly be thought that a humanitarian intervention would have been appropriate. Let it be stipulated that the activities of foreign powers in Northern Iraq (1991), Somalia (1992–93), Haiti (1994), Bosnia (1993–95), Kosovo (1999), East Timor (1999) and Sierra Leone (2000–01) can all be characterized as examples of humanitarian intervention in the sense that they were/are at least partly designed to prevent local authorities from perpetrating human rights abuses, committing ethnic cleansing and the like (even though in each case this characterization could be challenged). To this list could possibly be added the (January 2002) US action in Afghanistan, which although obviously motivated by the support given by that country's former rulers, the Taliban, to the perpetrators of the crimes of September 11 , 2001, nonetheless had a clear humanitarian dimension insofar as removing those same rulers from power improved the chances that human rights, particularly those of women, will be observed there.

Still, it is clear that this list covers only a small number of the recent occasions when large-scale human-rights abuses, up to and including genocide, have occurred. More human lives were lost in Rwanda in 1994 than in all the conflicts listed above taken together, and the only intervention that took place – *Operation Turquoise* by France in Western Rwanda – was effectively (albeit perhaps unintentionally) in support of the perpetrators of genocide rather than the victims.[4] Civil wars, foreign invasions and large-scale human-rights abuses in, *inter alia*, Angola, Zaire/Congo, Burundi, most of West Africa, Western Sahara, Palestine, Chechnya, Kashmir, Burma and so on have claimed more victims than most of the conflicts where interventions have taken place. So, how does it come about that interventions take place in one crisis but not in another – in particular, how can it be *morally* acceptable for the interveners to be so selective in their approach to intervention?

That this issue is raised with some frequency can be illustrated by examples drawn from commentary on NATO's war with Yugoslavia over Kosovo in 1999. From the left, Noam Chomsky's *The New Military Humanism* makes great play of the contrast between NATO's action in Kosovo and the human-rights abuses in Kurdistan committed by NATO member Turkey, while for Edward Said, the obvious point of contrast is US complicity in the Israeli occupation of Palestine.[5] From the other end of the political spectrum, Edward Luttwak makes the point very precisely albeit in more general terms: "What does it mean for the morality of a supposedly moral rule, when it is applied arbitrarily against some, but not others?"[6] The editors of *Commonweal* re-iterate this position in

October 1999 – "The principle of intervention should be universal and uncompromising."[7] It seems that this position is very widely held.

In short, doubts about the ethical implications of being selectively humanitarian are raised often enough to make this a suitable subject for analysis; in what follows the argument will be examined in three stages. First, it will be suggested that the usual responses to the charge of inconsistency are not particularly satisfactory – they are either based on false empirical premises, or they concede too much to the critics. On the other hand, and second, the critics themselves also characteristically offer unsatisfactory arguments in the sense that the logic of their position leads them down paths that most do not wish to take. The third stage of the argument will suggest that both sides of this debate mischaracterize the nature of the dilemma faced by policy-makers, largely because they understand moral behavior in terms of following a moral rule and this is not the most appropriate or helpful way of thinking about morality either in this case or, perhaps, more generally.

Two further preliminary points need to be made. First, although in order to simplify issues of presentation the focus here will be on *armed*, putatively humanitarian action, as opposed to the other forms of intervention mentioned above, such as economic sanctions, it should not be thought that armed interventions are necessarily more serious in their consequences than so-called peaceful methods. Far more innocent men women and children have died in Iraq over the past decades as a result of UN sanctions and the unwillingness of the Iraqi regime to cooperate with the UN than died in the course of the war that led to these sanctions; issues of selectivity obviously arise in this context as well as in the context of the employment of violence. In any event, whatever ideas come out of the discussion that follows will be relevant to non-violent as well as violent forms of sanctioning – the aim is to illuminate more generally the issues involved in deciding when to act and when not to act, regardless of the form that action takes. Following on from this, a second preliminary point that needs to be acknowledged is that many of those who charge the interveners with inconsistency actually have agendas of their own which are unconnected to this issue. Chomsky, for example, clearly would oppose *any* exercise of power by what he regards as the American Empire, and the charge of inconsistency is for the most part a rhetorical device designed to appeal to those who, while not accepting his wholesale critique of American society, are, nonetheless, concerned by the way in which American power is sometimes deployed. Still, the presumption of this chapter is that there is a valid issue concerning selectivity, and even if the motives of some of the people who raise this issue are sometimes suspect, their arguments can still be taken at face value and analyzed accordingly.

CONVENTIONAL DEFENSES OF SELECTIVITY

When charged with being inconsistent, those who have carried out or supported humanitarian interventions – insofar as they respond at all – offer a number of arguments that are superficially quite plausible but that, when examined in more depth, prove to be less than wholly convincing. The proviso in this sentence is important; it is actually relatively unusual for policy-makers to respond directly to this charge. One notable exception to this generalization can be found in a keynote speech by Britain's Prime Minister, Tony Blair, during the Kosovo War of 1999.[8] In the course of a speech on the wider issue of globalization, Blair attempted to shore up the moral case for the military action against Yugoslavia which, at the time, appeared not to be bringing results. His belief was that if it proved militarily necessary to escalate to a ground war, a precondition for success would be that NATO, and particularly American, public opinion became convinced of the moral rightness of the action – hence the insertion into of his speech of a section on the ethics of intervention (which, it is rumored, was drafted outside the British Foreign Office and without its approval).

The relevant section of this speech begins by arguing, unexceptionably, that the principle of non-intervention, while generally valid, must be qualified in cases of genocide and when acts of oppression create large-scale and destabilizing refugee flows; more controversially, he adds that when regimes are based on minority rule they lose legitimacy. No doubt aware of the extraordinarily broad implications of this position, he qualifies it immediately, recognizing that "if we wanted to right every wrong that we see in the modern world we would do little else than intervene in the affairs of other countries." He then goes on to set out five major considerations which have to be taken into account before intervening, asking rhetorically: are we sure of our case? have we exhausted all diplomatic options? on the basis of a practical assessment of the situation, are there military options we can sensibly and prudently undertake? are we prepared for the long term? do we have national interests involved?

Setting aside for the time being the last of these considerations, it is clear that what Blair has done here is first, to offer a quite plausible and sensible answer to the charge of being selective, and then, by the criteria he sets out in elaboration of this answer, to demonstrate inadvertently why the argument will not quite do the job he wants it to do. The proposition that it simply is not possible to "right every wrong" is obviously true – the number of situations in the world at any one time where human rights are being dramatically violated is, indeed, usually greater than could plausibly be responded to by those states with the ability and potential willingness to carry out humanitarian actions; even if this were not the case, the potential for instability and disorder that would follow from a policy of attempting to right every wrong would be enormous. Clearly, it is not possible to do everything that it might be good to do – but how is the choice made of which wrong to right? The first four considerations Blair sets out do *not* actually address this problem; on the contrary, they assume a choice has been made as to which wrong to right and instead focus on how the wrong should be righted, and, in particular, whether the use of force is the correct tactic. Setting the issue in its original context, Blair is attempting to explain why he believes that military force is the appropriate response to the Kosovo situation; from the perspective of arguments about selectivity, this is the wrong question – rather it should be asked why, given all the possible wrongs that could be righted, NATO decided to act in this particular case?

There is one possible answer to this question that would preserve the notion that the interveners were behaving consistently in accordance with some moral rule, and not simply selecting the case where they would intervene on the basis of non-moral criteria. Very crudely, it might be held that this particular case was chosen because it represented the most serious current violation of human rights or the situation where the most serious humanitarian disaster would follow from inaction – but this is, indeed, rather too crude because it ignores altogether issues of practicality. Better would be some notion of 'triage'; thus, one might divide the world's trouble spots into three categories – those where the difficulties are sufficiently minor such that forcible intervention would most likely always do more harm than good; those where the difficulties are of such magnitude that action would almost certainly be ineffective, either because of the scale of the problem (as, perhaps, with the civil wars in the Congo) or because they are caused by states who have the power to turn any external military intervention into a full-scale war (as with Chinese depredations in Tibet, or Russian in Chechnya); and third, those where outside forcible intervention is both a practical possibility and brings the prospect of actually improving the situation on the ground. If it could be argued that any particular action represented an attempt to right the most serious wrong to be found within this final category, then the interveners could legitimately claim to be acting in a non-arbitrary way, and thus to be preserving the sense that a moral rule was being followed, even if they were not actually addressing the most serious wrong overall.

The problem is that it is very difficult to argue that even this notion of what "addressing the worst wrong" might actually involve can be seen to be operating in the real world. Throughout the 1990s, the most appalling abuses of human rights, amounting in at least one case to genocide, took place in Africa, generally without effective external intervention, while, throughout the same period the West at least tried, intermittently, to do something about the less serious violations of human rights taking place in the Balkans. Even in 1999, it is by no means clear that the unfolding situation in Kosovo constituted more of a threat to human well-being than such long-running disasters as the civil war in Sierra Leone, the Indonesian occupation of East Timor, civil unrest and oppression in Kurdistan, Burma, Palestine, Afghanistan, and Kashmir, and wars in the southern Sudan, Burundi, and Angola to mention only a few of the possible candidates for the position of "most serious conflict where external intervention might have had a positive effect".

One of the features common to all of these latter cases – as opposed to Kosovo – is that, with the partial exception of the situation in Kurdistan, they are all located away from Europe and away from NATO's direct sphere of interest. Perhaps location is important, and one basis for selecting which wrong to right might be for the interveners to handle problems in their own neighborhood first – but is this really a *morally* defensible position? It might well be thought that the intensity of the wrong was rather more important than its location; other things being equal, it might make good sense to say that one should put out the fire in one's neighbor's house before turning to a similar conflagration elsewhere – but the conflagration in, say, Rwanda in 1994 was pretty clearly of a different order of magnitude to the fires which plagued Bosnia in that year, and the limited action in the latter case, as opposed to the total inaction in the former, cannot be justified *morally* by such an argument.

The term *morally* is emphasized here because it is quite clear that the actual reason why action was taken in one place and not in another does indeed have a great deal to do with "the neighborhood". This is where Tony Blair's fifth and final rhetorical question comes into

play – "do we have national interests involved?" The point he wanted
to make was that, unless interests are directly involved, intervention is
likely to be short-lived and ineffective – which is plausible enough –
but the same point has a locational dimension because such interests
are, on the face of it, more likely to arise when dealing with human
rights violations in one's own neighbourhood. West European leaders
such as Mr. Blair, Chancellor Schroeder and President Chirac were more
directly concerned with the conflict in Kosovo than with that, say, in
the Sudan because the refugees generated by this conflict would end up
in camps on their territory rather than in Uganda or Ethiopia. This is
understandable – but is this a moral position, as opposed to *Realpolitik*,
which is the charge directed against reasoning of this kind by figures
such as Chomsky and Luttwak? Do we have here the basis for a universal and uncompromising principle of intervention? In fact, it will be
argued below that the most appropriate way to make moral judgments
about intervention does indeed involve consideration of national interests (as well as many other factors) but this is a position which is not
easy to reconcile with the idea that behaving morally involves following a consistent universal rule. In order to get to a position in which
national interest arguments are morally legitimate it is necessary to develop a different conception of moral behavior. But before developing
this thought, it may be worth subjecting the arguments of critics of intervention to the same kind of scrutiny that has been devoted here to
the arguments of a representative supporter of action.

THE CRITICS OF SELECTIVE HUMANITARIANISM

So far the argument of this chapter has been favorable to the positions
of the Chomskys and Luttwaks but only because the logic of their own
positions has not yet been examined. Let it be supposed, for the purpose of this discussion, that they are right that current Western practice
follows no discernable *moral* rule, although it might reflect some other,
non-moral, calculus – what, then, must be done? What rule would the
critics consider to be morally appropriate for determining whether or
not to intervene?

Chomsky, at the end of his extensive critique of Western action in
Kosovo suggests that the appropriate rule that should govern external
action in cases where human rights are being violated is the Hippocratic
principle "do no harm".[9] If there is any possibility that by acting one
would do harm, one should not act. Since it is pretty much always the

case that forcible action will do harm, one way or another – it is, for example, difficult to imagine that an intervention to prevent genocide in Rwanda could have been "zero-casualty" on all sides – this maxim amounts to a blanket condemnation of all forms of military intervention. Indeed, it might well be taken to involve a condemnation of action altogether, since even non-violent interventions by state or non-state actors are likely to do *some* harm, although, to be more charitable to Chomsky than he usually is to his critics, it might be held that what he really means is something more like "do no direct physical harm" rather than the more extreme formulation. Either way, his position raises directly the classic problem of "dirty hands".

Debates over dirty hands concern the extent to which actions that may in themselves be morally dubious or even, from some perspectives, clearly wrong, may be justified in order to bring about a greater good; such debates have been found in the work of political theorists at least from the time of Machiavelli onwards, although the coinage "dirty hands" is more recent.[10] The central insight of these debates is that it is not possible to govern innocently, and Chomsky is probably right that the only way in which national leaders can preserve entirely clean hands is by abstaining from action. Most thinkers who have considered the issue regard such an abstention as too high a price to pay for clean hands, rejecting such moral extremism in favor of positions that pay at least some attention to the consequences of *inaction* as well as of action. It is certainly reasonable to stress that often, perhaps usually, forcible intervention will have adverse consequences which may overshadow any good achieved, but the proposition that the consequences of action in pursuit of the good are *always* more damaging than the consequences of inaction seems empirically implausible.

Chomsky's anarchism allows him to sweep aside the problem of dirty hands by making the assumption that, ultimately, government as such is unnecessary – but few even of his disciples are prepared to follow him in this, the latter preferring instead to stress the more specific, and less philosophically challenging, assault on US motives and intentions that characterizes his work. But, "always oppose interventions when conducted by the USA" can hardly be a candidate for a viable moral rule, unless one considers the United States to be some kind of satanic force in world affairs. Such a position, although held literally, for example, by Osama Bin Laden and the Al Qaeda network, can hardly form the basis for moral judgment on the part of those who do not, in general, adhere to an eschatological view of world politics. Certainly, the United States is the leading military and economic power in the world today, which means it has the largest stake in preserving the current global system, a system which is, at least in part, based on manifest inequalities and injustices. Moreover, US foreign policy has on occasion involved support for, indeed the establishment of, repressive regimes. Still, none of this amounts to support for the propositions that everything the United States does in the world must be morally contemptible, or that all oppressions can be traced back to its malign influence. Commonsense would suggest that, at least sometimes, the United States is on the right side of a moral argument, and the view that *all* global oppression is the product of American power and/or global capitalism is not worthy of respect.

Conventional realists such as Edward Luttwak reject the Chomskyan demonization of the US, but appear to share his absolutist account of moral behavior. As noted above, for Luttwak as for Chomsky, a moral rule is only a moral rule if it is applied in a non-arbitrary manner – however, as opposed to Chomsky, Luttwak and fellow realists such as Michael Mandelbaum and Colin Gray take this position to imply that, since arbitrariness is inevitable, decisions on the use of force ought to be based instead on allegedly non-moral notions such as the national interest.[11] Statespersons who stress morality are deceiving others (and perhaps themselves). From this perspective, the fact that states are selective in their decisions to intervene and that their choices cannot be accommodated under some moral rule is not, as such, problematic – what is problematic and misleading is the claim made by figures such as Tony Blair that they are, nonetheless, behaving morally by intervening. Such a claim is the product of a crusading mentality that is likely to override the cardinal realist virtues of prudence and restraint, or so it is argued.

The strength of this position need not be denied; the crusading mentality is indeed dangerous and realists are right to point to the probable consequences of disregarding national interests – as Gray crisply puts it, no good deed shall go unpunished. Where difficulties arise is rather in the fact that realist critics appear to believe that once reference is made to national interests, "morality" cannot be accommodated. As suggested at the end of the previous section, this is a position that needs to be challenged. With the appropriate notion of what constitutes moral behavior at least some of the insights of the realists can be accommodated; similarly, Blair's insistence that national interests be involved in any decision to intervene does not necessarily represent the retreat from morality that some have detected.

INCONSISTENCY, ARBITRARINESS, AND
MORAL JUDGMENT

If to behave morally it is necessary to follow a non-arbitrary moral rule, then humanitarian interventions appear not to fit the bill – such is the charge made by critics to the evident discomfiture of supporters. But is this an adequate account of moral behavior, and what does "following a rule" mean? And what kind of rules are under consideration here? It is always dangerous to generalize about moral intuitions, but it does actually seem widely believed that morality is about rule-following (the Ten Commandments, the 'Golden Rule', the Kantian Categorical Imperative and so on) and thus that there is something wrong with the idea that moral behavior could be arbitrary or inconsistent – and yet, when it comes to particular cases and actual practice, a degree of arbitrariness and inconsistency is much more common than this initial intuition would suggest. Is it always and necessarily wrong to be inconsistent or arbitrary in applying a moral principle? To answer this question it may be helpful to consider for illustrative purposes two examples from outside of the realm of international relations.

At present, in both the UK and the US, tobacco and alcohol are legal drugs while cannabis, heroin, and cocaine are not, even though there are quite good reasons for thinking that the latter substances are no more harmful to the user in the long run than the former – the case here is particularly strong with respect to cannabis but may well apply to the "harder" drugs as well. This is obviously not the place to argue this issue in detail, but let it be assumed, for the sake of argument, that the case has been made and that there is an inconsistency of treatment here that cannot be rationally defended. Should this inconsistency be eliminated, as it could be by either legalizing the illegal substances or criminalizing the legal? A case can be made along these lines, but it is certainly contestable whether this would be the right, or a sensible, thing to do. Given the difficulties involved in enforcing existing drug laws, and the history of Prohibition in the 1920s in the United States, very few people would argue that adding tobacco and alcohol to the list of banned substances would be sensible. On the other hand, given that cannabis, heroin, and cocaine actually are harmful, even though perhaps no more so than tobacco and alcohol, it may be sensible to discourage their use. The case here may be strengthened if there is good reason to think that legalization would have differential effects on different communities, as indeed there is, which is why many inner-city leaders are reluctant to back libertarian thought in this area. In short, although the present law may be both arbitrary and inconsistent, it may well be better, all things considered, than any alternative – and "better" in this case summarizes both moral and non-moral considerations.

Consider a second, slightly different, example – which I owe to Steven Clark of Liverpool University. Should one give money to sellers of *The Big Issue*?[12] It is possible to propose a moral rule here, but the only one that could be formulated in an easy and unambiguous way would be "never buy *The Big Issue*." Any alternative rule would be arbitrary in one way or another. It might be thought that one should buy the magazine but only from a deserving person, or a person in great need – but we have no way of knowing which of the potential *Big Issue*-sellers we encounter meet these criteria, and, in any event, it is not clear what exactly "deserving" or "great need" means. One might formulate a rule such as "buy from the first *Big Issue* seller you encounter," but it is difficult to see this injunction as actually incorporating a moral principle. In fact, it seems plausible that most people who buy the magazine, do so on whim, that is, on the spur of the moment and in response to a judgment that is difficult to put into words. Given the absence of sensible ways of determining from whom one should buy, this is not an irrational way to proceed.

The purpose of these two examples is to illustrate the point that consistency is perhaps not as prevalent in moral reasoning as might be expected, rather than to suggest that there are exact parallels at work here, although it is possible to see at least one point of contact with the cases with which we are concerned. In the second case – which comes closer to offering an analog to the decision on whether or not to engage in humanitarian intervention than the first – the only universal rule that can be formulated with ease is "don't buy," which clearly parallels both the non-intervention rule of the old international legal order, and the prohibition of "harm" which Chomsky wishes to see established. Or, to put the matter differently, in complex circumstances where drawing up rules of conduct is difficult, the easiest rule to formulate is a rule of abstention – it is always easier to find reasons for not doing something than to set down the circumstances under which action is morally permissible, even though the proposition that inaction is always morally preferable to action is itself difficult, if not impossible, to defend.

The more general point here is that the problems of drugs, street-magazine selling – and humanitarian intervention – call for the kind of ethical reasoning that follows the Aristotelian injunction, summarized by Stephen Toulmin, that "sound moral judgment always respects the detailed circumstances of specific kinds of cases."[13] Attempts to produce some kind of algorithm that will give a general answer to the question of what is right and what is wrong in such cases are unlikely to succeed. Moreover, this Aristotelian position applies more generally: the search for "universal and uncompromising" moral rules seems particularly fruitless in the cases discussed here, but this is simply illustrative of a wider problem with a great deal of contemporary moral reasoning. Toulmin has made this point very precisely; on his account, in the seventeenth century the moral insights of renaissance humanism and the classical world were put aside. Under the influence of Descartes and Hobbes, along with many lesser talents, formal logic came to displace rhetoric, general principles and abstract axioms were privileged over particular cases and concrete diversity, and the establishment of rules (or "laws") that were deemed of permanent as opposed to transitory applicability came to be seen as the task of the theorist. Toulmin suggests that at this time moral reasoning became "theory-centered" rather than "practically minded."[14] Moral reasoning became a matter of following a theoretically validated rule, rather than of making a practical judgment, and was impoverished thereby.

Of course, making a judgment is often more intellectually demanding than following a rule, and one of the attractive features of rule-based moral reasoning is that it appears to offer a degree of moral security to individuals in an uncertain age such as our own (or the early seventeenth century), some external assurance that they are doing the right thing. But this security is, for the most part, illusory, because "following a rule" itself generally involves the exercise of judgment. That this is so is sometimes missed because the notion of a moral rule is itself somewhat ambiguous. Possibly there are putative moral rules that can be understood algorithmically, in formal, logical terms, but others, the most important, cannot. Thus, a rightful concern over the harmful effects of drug-taking could result in the rule "ban all substances that cause harm" but the result of this process is absurd, since virtually any substance can be harmful under the wrong circumstances, and some very harmful substances can, under the right circumstances, have good effects (although the prevalence of health scares in recent years, which have led to a world in which virtually every foodstuff is suspect, suggests that this absurdity is not well understood). On the other hand, the much more defensible Kantian rule, "always treat human beings as ends and not solely as means" necessarily requires interpretation and the exercise of quite sophisticated moral judgment.

It is not unreasonable to suggest that the majority of putative moral rules require extensive interpretation before they can indicate a morally desirable course of action – and, in effect, it is the interpretation here, the exercise of judgment, that is doing the work not the rule as such. In dealing with complex situations, such as deciding whether it is right that one state should interfere forcibly in the affairs of another, there is no substitute for a form of moral reasoning that involves a judgment that takes into account the totality of circumstances, rather than seeks for a rule to apply. It is for this reason that the demand that the United States and other Western countries formulate an uncompromising and universal principle which will tell them when to intervene and when not to intervene, is fundamentally misconceived.

Lest this position be thought idiosyncratic, it should be noted that it is consistent with the most widely held contemporary moral philosophies. Kantianism is "deontological" in its approach – that is, it requires the establishment of rules that must be followed regardless of consequences – but this does not involve a denial that complex moral judgments are required on the part of actors. As noted above, what exactly the Kantian "Categorical Imperative" requires in particular cases may be as opaque as the notion of the greatest happiness is for utilitarians, to refer to another modern moral philosophy; both Kantianism and utilitarianism can be deployed to set out moral rules, but in neither case are these rules expected to act as *substitutes* for the exercise of judgment – rather they establish general principles and summarize past experience, thus forming the starting point for the exercise of judgment. On the other hand, it is certainly true that neither of these modern moral philosophies places the kind of emphasis on cultivating the facility for the making of moral judgments which was characteristic of older, pre-modern or classical moral philosophies.[15] This is one of the reasons why, in recent years, there has been a revival of interest in Greek moral theory, and, in particular, in the notion of the "virtues" – those qualities of mind that human beings can cultivate in order to enable them to be more effective moral agents.[16]

The virtues reflect an account of what a successful human life should look like, and purport to tell us what is necessary for human happiness. This is a perspective that may be very helpful for examining contemporary moral dilemmas, but there is an obvious difficulty in translating this kind of thinking into an account of how *states* ought to behave. Humanitarian interventions are carried out by states, although they may be ordered by particular statespersons, and it not obvious that much sense can be made out of the idea that states ought to cultivate the virtues, developing qualities of mind that will lead them to make the right decision when faced with difficult moral problems. States may have legal personality, they may even be "people" as Alexander Wendt suggests, but they do not have minds to cultivate.[17] This suggests that a *direct* application of agent-centered moral reasoning here is hardly possible, unless the institutional dimension of action is ignored and the individual decision-maker becomes the sole focus of attention. On the other hand, an *indirect* application of such moral reasoning is a much more viable proposition. Indeed, the categories employed by a great deal of classical thinking about international relations – from the "just war" tradition to the "righteous realism" of figures such as Hans Morgenthau – owe much more to classical moral thought than they do to modern moral philosophy, so the possibility of discussing the exercise of judgment by states is not as far-fetched as might initially be thought.[18] It is by developing this connection, that it may become possible to make sense of Tony Blair's inclusion of the national interest as one of the determinants of the decision to act in deciding whether to right a particular wrong, and to explain why Edward Luttwak's search for a non-arbitrary moral rule may not be true to the tradition he represents.

MORAL JUDGMENT AND HUMANITARIAN INTERVENTION

The obvious starting point for an examination of the morality of any particular intervention might well be taken to be the "Just War" tradition, which asks of any particular action whether the force employed is intended to right a wrong, is the last resort, is proportional to the offence, has reasonable prospects of success, is undertaken with proper authority, and with care being taken, as far as possible, to protect the innocent.[19] What is striking about these criteria – which date back to the medieval Catholic Natural Law tradition and, beyond that to Augustine and Aristotle – is the way in which they require us to make different *kinds* of judgment as part of the process of reaching a decision as to the justice of any particular action. "Right intention" requires an examination of the mental (perhaps spiritual) state of the intervener, while "proper authority" requires a combination of legal and ethical judgment.

Whether violence is actually the "last resort" can only be decided on the basis of a diplomatic–strategic judgment, likewise the issue of a "reasonable prospect of success." "Innocence" is a moral category, but whether proper care is taken to protect the innocent requires a different kind of judgment, and the application of complicated notions such as the doctrine of "double effect."[20]

In short, what we have here is *not* a pro-forma check-list of criteria whereby action is deemed just only if we are able to put a tick into each box – nor do we have a set of criteria that can be interpreted solely by theologians, ethicists, lawyers, or strategists. Rather, what is required is a practically minded judgment taken in the round based on all the circumstances of a particular case. Such a judgment will sometimes involve a tough-minded acknowledgment that there are wrongs that cannot be righted, but, equally, it will not allow the best to be the enemy of the good – what is required is a form of judgment that constitutes a creative interaction between the standard criteria and the full specifics of the particular case. Thus, to take a recent example, it is clear that the US bombing campaign in Afghanistan in support of the opponents of the Taliban has, inadvertently, resulted in civilian casualties, as such campaigns always will; does the doctrine of "double effect" – which holds that it may be permissible to perform a good act with the knowledge that bad consequences may ensue – apply in this case? This is a question that can only be answered by getting down to the details; were there alternative ways in which US could have assisted the Northern Alliance? As we have seen, "do no harm" – a moral principle that would certainly rule out bombing – is not a viable maxim in a world where dirty hands are the inevitable consequences of action, but this tells us little about this particular case. There is simply no substitute for the exercise of judgment here. Mine would be that bombing was, in this case, the right thing to do, but others will, and do, disagree – such is the nature of moral argumentation.

Still, the tendency to reduce these criteria to a set of rules which can substitute for the exercise of judgment here is clearly present in contemporary thinking, as is the reduction of the different kinds of reasoning they call for into some more easily manageable exercise. Thus, it is possible to turn "proper authority" and "innocence" into legal categories (say, a UN Security Council resolution and "non-combatant immunity"), while some ethicists and theologians seem to feel competent to judge whether or not some particular diplomatic initiative constitutes the "last resort." The point is that while these reductions may reflect the spirit of our age, they are not in the spirit of the original way of formulating the problem, which pointed to a less rule-based, more holistic process of judgment. It is here that the criteria set out in Tony Blair's "Doctrine of the International Community" speech start to make more sense; the practical questions he raises in that speech are fully in the spirit of the Just War tradition – and even the concern for the "national interest" is not as far away from that tradition as might be expected.

That the Just War tradition mandates "right intention" is a sign of its pre-modern, theological origins – contemporary legal versions of the Just War, such as Michael Walzer's "legalist paradigm," downplay radically this dimension of the tradition – but it is noteworthy that the requirement of an intent to right a wrong does *not* preclude the existence of *other* motives.[21] One of the effects – intended or not – of emphasizing the alleged desirability of non-arbitrary moral rules is to legitimize a black-and-white account of the moral universe under which actions are either wholly altruistic or wholly selfish – and since states are never *wholly* altruistic this move is usually the prelude to a denial that altruism can be a factor at all in the conduct of international affairs. Contrary to this absolutism, there is no reason to think that when states act to right a wrong they may not *also* be motivated by self-interest. Motivation is a complex process and about the only thing that can be said with certainty about it is that there is never simply one single reason why anyone does anything. The decision whether to act in a particular case rests on a judgment of the circumstances of that case, and those circumstances necessarily include interests – there is no reason to think that there is anything inherently immoral or non-moral about this, especially since self-interest may involve considerations that are not "selfish" in the usual sense of that term. Some realists – and some critics of realism – may assume that it is possible to have an account of national interests which would exclude in principle non-material factors such as the values we wish to see promoted in the world, but this position does not follow from the notion of self-interest as such. The desire to live in a world in which gross violations of human dignity do not take place, and a willingness to help to bring this about, is as legitimate a basis for self-interest as the defense of national borders or state sovereignty.

In fact, realists in particular ought to resist the conclusion that when interests affect conduct, morality is necessarily disregarded. Such a stark account of what is or is not moral would not have been endorsed by the majority of the thinkers who have shaped the realist mind-set over the centuries, or, for that matter, by some of the classical realists of the

twentieth century. The Augustinian tradition of realism has always focused upon how it is possible to behave morally in an imperfect world.
What that tradition denies is the notion that moral rules designed to regulate individual conduct can be applied directly to "immoral society" –
a position compatible with the point being made in this chapter.[22] From
this common ground it does not follow that moral judgment is impossible in international relations. The most compelling feature of the realist account of the world has always been its sensitivity to the issue of
"dirty hands," its strong sense that to act at all in a world gone wrong
is to sacrifice innocence – but there is no reason to translate this awareness of the tragic dimension to human existence into an endorsement
of a-moralism. When Luttwak and other realists deplore the absence of
a moral rule governing humanitarian intervention they are falling into
the trap so insightfully investigated by Hans Morgenthau in perhaps his
best work, *Scientific Man v. Power Politics*.[23] The desire to find abstract,
logical moral rules that will somehow enable the process of judgment
to be circumvented is very much part of the mind-set of "scientific
man," and fundamentally untrue to the texture of the moral life that
Morgenthau wished to illuminate.

CONCLUSION

And yet, precisely because the exercise of judgment is involved and
there are no hard-and-fast moral rules to be applied, critics such as
Luttwak, Gray, Mandelbaum (and Chomsky) might actually be right to
condemn intervention in Kosovo and on other occasions. The burden
of this chapter has been that there is no viable universal moral rule
that can tell statespersons what is the right thing to do in response
to particular circumstances. They must exercise their judgment as best
they can; sometimes their best may not be good enough and so criticism
of the kind offered by these writers may be appropriate. In the case
of Kosovo, it is arguable – and I have so argued[24] – that the leaders of
NATO did, in fact, get it more-or-less right, but, say, in the case of the
Rwanda genocide of 1994, the best judgment of the leaders of the West
was, clearly, nowhere near good enough. This was an occasion where
those who knew what was going on (and that includes the UN Secretary-
General, as well as the governments of the United States, France, and
Britain) were aware that a crime unprecedented since 1945 was being
committed, and yet hid behind obfuscations and lies in order to avoid
responding to this crime in the way that they should have.[25]

This was a failure of vision, a failure of will – and a failure for the kind of moral reasoning that refuses to pay attention to the specifics of particular cases. The sort of considerations of distance and the lack of a direct *material* national interest that might have been compelling in the case of a lesser crime have to be weighed against the awfulness of this particular crime – the international community has recognized in the Genocide Convention of 1948 that genocide has a special status even in the general context of "crimes against humanity." Those who were in a position to act ought to have realized that this was something out of the ordinary, that the kind of excessive concern for casualties that might be excusable in the case of an intervention without a clear purpose – such as that in Somalia in 1992/3 – was out of place here, and that the preservation of bureaucratic chains of command at the UN was no reason to allow nearly a million men, women, and children to be murdered. The only way to prevent a similar shameful denouement in the future is not to search for some illusory moral rule that will mandate intervention if such-and-such a set of conditions apply, but for those who have the power to act to develop the kind of moral sensitivity that will enable them to recognize what is the right thing to do in such appalling circumstances, and the strength of character to act upon this recognition.

NOTES

1 S. D. Krasner, *Sovereignty: Organized Hypocrisy* (Princeton NJ: Princeton University Press, 1999).

2 Useful general studies of humanitarian intervention in the 1990s include: O. Ramsbotham and T. Woodhouse, *Humanitarian Intervention in Contemporary Conflict* (Cambridge: Polity, 1996); R. Haass, *Intervention* 2nd edn. (Washington DC: The Brookings Institute, 2000); and N. J. Wheeler, *Saving Strangers* (Oxford: Oxford University Press, 2000). J. Moore (ed.) *Hard Choices: Moral Dilemmas in Humanitarian Intervention* (Lanham, MD: Rowman and Littlefield, 1998) is a valuable collection of essays by policy-makers and academics.

3 G. M. Lyons and M. Mastanduno, eds., *Beyond Westphalia?* (Baltimore MD: Johns Hopkins Press, 1995) is the best collection of theoretical essays contrasting the two sets of norms.

4 G. Prunier, *The Rwanda Crisis, 1959–94: History of a Genocide* (New York: Columbia University Press, 1995) is the best general account of Rwanda, 1994, while L. Melvern, *A People Betrayed: The Role of the West in Rwanda's Genocide* (London: Zed Books, 2000) is a powerful indictment of Western policy.

5 N. Chomsky, *The New Military Humanism* (London: Pluto Press, 1999); E. Said, "It's Time the World Stood up to the American Bully," *The Observer* (London, April 11, 1999).

6 E. Luttwak, "No-Score War," *Times Literary Supplement* 14 (July, 2000).

7 Cited from J. B. Elshtain, "Just War and Humanitarian Intervention," International Studies Association Annual Conference (Chicago, Feb, 2001).

8 T. Blair, "Doctrine of the International Community," Speech to the Economic Club, Chicago Hilton (April 22, 1999) http://www.fco.gov.uk/news/speechtext.asp?2316.

9 Chomsky, *The New Military Humanism*, p. 156.

10 See, for example M. Walzer, "Political Action: the Problem of Dirty Hands," *Philosophy and Public Affairs* 2 (1973), 160–80.

11 M. Mandelbaum, "A Perfect Failure," *Foreign Affairs* 78 (1999), 2–8; C. Gray, "No Good Deed Shall Go Unpunished," in Ken Booth, ed., *The Kosovo Tragedy: The Human Rights Dimension* (London: Frank Cass, 2001).

12 Or other similar magazine – the practice of the homeless raising money by selling a self-produced magazine seems to be common to most Western cities.

13 S. Toulmin, *Cosmopolis: The Hidden Agenda of Modernity* (Chicago: University of Chicago Press, 1990), p. 32.

14 *Ibid.*, p. 34.

15 This point has been made forcefully by Bernard Williams: see *Ethics and the Limits of Philosophy* (Cambridge: Cambridge University Press, 1985) and *Morality* (Cambridge: Cambridge University Press, 1993)

16 G. E. M. Anscombe, "Modern Moral Philosophy," *Philosophy* 33 (1958), 1–9; M. Nussbaum, "Non-Relative Virtues: An Aristotelian Approach," in Nussbaum and A. Sen, eds., *The Quality of Life* (Oxford: Oxford University Press, 1993). R. Crisp, ed., *How Should One Live? Essays on the Virtues* (Oxford: Oxford University Press, 1996). D. Statman, ed., *Virtue Ethics: A Critical Reader* (Edinburgh: Edinburgh University Press, 1997).

17 A. Wendt, *Social Theory of International Politics* (Cambridge: Cambridge University Press, 1999).

18 For accounts of classical realist thought stressing this point see J. Rosenthal, *Righteous Realists* (Baton Rouge, LA: University of Louisiana Press, 1991) and A. Murray, *Reconstructing Realism* (Edinburgh: University of Keele Press, 1996).

19 A classic study of just-war thinking is J. T. Johnson, *Just War Tradition and the Restraint of War* (Princeton: Princeton University Press, 1981), while M. Walzer, *Just and Unjust Wars*, 2nd edn. (New York: Basic Books, 1992) is a modern classic. J. B. Elshtain, ed., *Just War Theory* (Oxford: Blackwell, 1991) is a valuable collection of essays.

20 P. Woodward, ed., *The Doctrine of Double Effect* (Notre Dame, IN: University of Notre Dame Press, 2001) brings together classic articles and original material on this subject.

21 Walzer, *Just and Unjust Wars*.
22 R. Niebuhr, *Moral Man and Immoral Society* (New York: Charles Scribner's Sons, 1932) is the classic statement of this position.
23 H. J. Morgenthau, *Scientific Man v. Power Politics* (Chicago: University of Chicago Press, 1947).
24 Chris Brown, "A Qualified Defence of the Use of Force for 'Humanitarian' Reasons," in Booth *The Kosovo Tragedy*.
25 Melvern, *A People Betrayed*.

PART II

Just-war perspectives and limits

Chapter 4

Reciprocity, stability, and intervention: the ethics of disequilibrium

MICHAEL BLAKE

The current debates about foreign military intervention have several odd features.[1] One of the most notable, I think, is the degree to which the parties in the dispute are in agreement about conclusions. Commentators of widely different theoretical dispositions seem to agree in broad outline about what a theory of intervention ought to establish. It should defend, first, the moral permeability of state borders; in contrast to the nearly absolute sovereignty of traditional international law, theorists of foreign intervention agree that states can sometimes be made subject to international intervention by actions taken against their own citizens. A theory of intervention should also, however, be somewhat restrictive about when such intervention is justified. The fact that a state's action is unjust or illiberal is not, by itself, enough to justify intervention. That action must reach a certain level of moral evil before such intervention becomes morally permissible. Illegitimate restrictions in voting rights, then, likely cannot justify foreign intervention, even if we regard such restrictions as deeply abhorrent to liberal principles of political morality. Atrocities such as slavery or ethnic cleansing, by contrast, seem at least potentially to open the door for legitimate military intervention abroad.

All this, we seem to accept. What disagreement there is turns more on how we ought to defend these conclusions, and therefore with how the precise level of evil legitimating intervention ought to be determined. Any theory of intervention that did not accept these conclusions in broad outline – which did not, that is, defend a picture of state borders in which these borders are powerful but non-absolute barriers to intervention – would be unlikely to gain many adherents.

In what follows, I do not want to dispute these conclusions; I think they are correct. What I want to do is inquire about why they should be so; and why, in particular, we are reluctant to intervene in a foreign political community simply because that community's actions violate liberal precepts of justice. How can we justify the need for something more than simple injustice before intervention is legitimated?

One of the most cogent recent analyses of intervention rests on the notion of reciprocity, and takes its ability to answer this latter question as a strong reason to think that its analysis is correct. On this analysis, we ought to extend our liberal theories of politics to the international realm by seeking reciprocal agreement between the diverse political societies of the world. In this context, agreement could not be reached based upon any premises so controversial as the egalitarian guarantees we associate with liberalism in domestic politics. Thus, we ought to seek more restrictive and modest principles of international political morality, ones which could be accepted by all (or most) of those political communities found in the world today. On this analysis, liberals have a good reason for defending their restrictive conclusions about intervention. Indeed, liberals would be intolerant – would violate their own precepts seeking agreement under conditions of diversity – were they to arrive at any other conclusions in the area of international intervention.[2]

I believe this analysis to be mistaken. Liberals do have good reason to abide by the restrictive limits on intervention described above, but these limits do not derive from ideas of reciprocity or toleration. Rather, these limits stem from more homely restrictions on courses of action likely to prove useless, bloody, and counter-productive. There is nothing distinctively illiberal about seeking to defend and promote liberal values abroad; liberal states are not compelled by their liberalism to seek reciprocal agreement with those who deny the moral importance of individual dignity. We can develop a theory of intervention which matches the contours described above without abandoning our moral commitments in the international realm.

I will try to defend these conclusions in three sections. The first will discuss the nature of reciprocal agreement, and will seek to demonstrate that liberalism's extension of reciprocity to the international context creates a tragic dilemma. Liberals can seek stability, or respect for moral agency, but not both. The second will discuss the attempts made to overcome this tragedy, by seeking to defend reciprocal agreement between political communities as the moral equivalent of reciprocal agreement between individual citizens. This attempt, I argue, fails; to simply equate toleration abroad with toleration at home is to ignore differences in *what* is being tolerated in the two cases. Tolerating individual differences in plans of life is one thing; tolerating communities which seek to attack and repress such differences is quite another. While we might have reason to defend this latter sort of toleration, it cannot be derived in any easy manner from the former. The final part of the paper will seek to demonstrate that the tragic dilemma facing liberalism is not, perhaps, so tragic after all. We can abandon the search for reciprocally acceptable principles abroad, and seek to defend and promote liberal values of individual dignity. This commitment, however, does not compel us to act in a manner likely to denigrate these very values in the long run; and this, I think, is sufficient to establish that military intervention is generally to be disfavored. This, I think, means that we can establish the restriction on intervention we have sought, without having to abandon our moral commitment to individual dignity both at home and abroad. We will, however, have to develop a new understanding of political ethics abroad – what I call an ethics of disequilibrium, which does not privilege agreement between corporate entities such as states.[3]

RECIPROCITY AT HOME AND ABROAD

We might begin with a simple question: why should we even care about reciprocity? I mean this term to have a less specific meaning than the meanings given to it by Brian Barry and John Rawls; reciprocity, as I use it here, means simply the methodology of justifying political power with reference to principles acceptable to all those affected.[4] We need not concern ourselves at present with the precise means by which principles are determined to be so justifiable; I do not want to discuss how we ought to conceive of the situation of choice, nor the motivations of the parties. Our concern is with the structure of this methodology, which seeks to get justification through agreement. The methodology begins with what we already share – with the reasons and commitments we are already presumed to find motivating – and uses what is shared to provide us with reasons to support and defend principles of political justice. These principles are then used to justify and criticize those political institutions we share. Thus, political power is justified with reference to reasons we already share and accept; the realm of politics is ultimately justified with reference to individual agreement to be governed, however hypothetical this form of agreement might actually be.

Why, though, should this method be employed? To answer this question, we might begin with the domestic context. Here, the use of reciprocity provides two clear advantages. The first is that this methodology provides a mechanism guaranteeing stability. Political principles, however attractive, are unlikely to be of much use if they cannot form the foundation of a sustainable political community. In this way, stability is a virtue of political arrangements; if it is not itself of primary normative importance, it is at least a precondition without which other such normative values cannot be brought into the world. The use of reciprocity seems to provide a guarantee of stability in at least three ways. The first is in providing reasons to individual agents to comply with the principles governing the political system. Reciprocity is focused on giving reasons to those agents whose consent is required for the system of rules to work. A system of law cannot function based solely on coercive threat; individuals need to understand themselves as having reason to support and uphold the system itself. Reciprocity provides that reason, by demonstrating that the system is designed with reference to principles those individuals do or would accept. Reciprocity also provides, however, a guarantee to each citizen that *other* citizens will likely to motivated to act upon and abide by these political principles. Individuals can be assured that compliance with the political system will not subject them to a comparative disadvantage; cooperation is made to dominate over defection by the knowledge that other parties have been given reasons sufficient to motivate cooperative behavior. Reciprocity, finally, provides for stability through its normative significance; reciprocity, as will be shortly discussed, reflects a concern for the agency and dignity of those to whom it is addressed, giving reasons instead of simply demanding obedience. If we assume that individuals are at least partly motivated by the moral pull of such ideas, then the fact that the principles of political justice are acceptable to all parties creates incentive to comply. The fact that these principles are justified in this manner creates its own motivation to comply. Indeed, it is as a result of this last factor that we can understand reciprocally justified principles as forming an equilibrium result of justice. Any deviation from these principles will be met by contrary pressures, stemming from our normative commitments, to return to a situation in which reciprocal agreement is reestablished.

Reciprocity thus helps to ensure stability over time. The second advantage of reciprocity is more immediately normative, and begins from the moral commitments discussed above. Liberalism is motivated, at heart, by some idea of moral dignity and worth of persons. What makes liberalism distinctive – as well as attractive – is this notion that individual moral agents deserve to be treated with equal concern and respect. Liberals will differ in how this idea ought to be understood, and will disagree with each other about what such equality demands. These differences need not concern us now; what we can emphasize in the present context is that reciprocity offers a means by which we respect these notions of moral equality. Reciprocity seeks to give reasons to persons that they can be expected to endorse. As such, it treats individuals as equal moral agents, whose consent has moral gravity. If I wish you to support institutions giving me advantages, I must demonstrate that these institutions are in accord with principles you have reason to accept; I seek to transform a relationship of coercion into one approximating cooperation.[5] Reciprocity demonstrates respect for persons by insisting that institutions justify themselves to such persons; as such, reciprocity supports the moral ontology animating liberal thought.

What I want to notice here is that in the domestic context these two advantages come together. The two aspects of reciprocity are mutually supporting; liberal principles defended by reciprocity can be expected to be both just and stable, and stable because they are just. Those agents whose defection would destroy the system are given reason to support the system, so that its stability is guaranteed. The reasons given to ensure stability, moreover, are reasons which are acceptable to individual moral agents, so that the respect for moral agents necessarily follows from this method of gaining stability. In the domestic context, we get stability and justice as a package deal.

In the international context, however, things do not work quite so neatly. The agents whose consent must be gained to ensure stability are invariably corporate, collective agents; in our world, they are uniformly corporate and political agents such as states.[6] Stability thus requires the introduction of principles which would be reciprocally acceptable to the various states of the world.[7] If liberalism means anything, however, it means that individual moral agents have a moral status distinct from that given to collectives and institutional agents. Individual moral agents are taken by liberalism as having a moral status which entitles them to treatment as equal persons, with certain liberal rights guaranteed in virtue of this status. Individual moral agents have rights, on this account, which could never be negated by the choices of a collective. To abandon this idea in the international context would seem to rob liberalism of its most attractive element: the idea that individual agency is morally significant, so that individual persons have rights even against collective interest.

This means, I think, that there is a certain tragic element in the choices we can make in the international arena. If we wish to apply reciprocity, we must recognize that we can use it to attain stability, or justice between

individual moral agents, but not both. We can seek principles acceptable to states or "peoples," and so gain stability. Because the idea of
moral equality is controversial, however, such principles will not make
reference to the moral equality of persons or to the specific liberal rights
such status would produce. The most we could hope for is some more
modest set of principles governing mutual interactions; liberal states, if
they seek to govern their behavior by such principles, would be prohibited from certain actions intended to ensure or promote egalitarianism
abroad. We could, on the other hand, seek to defend the moral ontology
undergirding liberal thought, and develop a foreign policy whose aim
was to bring about a liberal world. The content of this world might
be developed with reference to reciprocity, but the relevant form of
reciprocal agreement would be that between individuals, rather than
states. Such a foreign policy would ensure that a liberal government's
actions were motivated by a consistent respect for human equality and
moral dignity – but it would preclude the possibility of state action being
governed by reciprocally acceptable international principles. A liberal
state choosing this horn of the dilemma would have to accept that international politics could never be governed by mutually acceptable
principles, so long as a diversity of political views obtains.

Thus, in the international world, stability and moral equality tear
apart, and the liberal state – like the liberal theorist – has a choice to make.
Because the agents in the international world are political communities
with coercive control over individuals, we can either seek justification to
individuals or international stability – but not both. We have to decide
which of these two benefits to pursue. This decision is rarely analyzed
in explicit terms; in the domestic arena, after all, the two values come
together, so we have no occasion to discuss in any detail their relative
importance.[8] Internationally, however, we must admit that there will be
some loss inherent in any methodological choice we make.

At this point, it seems wise to introduce a contrary argument: that
there is no tragedy here, because international reciprocity between states
produces both stability and the only sort of justice liberals are entitled to
pursue. On this analysis, liberals are commanded by their liberalism to
seek principles reciprocally acceptable to the various states or peoples
of the world; to do otherwise would be not simply imprudent but illiberal. I will deal with this argument in the following section, and hope
to demonstrate that this argument does not negate the tragic nature of
the choice I have outlined. In the final section, I will proceed to examine
the ways in which the tragedy of this choice might be minimized. The

prudential concerns which led us to seek agreement between states persist, I think, but can be reinterpreted as pragmatic blocks on otherwise acceptable action. A liberal state can pursue liberal values of individual dignity without thinking that this pursuit commits it to useless or counterproductive actions along the way.

INTERNATIONAL PLURALISM AND RECIPROCITY

The above dilemma forces a wedge between the moral notions animating liberalism and the prudential need for stable political structures. One method of eliminating the dilemma, I think, is to insist that the moral notions animating liberalism in fact *require* our international focus to be collective, rather than individual. Domestic reciprocity seeks stable political structures respecting individuals under conditions Rawls refers to as those of reasonable pluralism; under conditions of freedom, a variety of comprehensive doctrines are inevitable, and no agreement will be produced about religious truth or the most appropriate conception of the good.[9] Liberalism requires us, at home, to respect persons in part by respecting such difference, and refusing to ground political authority in any controversial doctrine.

If the international analogue to domestic tolerance looks to differences not in comprehensive doctrine but in political doctrine, then we might be pushed towards reciprocal agreement of states both for reasons of prudence *and* reasons of political morality. The reasoning proceeds analogically: people, with their distinct conceptions of the good, become peoples, with their distinct ways of life; the property held by individuals can be analogized to the territorial resources over which the people's government has sovereignty; and so on. The outcome of this process of reasoning will be principles which mandate respect for illiberal societies and thereby restrict intervention on behalf of liberalism – not simply because such intervention is usually a bad idea, but because this intervention is itself *illiberal*. Liberal states are to limit their actions to those which are in accordance with principles acceptable to all such states; they are, in particular, precluded from exercising political sanctions – whether economic, military, or diplomatic – to bring about the liberalization of illiberal states. With this analogy in place, liberal tolerance extends inevitably to the toleration of illiberal practices. The dilemma given above is dissolved; liberals face no tragic choice in the international realm, since only one horn of their dilemma – that premised upon reciprocal agreement of states – is available to a liberal theorist.

This analogy, however, does not suffice to overcome the dilemma given earlier. To see this, we have to examine in more detail the reasons why reciprocal agreement is methodologically useful in the domestic context. If we pay more attention to the relationship between reciprocity and disagreement, I think, we will be forced to the conclusion that liberals still have a choice to make in the international arena. There is nothing inherently illiberal or intolerant about insisting upon liberalism as a valid aim of foreign policy. We are not precluded by liberal toleration from acting upon liberal principles – even when such principles are, as they inevitably will be, controversial and unacceptable to many of the world's states.

We may begin to see this by examining what happens when liberal theory encounters pluralism in all its various guises. How does a liberal theorist, concerned to give reciprocally acceptable reasons to all, react when in face of a disagreement between free and equal persons? There are, I think, two possible responses. The first is to bracket that which is the subject of disagreement, and refuse to take what is controversial as foundational for political justice. To do this, of course, is to make reference to something about which the parties to the disagreement actually do agree; it is to negate disagreement with reference to some higher-order agreement. In the domestic political context, religious difference has this character. You and I may disagree about the nature of religious truth, but because of some higher-order beliefs about political morality, we agree that neither one of us will or should attempt to enforce our beliefs by political means. If we did not share some such beliefs, the very project of reciprocal agreement would be impossible; reciprocal agreement cannot grow without some common links of political morality.

The second response to disagreement, however, is to refuse to take this step, and to insist that one party has the better of the dispute. Where this response is legitimate, the liberal theorist is entitled to ground political justice even upon what is controversial. This response has an aura of paradox about it; could a liberal insist upon orthodoxy in the face of disagreement? The paradox, however, is largely an illusion. All liberal theorists, including Rawls, take some points of disagreement as being beyond the pale for liberal justification. In the domestic arena, we might note the existence of certain illiberal persons – say, sincere believers in the moral superiority of the Aryan Nations – whose refusal to endorse any aspect of the liberal project certainly counts as a form of disagreement. In the face of such disagreement, liberal theory is certainly not commanded to become neutral about its own validity at home. Liberals can still insist upon liberalism even in face of domestic disagreement; the existence of illiberal views and beliefs does not cause us to seek agreement at some higher level between liberals and their enemies. Treating certain sorts of disagreement as an aspect of the political world to be dealt with, but not necessarily treated as a matter of reasonable disagreement, is an entirely respectable option for a liberal theorist.

But if this is true, then what distinguishes the cases in which each of these responses is appropriate? Sometimes, the existence of disagreement causes us to seek agreement at a higher level, and in particular an agreement not to found political power upon that about which we disagree. Other times, disagreement does not lead to restrictions on legitimate political actions; while sincere Nazi believers have certain basic political rights, we do not believe our political institutions ought to remain neutral between their views and those espoused by liberals. Religious diversity provokes us to refuse to enforce religious orthodoxy; but the mere existence of diversity does not always motivate neutrality. Why do we treat these two cases in such disparate ways? How do we decide what sorts of disagreement are sufficient to motivate reciprocal agreement between those who disagree?

There are two possible answers to this question, I believe, mirroring the two functions given for reciprocity above. One way of dividing the two is simply to use reciprocity as a tool for stability, and seek to avoid controversial premises wherever the use of such premises would engender a lack of social peace. There is, in Rawls' political liberalism, some element of such an interpretation of liberalism. I do not think, however, that it is sufficient as an interpretation of how liberalism ought to understand itself. On this analysis, liberalism is left without any determinate content; what it can insist upon is dependent upon the content of disagreement in that world in which it is applied. Liberalism's implications now wait upon the sorts of diversity and pluralism we encounter. As the content of agreement shifts, liberalism's content shifts as well; liberalism, under some unhappy circumstances, would be able to defend only certain minimal conclusions most liberals would regard as utterly inadequate.

Another way of answering the question would be to take some aspect of liberalism as being itself morally privileged. On this analysis, we can legitimately insist that neither side in the religious conflict has the right to use political power to enforce religious orthodoxy. This would be true, however, not simply because the alternative is unstable, but because that higher-level principle we are presumed to endorse – that persons are equal sources of moral value, and so have some right to moral independence – is taken as being true, or uniquely plausible, or in some other way privileged. This analysis would regard liberalism as having some determinate content; liberalism defends certain sorts of individual moral equality, and we are able to use this shared belief in equality to insist upon certain political conclusions. But here, as before, the purpose of liberalism is to create political structures justifiable to individual persons, because liberals believe that individual persons are entitled to be treated as moral equals. This has the consequence domestically of ensuring stability, but stability itself is not the motivation for the project.

All of this is intended only to establish one thing: the fact of disagreement does not necessarily motivate a liberal to seek accommodation. Domestically, there are disagreements which do not issue in a legitimate demand for reciprocal agreement between the disagreeing parties. It is certainly possible that such circumstances occur internationally as well; indeed, Rawls insists that certain states have beliefs such that they are not entitled to justification through reciprocal agreement. But what distinguishes the two cases? Once again, the question arises whether we favor individual moral agency, or stability. If our task is searching for principles which might create stability, we have reason to search for principles acceptable to most of the world's diverse peoples and states. But, just as liberals can sometimes insist that one party to a dispute is wrong in the domestic context, liberals are not precluded by liberalism from insisting upon moral equality abroad. The fact of controversy is not sufficient to motivate the demand for reciprocal agreement.

What this means, I think, is that our dilemma persists. Liberalism in the domestic context creates stability and moral equality and creates them together; we have no occasion to choose between the two, because those principles acceptable to most are (we presume) those guaranteeing the moral equality of persons. Liberalism in the international context, however, does seem to demand a choice between these two values. We may seek reciprocal agreement between states, or stand on the moral beliefs animating liberal thought, but we cannot do both.

We can return now to the analogy between states and persons discussed above. If we respect difference, it was argued, we are compelled to respect it at home and abroad; given that the differences we see internationally deal with modes of collective political organization, we are therefore compelled to tolerate and respect illiberal states by liberalism itself. I think we are now in a position to realize now that this easy equation is too simple. From the fact of difference, nothing yet follows about how a liberal ought to react. We now need a story about why liberal theorists should not insist upon liberal values in face of this diversity; why, that is, we ought to seek agreement which is reciprocally acceptable to liberal and non-liberal states alike. It is not always illiberal to insist that one side of the debate has it right. What sort of story might we offer to support the idea that it is illiberal to insist upon liberal values, when faced with opposition from those who disagree?

This question is not frequently asked in any explicit way, and still more infrequently given a reply. The answer, I think, stems as much from our intuitive sense that to insist upon liberalism would be, in practice, to insist upon a sort of institutionalized moral superiority[10] – in which our current moral beliefs, warts and all, are to be exported forcibly to an unwilling and dismayed foreign populace. As I will explain in the next section, I think our displeasure at this prospect is entirely justified, and provides us with good reason to refrain from military adventurism in all but the most egregious cases. But I do not think this intuition can establish that liberals ought to regard liberal values abroad as akin to religious beliefs at home. We are not compelled to seek principles reciprocally acceptable to all states, liberal and otherwise; we can seek to promote and defend liberal values, so long as we bear certain homely moral truths in mind.

But let us give this alternative a hearing. The image created by those who defend this need for reciprocity is of a people unified in their political beliefs, which are in tension with liberal values. In Rawls' memorable description of a hypothetical illiberal society, its citizens "accept certain inequalities among themselves."[11] If they agree with this illiberal practice or principle, who are we to argue? This seems to create an image of a national consensus on inequality, so that respecting illiberal institutions now seems to be a result of, rather than in conflict with, respect for persons. It would seem, on this analysis, illiberal – not to mention foolish – to insist upon the liberal justice when those facing the inequality themselves support its imposition. To insist upon liberalism would be to refuse any accommodation to deep and persistent disagreement about value; it would be, in other words, very much like insisting upon religious orthodoxy at home.

What we should notice about this idea is that it seems to trade on a specifically liberal notion of justification through consent. The fact that the inhabitants of the society defend and support the illiberal practices is central to our defense of the need to tolerate such practices. As such, this method of justification seeks to enlist our support for liberal concerns of justification, but use this support on behalf of illiberal institutions and practices. It is far from clear that this can be done. In the first place, it is not clear that this sort of consent is sufficient in either method or content to enlist our liberal ideals of justification. We are faced with here not an ongoing process of consent, given from an appropriate situation of free choice; rather, we have simply an assumed act of agreement to inequality, which, if it exists, is as likely to result from adaptive preferences, indoctrination, an ignorance of alternatives, and so on, than anything more morally reputable. The liberal can take this sort of consent on board as a reason to avoid intervention without thereby thinking that such inequality has been given a sanction from within liberal thought itself. Moreover, remember that the *content* of what is agreed to here is, ultimately, the proposition that around here not everyone's consent matters equally. Even if everyone is supposed to have consented to such a proposition, it is not clear that this sort of proposition could ever be consistently defended from within liberal thought.

At the very least, once resistance to such unequal treatment begins, it is far from clear that a consistent liberal could defend the illiberal majority against the disfavored minority. This, in turn, raises the most important of the reasons to reject this analysis of liberal toleration: the simple fact that agreement to inequality is more likely a useful fiction than a morally salient reality. It is frequently useful for governments to insist that their citizens do not desire liberal political guarantees, or that their cultural traditions preclude such liberal political structures. It is as frequently true, however, that dissent exists within that society, and this dissent often takes the form of an insistence upon the right to some version of liberal politics. Insisting that an international interpretation of liberalism should take the voice of the government as the official voice of the people, and ignore the existence of dissent and disagreement, strikes me as a problematic move for a liberal to make. I think it should be clear that such a move could only be motivated by concern for international stability, rather than concern for liberal justice itself.

To sum up: states are not natural persons. They are corporate entities with political power over natural persons. Where states disagree is not over the proper conception of the good, but over whether or not a diversity of such conceptions ought to be tolerated in the first place. Because of this, I suggest, we are not compelled to seek reciprocal agreement between states as an implication of liberal toleration. If we defend the individualistic moral principle animating such agreement domestically, then we might also do so abroad. Liberals can interpret their liberalism as a substantive position about the importance of moral equality – as a fighting creed, in Charles Taylor's memorable phrase[12] – and refuse to take reciprocal agreement between states as morally significant.

There is, nonetheless, something quite worrisome about the results at which we have now arrived. If we are not to seek reciprocity between states, then what is left? In what follows, I hope to demonstrate how our worries can be defused. We can, I think, seek to promote and defend liberalism abroad; we are not thereby compelled to be arrogant, rude, violent, and stupid in the attempt. We have good reason to be modest, and careful, in actions otherwise permissible on a liberal theory; this simple fact may suffice to dispel our concerns that a liberalism committed to equality is thereby committed to widespread and careless intervention.

RESTRICTIONS ON INTERVENTION: PRINCIPLED AND PRAGMATIC

What is disheartening about the analysis above is that it argues against the possibility of a liberal theorist endorsing an equilibrium solution to the problem of global justice. We can, that is, seek to defend and promote individual dignity, but must then accept that we will not be able to endorse principles reciprocally acceptable to all states. We could, instead, seek to develop such principles, but would have to accept that they would represent at best pragmatic deviations from liberalism. At any rate, it seems as if liberals cannot consistently pursue both individual dignity and stability through reciprocity. And this fact seems deeply regrettable in a world which seems desperately in need of stability and order. If would be a disheartening conclusion if liberals were forced to choose between principles and peace.

In what remains of this paper, I want to establish that this tragedy is not, perhaps, as awful as we might otherwise think. Liberals can take themselves to be committed to acting in defense of liberal values abroad, and can therefore refuse to take the interests and programs of states as morally salient. But this commitment demands that liberal states act in a manner which will actually bring about a world in which these values are respected. And this, I think, will tend to produce significant limits on what sorts of actions could be taken in defense of liberal values abroad. It will, I think, produce quite dramatic restrictions on the permissible use of military force abroad. In this manner, I think we might end up

defending stability without invoking reciprocity; there will be no equilibrium solution in the international realm, but we might nonetheless
find reasons sufficient to guarantee peace.[13]

To begin with the obvious: military intervention involves the use of
deadly force. The use of such force requires justification. Such justification cannot be provided, I think, if the practices to which this intervention is directed do not represent an evil sufficient to warrant the risk of
killing and being killed. I do not want to address precisely how such
a level of evil might be determined; all I would insist upon is that the
pain and horror of warfare is sufficient to make military intervention
illegitimate in all but the most egregious of cases. This is, perhaps, not
a theoretically interesting way of restricting intervention, but I think its
importance cannot be overestimated. From the fact that liberal intervention is not inherently illiberal, it does not follow that liberals have a
blanket permission to make war in the name of justice. Intervention is
prohibited where the costs of such intervention would not be justified
by the good to be accomplished.

Nor, for that matter, is it permissible if there is any less extreme
method by which the same results might be achieved. This limitation on
intervention, it is true, has a certain prudential cast to it. But prudential
considerations can rise to the level of moral constraints. It is morally impermissible to use violent means to right a wrong when peaceful means
could accomplish the same end; there are obvious moral constraints on
unnecessary creation of death and destruction. We have no reason to
fear that liberals will, if not prevented by reciprocal agreement, take
themselves as licensed to export liberalism abroad at the end of a gun.
Reciprocal agreement is not needed to prevent this because this sort of
imposition is prevented by more simple and local moral concerns. We
have no need to invoke reciprocity to tell us why we ought not use the
military to correct minor deviations from liberal values abroad.

This last idea leads to a more general set of concerns regarding the
effectiveness of intervention. Intervention in the name of liberal justice
is not inherently illiberal. But intervention nonetheless needs justification; at the very least, it must be established that it will likely prove an
effective remedy for the evils it addresses. This will, I think, often prove
difficult to do. The reasons for this, I think, are many, and empirical
analyses of politics may be more helpful than philosophy in determining what those reasons are. But I will here mention one obvious problem.
Liberal governance, I have argued, requires not simply liberal institutions, but that citizens understand those institutions and accept them

as legitimate. Liberalism thus requires not simply political institutions, but public norms. While the former can sometimes be imposed from outside, the latter will always prove much more elusive. If intervention could only be justified with reference to its ability to create liberal justice, we have to face up to the fact that outsider intervention cannot always accomplish this task. Indeed, in many cases it will prove counter-productive. The perception of condescension and humiliation attendant on foreign intervention may well create more support for the local despot, rather than less. Intervention, then, is generally to be disfavored. The long-term interests of liberal justice are usually better served by restraint and dialogue than military force.

All this is intended to support the proposition that liberals should not treat a commitment to liberal values as a license to intervene. I want to conclude with a final set of reasons to support a restrictive view of intervention. This set of reasons stems, in different ways, from the difficulties inherent in interpretation. It is difficult, in the first instance, to offer any single interpretation of the abstract liberal idea of individual dignity. Indeed, philosophers disagree wildly about what implications such ideas have. It is therefore wise, I think, for a state to be modest and restrictive in which injustices it regards as sufficient to license intervention. To put things bluntly: if we cannot agree about what liberal justice demands, it makes sense to avoid intervention in all but the most obvious and clear cases of injustice.

If liberalism is difficult to interpret, then foreign political practices will prove even more recalcitrant and difficult to understand. But before intervention can be legitimate, the meaning and function of such foreign practices must be understood. Part of our distaste at the prospect of intervention, I think, stems from a worry that we will intervene in societies we do not comprehend, condemning as illiberal practices we do not fully understand. This worry is, I think, completely justified, and provides a reason for liberals to be restrictive and careful in what cases of intervention they are willing to countenance. The history of relations between developing and industrialized nations is sufficient to demonstrate that cross-cultural understanding is difficult to establish. Liberals therefore have good reason to restrict intervention to cases of grave injustice, whose status as evil can be established beyond question.

It is, finally, even more difficult for an observer to interpret the trajectory of a foreign political community as a whole. As I have noted above, there is never only one voice present within a political community. There are liberal movements within all existing societies. Liberals do not have to be neutral between these movements and those who oppose them; we should be unembarrassed to support democracy over despotism. But intervention acts to stop the political dialectic within a society, and replaces that dialogue with one written abroad. I think we have good reason to think of that as a last resort. To insert a political system into another society when a just political order might have developed there spontaneously is a deeply misguided idea. It is, in a way, insulting; it suggests that we have no confidence in the strength of those who struggle against tyranny abroad. But in a more practical sense, it is counter-productive. Political systems that develop locally have more chance to survive in the long run. Liberals have reason to support liberal political systems abroad; but, more often, that support can be most effectively expressed without the use of military might.

All of this, I think, is enough to establish that the rough conclusions introduced at the beginning – in particular, the restrictive analysis of intervention – can be made harmonious with a political theory that refuses to privilege agreement between states. Although there is a tragic element to our international political situation, the tragedy is perhaps not quite so bad as we have thought. Liberal states have no reason to abide by reciprocally accepted principles, but for all that they have no license to become bullies in the name of justice. They have reason to work for peace and stability in the world community, even as they work for liberal values abroad. Indeed, it is worth noting that nothing I have said here precludes liberal states from entering into treaty relationships with other societies, nor with endorsing and obeying rules of international law.

But if that is true, then what has changed? Only, I think, the *nature* of the agreements states make with one another. For those who endorse reciprocity, agreement between states – agreement, that is, at the level of principle – is taken as foundational. What I have argued here is that no such agreement is required. Liberal societies take themselves as having responsibility to individual moral agents. While agreement with other states may be helpful on the road to that goal, such agreement is not itself of primary moral importance. Thus, while the absence of reciprocal agreement will not lead to widespread intervention or military adventurism, it will require us to rethink how we understand the nature of liberal politics in the international arena.

In particular, I think what I have argued for here demonstrates the need for a new approach to international liberal justice. What we need, I think, is a way of thinking about how a liberal state ought to act if it is not to seek reciprocal agreement with illiberal states. What we need, that is, is an analysis of political ethics which does not begin from the assumption that all the agents will be in agreement; an ethics, that is, of disequilibrium. Given how entrenched the idea of equilibrium is within traditional liberal uses of reciprocity, this may prove to be a difficult task. But the conclusions endorsed by an ethics of disequilibrium, I have argued, will not be as bad as we might at first have thought; and only such an analysis, I think, can do justice to the basic commitments of liberal thought.

NOTES

I am grateful to audiences at Columbia University and SUNY Albany for their comments on previous versions of this essay. I am especially grateful to Henry Shue, both for his comments and for his patience in listening to my ideas as they developed.

1 In this essay, I focus on intervention abroad which is (i) military in character, and (ii) humanitarian in intent. This is not to dispute the importance on non-military intervention, nor is it to deny that little interstate action in the real world is motivated by humanitarian concern. I want to focus on humanitarian military intervention as a limit case of principled state action abroad. I hope that what moral constraints exist upon this form of action may also prove relevant as a constraint upon less altruistic forms of foreign intervention. I hope that what I say will also have implications for non-military forms of interstate action, such as favored trading relationships, conditional foreign aid, and so on, although I will not attempt to spell out such implications here.

2 I have in mind here, of course, John Rawls' *The Law of Peoples* (Cambridge: Harvard University Press, 1999), although similar ideas can be found elsewhere. See, for example, Will Kymlicka, *Multicultural Citizenship* (Oxford: Clarendon Press, 1999), pp. 163–72, and Thomas Pogge, *Realizing Rawls* (Ithaca: Cornell University Press, 1987).

3 I owe this felicitous phrasing to Sanjay Reddy.

4 For more specific conceptions of reciprocity, see John Rawls, *Political Liberalism* (New York: Columbia University Press, 1993), p. 17, and Brian Barry, *Justice as Impartiality* (Oxford: Oxford University Press, 1995), pp. 46–52.

5 John Rawls' political liberalism, for one, emphasizes the role of reciprocal agreement in transforming politics from coercion to cooperation. See Rawls, *Political Liberalism*, pp. 212–20.

6 This idea is, I think, given some support by the aftermath of the events of September 11, 2001. While non-state agents such as Al Qaeda can clearly affect the course of international politics, state action – including military action – is still conceptualized as a matter of relationships between states. We are accustomed to thinking of international rules as applying between

states; it is difficult to understand international principles except with reference to national powers. This, I think, explains our recent difficulties in understanding military action against terrorist groups. It is not easy to adapt the interstate language of warfare to apply to non-state actors such as Al Qaeda. Our ideas of warfare have thus slipped uneasily between literal warfare and metaphoric forms of warfare (such as the "war on drugs," "war on poverty," and so on), given that Al Qaeda has the military aspect of a state without the traditional aspects of state sovereignty. In all this, I believe the existence of Afghanistan may have helped defer some vexing conceptual questions, by providing a state against which traditional international military action might be taken.

7 Henry Shue has pointed out to me that some international rules can be understood as humanitarian in intent; such rules – like non-combatant immunity – would seem to blur the distinction between states and persons here. I think this is right, but would note that even such rules can be understood as agreements between states not to do certain things to individuals. Individuals, in such an analysis, are the objects of agreement, not parties to that agreement. Such rules do not make them agents in international law, any more than environmental treaties give a voice to ecological communities.

8 Indeed, I believe Rawls' idea of political liberalism is undermined by the possibility that stability and individual political justice might diverge under certain conditions. If our political conception of justice is uniquely privileged to serve as the object of overlapping consensus, then it is perhaps more appropriate to regard it as true than as merely plausible or useful. If this conception is simply one means among many to get social stability, then it is unclear that Rawls' political methodology is necessarily a liberal one even in the domestic arena. In this respect, the widespread negative reaction to the *Law of Peoples* can be understood to result from that book's willingness to make explicit what *Political Liberalism* does not: that there is nothing in Rawls' methodology which necessarily endorses the liberal rights and values Rawls himself so eloquently defends. These rights and values become the solution to the problem of political justice in certain specific circumstances, which may or may not obtain in any given case. It is understandable that many theorists would be disheartened by a theory which so demotes what is often taken as the animating core of liberal thought.

9 See Rawls, *Political Liberalism*, pp. 36–38.

10 I am grateful to John Mandle for discussions regarding this analysis.

11 Rawls, "The Law of Peoples," in Stephen Shute and Susan Hurley, eds., *On Human Rights* (New York: Basic Books, 1993).

12 See Charles Taylor, "Multiculturalism and the Politics of Recognition," in Amy Gutmann, ed., *Multiculturalism: Examining the Politics of Recognition* (Princeton: Princeton University Press, 1994).

13 One question which now arises: is what is being proposed here simply a *modus vivendi*? If liberal states do not seek to abide by principles acceptable to illiberal states, is the relationship between the two now reduced to that of prudential jockeying for position? The answer is, I think, no – so long as a *modus vivendi* is understood in the traditional way, as a temporary balance of power between adversaries who recognize no moral principles limiting their actions towards one another. The goal of a liberal society, in what is imagined here, is not power over other societies, but a situation in which power everywhere – at home and abroad – is rendered transparent; in which, that is, all individuals face only forms of political power which respect and defend their dignity. To equate this situation with a prudential agreement between rival expansionist empires is, I think, entirely misleading. The two are equivalent only if liberal values are understood simply as local traditions – things we do here, and would like you to do over *there*. But we do not, and should not, look upon liberal ideas in this way. Liberal ideas are not simply local traditions, but normative commitments demanding that people not be used in certain ways. To insist upon liberalism abroad is only to insist that citizens of foreign states not face treatment which disrespects this moral status. To equate this commitment with a desire for mercantile control over another society, I think, is to misunderstand the nature of the liberal project in an important way.

Chapter 5

From *jus ad bellum* to *jus ad pacem*: re-thinking just-war criteria for the use of military force for humanitarian ends

GEORGE R. LUCAS, JR.

During the decade prior to September 11, 2001, many analysts in ethics and international relations had begun to envision a post-Cold War era in which the principal need for military force would come to be the rendering of international humanitarian assistance. Humanitarian tragedies in Somalia and Rwanda, and at least partially successful military interventions to prevent or halt atrocities in Bosnia and Kosovo, had prompted this significant new attention to the problem of using military force for humanitarian purposes in international relations.

The events of that day served as grim reminder that, humanitarian causes notwithstanding, nations equip and support military forces primarily for the purpose of defending their own borders and protecting their own citizens from unprovoked attacks from abroad. It is nonetheless a sign of the growing importance of this relatively new-found interest in the humanitarian use of military force that military intervention by the United States and Great Britain in Afghanistan (ostensibly to seek out and punish terrorists and destroy their paramilitary organizations) swiftly came to be represented to the world as a humanitarian intervention as well. The recent Afghan campaign was characterized in broad and quite plausible terms as an effort to liberate citizens from an oppressive and unrepresentative regime, restore human rights (primarily to women who had egregiously been denied them), and prevent some of the worst effects of poverty and starvation in a troubled and long-suffering region of the world.

Notwithstanding all this attention to the problem, the criteria governing the justifiable use of military force for humanitarian purposes remain quite vague. Of those analysts who have attempted to address this issue, some, like James Turner Johnson and Paul Christopher,[1] represent humanitarian interventions as an extension of traditional just-war theory because they still involve the use of military force for coercive purposes. Others, like Michael Walzer,[2] have long argued that various caveats and qualifications need to be added to the baseline legalist paradigm in international relations in order to cover extenuating or emergency situations, including massive violations of human rights within what we are now coming to call "failed states." Still others, like Stanley Hoffman, have argued that the humanitarian use of military force represents an emerging new paradigm in international relations that calls into question some of the basic assumptions regarding the sovereignty of nations, thus requiring a set of justifications all its own.[3]

I will suggest that the attempt simply to assimilate or subsume humanitarian uses of military force under traditional just war criteria fails because the use of military force in humanitarian cases is far closer to the use of force in domestic law enforcement and peacekeeping, and so subject to far more stringent restrictions in certain respects than traditional *jus in bello* normally entails. It is not, for example, sufficient that humanitarian military forces (any more than domestic police forces) simply refrain from excessive collateral damage, or merely refrain from the deliberate targeting of non-combatants. In fact, the very nature of intervention suggests that the international military "police-like" forces (like actual police forces) must incur considerable additional risk, even from suspected guilty parties, in order to uphold and enforce the law without themselves engaging in violations of the law.

The second strategy for encompassing humanitarian use of military force is represented in Michael Walzer's longstanding attempts to revise and reform our understanding of international law in lieu of relying on the vagaries of moral reasoning alone. This strategy, however, does not address the underlying conceptual incoherence involved in making the autonomous nation-state the unit of analysis in international law. Humanitarian interventions are not undertaken to address solely the political problems of "failed" states (of which Rwanda and Somalia are examples), nor only to contain or discipline the behavior of "rogue" states (such as Yugoslavia and Iraq). Instead, such interventions are necessary even more frequently to address the substantial pressures placed upon the international community by the behaviors of what might be termed "inept" states (of which Afghanistan, Congo, the Sudan, and many others are examples). "Inept" states are those nations with recognizable but ineffective governments unable to provide for the security and welfare of citizens, secure the normal functioning of the institutions of civil society, or maintain secure borders sufficient to control the operations of criminal elements in their midst. None of Walzer's earliest qualifications of the baseline legalist paradigm in *Just and Unjust Wars* (1977), let alone his more recent elaborations of his reformed legalist paradigm,[4] addresses this dilemma successfully, or explains whether we have either the right or responsibility to do (for example) what the United States and Britain are currently doing in Afghanistan. As mentioned, this current exercise includes not only pursuing and destroying international terrorist networks and apprehending international criminals, but assisting in liberating – and in providing food, humanitarian assistance, and political support in nation-building – for the multi-ethnic citizens of a country held for years in virtual slavery by their own, internationally-recognized government, the Taliban. In what follows, I propose to address the unique and problematic features of *jus ad pacem* and *jus in pace*, by spelling out specific criteria and explanations and justifications for each.

BACKGROUND: "ON THE VERY IDEA OF *JUS AD PACEM* AND *JUS IN PACE*"

Jus ad pacem (or *jus ad interventionem*) refers to the justification of the use of force for humanitarian or peaceful ends.[5] The concept of this use of military force has been much discussed as incidents of it have proliferated since 1990. The discussions of justification, however, have focused mainly upon legitimacy (legality) and legitimate authority: that is, upon analysis of the sorts of entities that might theoretically have the right to use force across established national boundaries in order to restore peace, maintain order, respond to natural disasters, prevent humanitarian tragedies, or attempt to re-build so-called "failed" states.[6] Political legitimacy or "legitimate authority" was originally the paramount criterion of just war doctrine as explicated by Aquinas. It has once again been restored to its pre-eminent status[7] as nations cope with the havoc wreaked by semi-autonomous "non-state entities" (organizations like Hamas and Al Qaeda), as well as to the attempts by such entities to justify their alleged right to violate time-honored principles of *jus in bello* by targeting non-combatants who dwell in regions of the world far removed from their spheres of concern, and who are utterly innocent of any kind of involvement in the political affairs with which they claim to express grievances.

Given the extent of the interest in this topic, and the increasing demands made on military forces for this purpose, from Somalia and

Rwanda to Bosnia, Kosovo, and arguably now even Afghanistan, these discussions and resulting analyses have been surprisingly unfocused, inchoate, and inconclusive. Many authors seem to treat the use of military force for humanitarian purposes as a novel development of the post-Cold War era, when in fact this use of the military has a long and noble history.[8] Other writers and analysts, suspicious of the use of military force for any purpose whatever, have been reluctant to re-consider their selective anti-military bias (forged in the aftermath of the Vietnam war), let alone embrace the emerging notion that national militaries do now, and will, for the foreseeable future, continue to have a positive and important role to play in enforcing justice, protecting individual liberty, and defending fundamental human rights, as well as in performing their more traditional role of defending national borders and protecting the welfare of their own citizens.

What is often overlooked is that *the prospective need for humanitarian military interventions is rapidly becoming the principal justification for raising, equipping, training and deploying a nation's military force.* What we might call the "interventionist imperative" lies at the core of the policy first officially formulated by former Secretary of State Madeline K. Albright in a speech at the US Naval Academy early in 1997. Secretary Albright's position at the time seemed to assert the following moral principle: "When a clearly recognizable injustice is in progress, and when we as international bystanders are in a position to intervene to prevent it, then it follows that we are under a *prima facie* obligation to do so . . . in Kantian terminology, [the interventionist imperative] amounts to an "imperfect duty" of beneficence: we have a duty to prevent harm and injustice when we are able and in a position to do so, but what actions we choose to perform or strategies we choose to devise to carry out this imperative, and the beneficiaries of our protection, are not specified."[9]

Military forces have been used sporadically for centuries for the decidedly secondary purpose of peacekeeping and nation-building in their own nation's political or economic interest. It is extraordinary and utterly without historical precedent, however, to appeal to humanitarian exercises in behalf of this interventionist imperative, rather than to national self-defense or the defense of vital national interests, as the primary justification for the use of military force. It is not at all clear that nations and their citizens, once fully apprised of this reversal or subordination of the traditional ranking of priorities regarding the use of their military, will be willing to provide the human and financial resources for such exercises in the absence of accompanying, and clearly defined national interests. The abysmal failures of United Nations coalition forces in Rwanda and Bosnia dramatically illustrate this problem.

Even if nations (such as the United States and the nations of Western Europe) are willing to accept some variation of the interventionist imperative, the acceptance of this obligation results in a fundamental and profound renegotiation of the implicit "military–civilian contract." I will not rehearse here the traditional terms of that contract, or comment on the nature of the substantial alterations introduced into it by acceptance of the interventionist imperative.[10] Suffice it to say that the terms of the renegotiation are sufficiently substantial to have prompted an ongoing debate within our own nation's military at present, to have evoked a great deal of uneasy criticism and even a few isolated protests (such as military personnel refusing to comply with the uniform dress codes of coalition forces, or refusing to subject themselves to a chain of command outside the direct jurisdiction of their own national leaders), and to have prompted senior military leaders to suggest that a distinct humanitarian and peacekeeping division of our existing military forces should be established and separately maintained.[11]

The final dilemma (again, still incompletely diagnosed) is the unavoidable ambiguity inherent in humanitarian military missions. While it has become popular since the inception of the so-called "Weinberger Doctrine"[12] for military and civilian strategic planners to demand clearly articulated performance goals and well-defined "mission end-states" prior to consenting to the deployment of military force, I have argued that such goals and end-states will always be elusive in the case of humanitarian exercises patterned after what we might label, in contrast, the "Albright Doctrine." This is a problem altogether different from that of claiming that the *imperative* to intervene may be unclear or non-binding. Rather, as in the case of Rwanda, the imperative to intervene may be all too clear, and the attendant obligation "to do something to help those unfortunate people" might be quite strong, but *the means, methods, goals, strategy, and definition of the mission and its successful accomplishment* will remain difficult to define beyond some initial and desperate preliminary aim (to prevent, or to halt, the impending genocide, for example).

ESTABLISHING CRITERIA FOR *JUS AD PACEM*

The foregoing summary of the complicated issues and problems associated with humanitarian military intervention is meant to suggest that such operations are sufficiently unique as to demand their own form of justification, and their own regulations or limitations governing the acceptable use of force (*jus in pace*, or *jus in interventione*). There is a straightforward, almost pedestrian, sense in which *jus ad bellum* does not apply to humanitarian operations: they are not, nor are they intended to be, acts of war on the part of the intervening forces.

There is a profound difference in the expectations and obligations laid upon combatants during conventional hostilities between military adversaries, and intervention with a humanitarian motive. For example, what Michael Walzer terms the "war convention" grants at least a limited license to combatants to act so as to minimize risk to themselves *vis à vis* the enemy, and so to preserve their lives in combat. The same latitude does not carry over so clearly to humanitarian exercises. Should NATO ground troops have been deployed in Kosovo, for example, their mission would clearly not have been simply to make war upon the Serbian military forces in a conventional manner, but to prevent those forces by whatever means necessary from harming unarmed Kosovar civilian noncombatants, and to prevent (insofar as possible) exchanges of fire between the Serbs and the Kosovar separatist militia. Belgian troops in Rwanda were not sent to fight against a hostile army; they were certainly not expected nor licensed simply to destroy marauding Hutu militants, but to prevent them from doing harm to unarmed Tutsis (which might require, but did not necessarily require, their own destruction). We might say that the justification for such actions to begin with, and the subsequent prospects for their enduring legitimacy, rest upon understanding the purpose of the intervening forces as primarily the enforcement of justice, the protection of rights and liberties currently in jeopardy, and the restoration of law and order, rather than straightforwardly defeating (let alone destroying) an opposing military force.

This marked difference in objective means that humanitarian missions are quite unlike conventional combat, in which the main mission is precisely to destroy or render ineffective an opposing army. Instead, the humanitarian moral and legal objectives that putatively provide a justification for overriding national sovereignty through the involuntary imposition of a multi-national military force are seriously compromised if the intervening forces themselves deliberately, or even inadvertently, behave unjustly, violate rights, infringe liberty, or destroy the rule of law. The situation of this intervening military is more to be compared to domestic police forces protecting the innocent public from criminals, rather than to one of two, morally equivalent opposing armies.

77

As a result, military personnel engaged in humanitarian actions may not be entitled simply to protect themselves at all costs from harm, or even to inflict unintentional collateral damage on non-military targets or personnel by the principle of double effect, even though both of these eventualities are commonly excusable under the "war convention" in traditional combatant roles. Rather, humanitarian military forces are expected instead to incur some risk to themselves, and surely *to avoid even inadvertent commission of the kinds of acts they are intervening to prevent.*

This last observation is critical, in that it represents a demand for consistency of means and ends that is essential to the moral justification of these specific kinds of military actions. Everything adduced thus far about the differences of humanitarian intervention from traditional *jus ad bellum* follows from this demand for consistency. Otherwise, for example, one might argue that the role of foreign nationals called in to make peace or keep the peace between warring belligerents was more like that of a helpful stranger coming to the aid of an accident victim, than like that of domestic peace keeping forces fulfilling a solemn oath of office. The former would be under far less strong an obligation to incur risk of harm to self in effecting aid or rescue than would the latter. Neither, however, would be released from the demands of consistency of means and ends: not even the helpful stranger, for example, simply to avoid incurring risk to self, would be excused from pursuing means of rescue that inflicted risk of harm – let alone actual "collateral" harm – upon other bystanders or upon the accident victim in order to carry out the proposed rescue more easily! In the "war convention," during traditional combat, by contrast, the individual soldier is entitled precisely to transfer a substantial (through presumably not an unlimited) amount of risk away from himself and onto the opposing military forces, and even (if unintentionally and otherwise unavoidably) onto the enemy's non-combatants in order to fulfill his mission and preserve his own life, as Walzer's ample and substantive case studies illustrate. It is this difference from traditional warfare, which applies consistently to interventions designed to make or keep peace, and even to those designed eventually to rebuild nations, that I am at pains to highlight.[13]

That said, the practice of humanitarian interventions to date has often diverged significantly from the obligations imposed by this unique, *jus in pace* constraint. Given the aforementioned absence of clarity and purpose of mission in terms of traditional national interests, military and civilian leaders have been led to formulate policy on the fly, with unfortunate results. Beginning with Michael Ignatieff,[14] many commentators have come to lament the resulting emergence of a battlefield doctrine termed "radical force protection," in which field commanders are ordered to suffer few or even no casualties, for fear that public support for a "humanitarian" mission will quickly erode when a nation's own precious human resources begin to be consumed in its pursuit. Many military and civilian analysts have commented upon the unfortunate and paradoxical qualities of this doctrine, in which military forces are willing to kill but not willing to incur risk, and have rightly lamented the unintended success of sophisticated battlefield tactics and "hi-tech" weaponry in exporting most, if not all, of the risk of armed combat to non-combatants. Martin L. Cook laments the sense in which both asymmetric warfare (the possession of vastly superior forces and matériele), and precision-guided weaponry – both of which should have made discrimination between military and non-military targets possible and more precise – have had precisely the opposite effect. The paradoxical quality of "immaculate" or "riskless" war is that it is comparatively "riskless" only for the combatants with superior forces, exporting virtually all risk of harm or death to non-combatants.[15]

The growth of the doctrine of "radical force protection" is a logical outgrowth of the application of conventional just-war doctrine to a situation in which it is clearly inadequate. The doctrine seems to be a reasonable interpretation of the war convention in an instance in which military objectives are poorly defined, and national interests elusive or non-existent (as occurred, for example, in Vietnam). But even the cursory rationale for *humanitarian* military intervention provided above leads to precisely the opposite conclusion: namely, that military forces should expect to incur at least as much, if not more, rather than less risks, for the sake of enforcing international law and establishing peace.

One final feature of the advent of humanitarian uses of force as a principal, if not primary, justification for the retention and use of national militaries is to call into question the notion of the "nation state" as the primary unit of analysis in international relations. Here again, Martin L. Cook makes reference to this profound change in established ways of thinking about international relations since the Peace of Westphalia in 1643.[16] Likewise, Stanley Hoffman has excoriated the "political realists" in international relations for their uncritical and unreflective reliance on this artifice as clearly inadequate to the tasks of thinking about the protection of the lives, liberties, and rights of real biological individuals within the borders of such entities whose normal operations have clearly "gone awry."[17]

While it provides appropriate analysis and response to the behavior of "rogue" or "criminal" states, the legalist model of international relations is largely ineffective in delineating appropriate responses to "failed states," and utterly collapses in the case of "inept" states. International law, grounded in national sovereignty and the protection of identifiable national entities against aggression, is readily able to identify and condemn the behavior of "rogue" states in clear and unambiguous legal terms. Unlike the case of inter-state aggression, however, it is not "against the law" for a nation to "fail," or to prove inept in providing for the welfare of its own citizens.[18] In the case of true failure, as in Rwanda, there are at least reasonably clear guidelines for peacekeeping established within the United Nations Charter that *permit* (but do not, as we have unfortunately discovered, *require*) outside intervention to restore peace and order.[19] It is the robustness and moral force of these legal permissions that Walzer seeks to clarify and strengthen in order to encompass a situation like Rwanda more effectively.

By contrast, it is neither illegal to be, nor do we have guidelines in international law to delineate appropriate responses to, an "inept" state. This is a troublesome lacuna, for "inept" states (unlike "failed" states) retain the semblance of viability, but harbor within (or are powerless to resist from without) terrorism, insurrection, border violations, and countless flagrant violations of civil law that collectively lead to the kinds of problems that require humanitarian intervention.[20]

Inept states constitute a severe problem for the legalist paradigm. Michael Walzer can alternately be thought of as the principal defender of this conception – given his advocacy of legal rather than moral reasoning in international relations – or as a severe critic of this conception – given his profound revisions of its implicit "baseline" usage as that has evolved since the seventeenth century. He is certainly not an uncritical acolyte of the sovereign nation-state. What Walzer clearly does wish to defend is a robust notion of international law, in which sovereign nations as the primary units of analysis can be held strictly accountable in clearly defined, legal terminology for violations of clearly established legal statutes. This he holds to be a vastly superior mode of analysis to case-based moral reasoning characterizing the older rubrics of the just-war tradition. Law is stipulative, while moral reasoning is argumentative. The former is clear (if quite limited in scope), while the latter is inherently vague, even if far-reaching in scope.

The very important qualifications to the baseline model he then proposes, however, in order to generate conditions justifying an international response to terrorism, natural or political disasters, or massive violations of human rights and genocide (for example) seem sharply at odds with the importance he elsewhere attaches to the functional role of the state, and to the justification for the existence of sovereignty he famously develops in *Just and Unjust Wars*. The substantial qualifications he introduces there and subsequently to handle humanitarian disasters returns the focus of moral analysis to the *biological* individuals (their needs and rights) for the sake of whom nations are said to exist. The fate of individuals and their nations in international law rests upon a powerful analogy with domestic law, in which such individuals *themselves* are the primary unit of analysis.[21] In the domestic instance, however, the fundamental equivocation over moral or legal considerability (that is, over what sorts of entities "count," or are protected, in law or morality) is largely absent, arising only in the deliberate decision to treat corporate entities (like businesses, organizations, or local governments) as "fictional persons" under very clearly defined and limited situations. Such equivocation, however, lies at the heart of the international legal dilemma. When do we privilege nations, and when do we privilege their inhabitants? To do the latter almost always involves violations of international statutes and conventions designed to protect the sovereignty of the nation-state precisely for the sake of the peace and security of its inhabitants. This is the heart of what Cook cites as the Westphalian paradigm, and (as he argues) this was all along the carefully concealed source of its fundamental incoherence.

I am now claiming that this dilemma, this equivocation over moral and legal considerability, is most pronounced in the case of inept states. In the case of "rogue" states, the analogy with the behavior of individual criminals in domestic law covers the range of our responses, at least up to the point of punishment (how do we "punish" criminal states like Iraq without harming their innocent inhabitants, for example?). In the case of "failed" states, like Rwanda, there is (at least temporarily), no government or established, defensible borders any longer to recognize in any meaningful way, as their dissolution is what has provoked the crisis to which the international community responds. We do no discernable harm to "Rwanda" if we intervene militarily to prevent factions of its citizenry from destroying one another.

All of this is much less clear in the case of "inept" states like Congo, Sudan, Haiti, or (now very dramatically) Afghanistan. The borders, and the presumably "legitimate" government, are intact, as was the case with the Taliban in Afghanistan. The behaviors that provoke concern (harboring terrorists in Afghanistan, or permitting drug-running, diamond-smuggling, slavery, torture, and extortion in Congo) are not necessarily the acts of the government, let alone do these actions represent the collective will of the people of the nation themselves (in which case they would simply be classified as "rogue states"). Rather, the problem lies instead in the inability or unwillingness (usually the former) of the governments in question to enforce the rule of law or maintain the normal workings of civil society within their own, sovereign borders. These glaring inadequacies of "inept" states, in turn, permit insurgent forces or shadowy international organizations to penetrate and operate within their borders at will, often wreaking as much havoc for the nation's own citizens (as occurred in both Congo and Afghanistan) as for innocents abroad.

It is not "against international law" for a nation to lack the resources to field an effective Coast Guard to ward off terrorists or smugglers (as in Yemen), nor is it against the law for desperately impoverished or ineffective governments to find themselves powerless to prevent terrorist organizations from operating within their borders (as in Sudan and Afghanistan). These are very different situations from promoting or encouraging terrorism, or providing aid and comfort to international criminals, as Iraq, Libya, Iran, and North Korea have been on occasion accused of doing, and which are definable and theoretically punishable offenses under international law. By contrast, it is not clear we can "punish" entities for being poor, or even for being incompetent! Yet the poverty and/or incompetence, when it results in the terrorizing and savage mutilation of citizens by insurgent armies in Congo, or the senseless destruction of innocent workers in the New York Trade Center by tragically misguided fanatics trained on Afghan soil, clearly results in a situation in which some sort of firm response is justified. When one finds oneself, as Walzer does, consistently called upon to invent exceptions to the rules to encompass such situations, it seems to me a clear indication that something is fundamentally wrong with the underlying conceptions to which the exceptions must be granted.

Perhaps we might preserve Walzer's underlying perspective by arguing that an inept state, facing some of the difficulties described above, could request outside forces to come in to help it clear up the drug cartel, or put down the insurgent forces, or root out the terrorists. (The US government pointedly asked the Taliban numerous times for permission to provide assistance to them in expelling Al Qaeda, for example, and in taking its leadership into international custody.) If outside forces are invited in by this inept (legitimate but weak) state, then the use of military force does not constitute an involuntary intervention, and so is not a *prima facie* violation of international law. "Intervention," in the context of international affairs, applies only to a coercive action of some kind by an outside party that takes place within a sovereign state irrespective of the wishes of that state's legitimate government. On the other hand, if the inept state does not agree to call in outside help when help is offered, then it risks becoming a culpable accomplice to the evil within; it loses its legitimacy and becomes a rogue state, even if it is also a weak and ineffectual one, and Walzer's provisions regarding the punishment of rogue states by the international community would then apply.

PRINCIPLES OF *JUS AD PACEM*

Stanley Hoffman has proposed two versions of what he terms a "universal maxim" of *jus ad interventionem*:

(1) collective intervention is justified whenever a nation-state's condition or behavior results in grave threats to other states' and other peoples' peace and security, and in grave and massive violations of human rights;
(2) sovereignty may be overridden whenever the behavior of the state in question, even within its own territory, threatens the existence of elementary human rights abroad, and whenever the protection of the rights of its own members can be assured only from the outside.[22]

These proposals deserve careful consideration, not only on account of the distinguished credentials of their author, but because this two-part proposal constitutes the only substantive criterion thus far put forward to guide and clarify the justification for humanitarian military actions. The first version seems designed to define something akin to "just cause" in classical just-war theory, and applies to events ranging from the Holocaust to the genocidal acts in Bosnia, Kosovo, and Rwanda. The wording, however, appears to tie "threats to other states' and other peoples' peace and security" with "grave and massive violations of human rights" (presumably occurring within the affected nation's borders and not necessarily constituting an external threat). The first clause represents the traditional perspective on a state's behavior within the nation-state system; the second adds an additional provision, similar to Walzer's concern for behavior that "shocks the conscience of humanity." Simply replacing the final "and" with "or" would clarify that one or the other objectionable behavior, and not both simultaneously, are sufficient to invoke justification for armed intervention.

In the second version of his "universal maxim," Hoffman addresses the sovereignty problem explicitly. He seems to be attempting to address at least partially the notion of "legitimate authority." Both versions of the maxim seem to imply that legitimate authority in humanitarian interventions is restricted to "the international community" or to collectivities of some sort.

This raises in turn the most vexing aspect of intervention. Why should not a country (India, or Tanzania, or Vietnam, for example) be empowered to "invade" a neighbor (East Pakistan, Uganda, or Cambodia, respectively) engaged in massive violations of human rights carried out against its own citizens? And why should the "international community" be obliged to wait to prevent what Walzer also describes as "gross and massive" violations of human rights like this until some perceived threat to other states' freedom and security is detected? Hoffman's phrasing of (2) accurately reflects current agreements and UN policies on collective security, but for those who found the UN debacles in Bosnia and Rwanda less than satisfying, it is worth reminding ourselves that these collective humanitarian actions were carried out under the constraints imposed by such existing agreements and conventions.[23]

At present, the criterion of "legitimate authority" appears to be largely taken for granted: all legitimate humanitarian interventions, it would appear, should come about through multilateral debate and decision, and should reflect the collective will of the international community. Unilateral interventions should be prohibited. Does this, however, mean that the international community cannot appoint a single nation to act as its agent (and perhaps should have in the cases cited above)? Likewise, the role of regional security organizations, like NATO, needs to be more carefully explored as a possible legitimate agency. Interventions carried out by such regional security collectivities would neither be unilateral (and so not strictly proscribed) nor sufficiently multi-lateral to qualify as legitimate authorities under conventional understandings of that concept. Perhaps language should be included within any new *jus ad pacem* rubric to address problems, like Bosnia and Kosovo, that seem to fall as responsibilities primarily to a region (that is, Western Europe) rather than to the international community as a whole, permitting the affected region's security and cooperation organization to act as the legitimate authority in such a case.

These questions and problems suggest that it is high time to formulate a more complete list of *jus ad pacem* or *jus ad interventionem* (including some preliminary provisions for restrictions on battlefield conduct, or *jus in pace*), sufficient to govern involvement in humanitarian exercises. While there is no compelling need to require that such criteria perfectly match the seven conventional provisions of just-war doctrine, it will help guide our discussion and ensure a full and comprehensive treatment of the problem if we use the traditional provisions as guideposts for our proposed new formulations.

Justifiable cause for intervention

Let us begin with the humanitarian equivalent of "just cause":

Humanitarian intervention is justified whenever a nation-state's behavior results in grave and massive violations of human rights.

From my comments above, it is apparent that this needs to be understood in two senses:

(a) intervention is justified when these behaviors result in grave threats to the peace and security of other states and other peoples, and
(b) intervention *need not be restricted to such cases*, but may be justified when the threats to human rights are wholly contained within the borders of the state in question.

Legitimate authority

We must ask what, if anything, gives the interventionists the right to ignore international borders and nation-state sovereignty in order to respond to the clear humanitarian emergencies cited in the first provision pertaining to "just cause."

Sovereignty may be overridden whenever the protection of the rights of that states' own citizens can be assured only from the outside.

Hoffman's formulation above contains two additional clarifications:

(a) sovereignty may be overridden whenever the behavior of the state in question, even within its own territory, threatens the existence of elementary human rights abroad;

(b) sovereignty may be overridden even when there is no threat to human rights outside the borders of the state in question, providing the threat to that state's own citizens are real and immediate.

This still leaves the question of "who" is to determine whether such threats are "real and immediate?" Here I propose a second clause that seems to capture widespread concern on the part of most commentators on this problem that such judgments should be collective rather than unilateral, in order to ensure "right intentions" (see below) and exclude ulterior, self-interested motives.

The decision to override sovereignty and intervene must be made by an appropriate collective international body.

This does not, however, mean that the intervention itself must constitute a collective military action, although there are ample grounds for finding that preferable. Instead, in light of our recent experience and the analysis above, this legitimacy provision seems to entail:

(a) The *decision* to intervene can never be undertaken unilaterally; however
(b) a unilateral agent of intervention may be authorized by an appropriate international tribunal; and also
(c) a regional security organization may be authorized by an appropriate international tribunal to undertake a military intervention for humanitarian purposes.

Right intention

Much of the concern over multi-lateralism and collective action concerns the possibility of conflicted and self-interested motives. Paul Christopher notes that Hugo Grotius originally licensed military interventions for clear humanitarian purposes (such as the prevention of cannibalism, rape, abuse of the elderly, and piracy), and simultaneously warned against the likelihood of hidden and less noble agendas, such as greed, religious and cultural differences, and national self-interest, poisoning the presumptive humanitarian and disinterested motivations.[24] These considerations lead straightforwardly to the following restrictions on the use of force for humanitarian purposes:

The intention in using force must be restricted without exception to purely humanitarian concerns, such as the restoration of law and order in the face of natural disaster, or to the protection of the rights and liberties of vulnerable peoples (as defined in the United Nations Charter and the Universal Declaration of Human Rights).

Furthermore, the intentions must be publicly proclaimed and clearly evident without conflict of interest to the international community. Intervening nations and their militaries should possess no financial, political or material interests in the outcome of the intervention, other than the publicly proclaimed humanitarian ends described above, nor should they stand to gain in any way from the outcome of the intervention, other than from the general welfare sustained by having justice served, innocent peoples protected from harm, and peace and order restored. A useful protection against abuse of this provision is for the intervening powers not only to state clearly and publicly their humanitarian ends, but also to set forth a set of conditions under which the need for intervention will have been satisfied, together with a reasonable timetable for achieving their humanitarian goals. Suspicion of possible ulterior motives might be further allayed not only by ensuring the trans-national character of the intervention, but by providing (in the publicly stated proposal to undertake it) for periodic rotation, where feasible, of the specific nationalities involved in carrying out the action.[25]

Last resort

Military intervention may be resorted to for humanitarian purposes only when all other options have been exhausted.

What this means is that good faith efforts by the international community must be made to avert humanitarian disasters within the borders of a sovereign state through diplomatic negotiation, economic sanction, United Nations censure, and other non-military means as appropriate. In practice, this is easier said than done, and could result (as in Rwanda and Bosnia) in delaying necessary deployment of force to prevent a humanitarian tragedy while the "international community" wrings its collective hands ineffectually, worrying whether all other available options have been satisfied. Paul Christopher's sensible proposal from the standpoint of just war theory, applied to humanitarian cases, is that "[this] condition is met when reasonable nonviolent efforts have been unsuccessful and there is no indication that future attempts will fare any better."[26]

Likelihood of success

Johnson and Christopher tend to collapse or blend their concerns for the criterion of likely success into others treating everything from last resort and legitimate authority to the proportionality of war to its stated ends. I favor keeping this criterion distinct, as providing a unique and important constraint on the decision to deploy force for humanitarian reasons.

Military force may be utilized for humanitarian purposes only when there is a reasonable likelihood that the application of force will meet with success in averting a humanitarian tragedy.

This seemingly obvious provision in fact imposes something like Weinberger Doctrine constraints on those whose moral outrage or righteous zeal might tempt them into military adventures for which the intervening powers are ill-prepared and unsuited, or which might make an already-bad situation even worse. Specifically:

(a) a resort to military force may not be invoked when there is a real probability that the use of such force will prove ineffective, or may actually worsen the prospects for a peaceful resolution of the crisis; and

(b) military force may not be employed, even for humanitarian ends, when the international community is unable to define or determine straightforward and feasible goals to be achieved by the application of force.

These Weinberger-like constraints are also important as reassurances to those political representatives of that camp who have been extremely reluctant to embrace what otherwise appears to be an international moral obligation to render humanitarian assistance or prevent avoidable tragedies when we as bystanders are in a position to do so (the "interventionist imperative").

General Anthony Zinni, speaking of his experiences in Somalia,[27] warns us that this traditional criterion limiting military force has a special urgency and ambiguity in the humanitarian instance. Militaries, including the American military, are not primarily oriented or necessarily well-suited to carry out the varieties of tasks a true humanitarian exercise may require. It is difficult in advance to predict just what sorts of activities these may comprise, but they certainly transcend the straight-forward projection of lethal force to include also civil engineering, police and law enforcement, and other functions of a stable civil society. In some instances, military experts on hand may perform, say, civil engineering functions (such as water purification, distribution of food rations, or bridge and road construction) as or even more readily and ably than civilian counterparts. In other instances, as occurred in Somalia, the need to resurrect a moribund legal system and to re-establish police, courts, and a working prison system may push the intervening forces into roles they are ill-prepared and ill-equipped to play, with disastrous consequences. Yet, as Zinni notes, any attempt to avoid engaging in these necessary nation-building exercises is likely to doom the humanitarian mission to failure.

Proportionality of ends

It is not sufficient, however, to demand that military intervention be successful, or that it merely refrain from worsening a bad situation. The NATO air campaign in Kosovo satisfied both constraints, but concerns abound regarding the consequences of the aforementioned doctrine of force protection, and the resulting civilian casualties sustained (for example, from height restrictions imposed on attacking aircraft).

The lives, welfare, rights and liberties to be protected must bear some reasonable proportion to the risks of harm incurred, and the damage one might reasonably expect to inflict in pursuit of humanitarian ends.

In the end, the debates over this aspect of the Kosovo air campaign come down to this provision, although the question of whether to engage in that intervention initially focused on what amounted to discussion of the likelihood of success, as outlined above. Post-mortems and contin-uing analysis of the results of that intervention now routinely raise the question of whether the damage inflicted in an effort to stop the threat-ened genocide by Serbian troops against Kosovars (as a result of force-protection measures imposed, including the unwillingness to commit ground troops to the exercise) was, in the end, unduly large.[28]

It is at this stage that discussions of justifiable military intervention for humanitarian ends shift from the actual discussion of the justification of such intervention, to discussions, similar in some respects to tradi-tional law of armed combat (*jus in bello*), governing the manner in which intervening forces may operate and conduct themselves. The Kosovo debate illustrates this ambiguity clearly. Given what was known of Serbian intentions within the province of Kosovo, based upon substantial prior experience elsewhere in the region (in Bosnia and Herzegovina, for example), there was every reason to expect that the anticipated casualties to be suffered by innocents in the absence of armed intervention of whatever sort would vastly outweigh any foreseeable "collateral damage" that the intervening forces might inadvertently inflict themselves. While any attempt to engage in such calculus is necessarily fraught with difficulty, it seems that most observers agree that this condition (taken as a constraint to be satisfied in the initial decision to deploy military force) was amply satisfied.

What is being debated after the fact, then, is no longer the initial justification of the intervention, but the manner in which it was ultimately carried out. *Jus ad pacem* demands that a reasonable evaluation of the likely overall outcomes (including necessary forms of military deployment and conduct during the intervention) be undertaken before deciding whether to undertake the mission. By contrast, what is now being debated is whether, during a justifiable humanitarian mission, reasonable resulting constraints on the conduct of military forces during the humanitarian mission were violated in selected instances.

Just means, moral means (or, proportionality of means)

The concern that remains unaddressed is something equivalent to the traditional *jus ad bellum* requirement that justifiable wars must be prosecuted by just means. There are a variety of ways of capturing this essential insight, which may well be the most important and difficult provision to achieve in practice for otherwise justifiable, if not downright obligatory, military interventions. This would not be surprising, as strict compliance with *jus in bello*, particularly the principle of discrimination between combatants and non-combatants, remains the most elusive component of just-war theory generally.[29]

The morality of the means employed to carry out a humanitarian intervention, or to achieve its stated goals, must be commensurate with, or proportional to, the morality of the cause or ends for the sake of which the intervention is conducted. Transparently, a military intervention conducted for the sake of protecting human rights or averting a humanitarian tragedy cannot itself rely upon military means of intervention or modes of conduct by military personnel which themselves violate the very rights the interventionists sought to protect, or which provoke a humanitarian tragedy of dimensions similar to the original impending tragedy the interventionists sought to avert.

The last phrase in particular captures the concerns of critics of the NATO bombing strategy, and the concomitant decision against using low-flying Apache combat helicopters or ground forces, for the sake of force protection and the minimization of allied combat casualties in Kosovo. The critics, both military and civilian, are not quibbling about proportionality with the advantage of hindsight, so much as calling attention to this paradoxical feature of the use of deadly force for humanitarian purposes, the details of which I have collectively labeled *jus in pace* or *jus in interventione*.

Humanitarian intervention can never be pursued via military means that themselves are deemed illegal or immoral.

As I have suggested throughout this essay, the provisions and restrictions upon the conduct of military forces that this final provision imposes are not well understood, but are certainly more, rather than less, constraining than traditional *jus in bello* or law of armed combat, while including those tradition provisions as well. Specifically:

(a) captured belligerents must be treated as prisoners of war according to established international conventions, and may not be mistreated or subject to trial or sentence by the intervening forces;
(b) prisoners of war accused of humanitarian crimes and abuses may be bound over for trial by an appropriate international tribunal;
(c) civilian non-combatants must never be deliberately targeted during a humanitarian military operation;[30]
(d) military necessity during humanitarian operations can never excuse the use of weapons, or pursuit of battlefield tactics, already proscribed as illegal under established international treaties and conventional law of armed combat;
(e) finally, military necessity during humanitarian operations cannot excuse tactics or policies, such as "force protection," *that knowingly, deliberately, and disproportionately reallocate risk of harm from the peace keeping forces and belligerents to non-combatants*. It is not sufficient that humanitarian military forces simply refrain from excessive collateral damage, or merely refrain from the deliberate targeting of non-combatants. The very nature of intervention suggests that the international military forces (like domestic law enforcement

personnel) must incur considerable additional risk, even from suspected guilty parties, in order to uphold and enforce the law without
themselves engaging in violations of the law.

Paragraphs (a) and (c), and (d) capture the conventional constraints
characteristic of *jus in bello*. Paragraph (b), however, begins to suggest
the character of law enforcement that humanitarian interventions may
entail. Paragraph (b) implies that the intervening forces are not, in the
name of protecting or minimizing casualties among their own personnel, permitted to turn a blind eye toward international criminals operating in their midst, but have the same obligations to apprehend criminals
and enforce justice that their domestic peacekeeping counterparts do.
Moreover, it explicitly states that if, during the course of an armed intervention or afterwards, an apparent perpetrator of criminal actions
such as Slobodan Milosevic or Osama bin Laden is apprehended, then
(as with conventional domestic criminals) the duty of the intervening
forces is to ensure that the accused is properly treated and bound over
for trial in a legal manner.

Why do I suggest this? Let me hasten to say that it is not because
I believe that murderous Yugoslavian thugs or spoiled, vain, and destructive miscreants like bin Laden are somehow especially entitled to
avail themselves of the protections of the law which they have otherwise scorned. Instead, there is an important practical element at work
in this provision. It properly classifies terrorism and its proponents as
"criminals" carrying out "crimes against humanity," rather than digni-
fying their actions as quasi-legitimate acts of "war," or otherwise confer-
ring upon their perpetrators and their shadowy, non-state organizations
the status of statehood. The important domestic analogy is the continuing struggle to avoid "romanticizing" the activities of organized crime
or dissident factions within a nation-state with a quasi-cultural status as
"acts of war," lest we seem to be sanctioning or excusing the resulting
violence and threats to legitimate and established order. No matter how
legitimate the *grievances* of such individuals and organizations may otherwise be found to be, it is vital not to permit them or ourselves to fall
into the fatal trap of somehow legitimating *criminal actions* (whether of
Timothy McVeigh or Osama bin Laden) as if these were some sort of
populist redress of grievance or otherwise-justifiable protest against the
injustices they purport to cite.

It is precisely this recognition of the radically different moral status
of these criminals, and of the international society against which they

have set their faces and directed their actions, that imposes special burdens and responsibilities on the decorum and behavior of intervening forces, sent to enforce and uphold the law. Paragraph (e) thus directly enjoins the as-yet-unresolved paradox posed by the increasing tendency toward force protection in the course of carrying out humanitarian interventions. I suggested in the preceding pages that such tactics evolve as a result of thinking dictated by conventional just-war theory and international relations, according to which national sovereignty and national interests are the primary units of analysis. These serve to define the nature of the limitations placed upon an individual's self-sacrifice during wartime, as described in Walzer's "war convention." Since these provisions are almost always lacking in truly justifiable humanitarian interventions, the concerns they engender, while understandable, are seriously misplaced.

What we require of the intervening forces is not merely that their controlling interests and command structures lack any personal conflicts of interest in the enforcement of justice, protection of rights, and establishment of peace, but that they be willing to incur risk and put themselves in harm's way for the sake of these moral ideals, and with an end of securing (and certainly not themselves threatening or destroying) the blessings of rights and liberty to the vulnerable and endangered victims whose desperate plight initially prompts the international call for military intervention. This is not an imposition of lofty moral idealism, but a simple requirement for consistency of purpose that civilized society routinely imposes upon itself, and particularly upon those who choose to uphold and defend civilization's highest ideals and most essential governing principles. *In humanitarian interventions, as in domestic law enforcement, we cannot and we do not forsake our laws and moral principles in order to enforce and protect them.*

These *jus in pace* criteria, and especially this final provision, are not as strange, stringent, or unreasonable as they may at first seem, since we ask precisely these same commitments of any domestic law enforcement agency or authority. It is, I have argued, in the nature of humanitarian intervention that it not only restores a legitimate role to morality in foreign policy, but that it begins to import some of the more cherished securities and civilizing protections of domestic civil society into the international arena precisely to supplant the anarchy, ruthlessness, and terror that still too often flourish in the darker regions of our new global order.

NOTES

1 James Turner Johnson, *Morality and Contemporary Warfare* (New Haven, CT: Yale University Press, 1999); and "The Just-War Idea and the Ethics of Intervention," in *The Leader's Imperative: Ethics, Integrity and Responsibility*, ed. J. Carl Ficarrotta (Lafayette, IN: Purdue University Press, 2001); Paul Christopher, *The Ethics of War and Peace*, 2nd edition (Upper Saddle River, NJ: Prentice-Hall, 1999). Hereafter cited as EWP.

2 *Just and Unjust Wars*, 3rd edition (New York: Basic Books, 2000), ch. 6.

3 Stanley Hoffman, *The Ethics and Politics of Humanitarian Intervention* (Notre Dame, IN: Notre Dame University Press, 1996). Hereafter cited as EPHI.

4 "The Politics of Rescue," *Dissent* 42, no. 1 (1995), 35–41; "Emergency Ethics," in J. Carl Ficarrotta, *The Leader's Imperative*, pp. 126–39, and *Nation and Universe*, "The Tanner Lectures on Human Values, Volume XI" (Lake City, UT: University of Utah Press, 1990).

5 George R. Lucas, Jr., *Perspectives on Humanitarian Military Intervention* (Berkeley, CA: University of California/Public Policy Press, 2001), pp. 4ff.

6 A state "fails" when its ability to guarantee basic rights and liberties, provide fundamental essential services that constitute a civil society (such as basic medical care, education, banking, commerce, agriculture, and a dependable food supply), and enforce the rule of law *completely evaporates*. This contrasts with the behavior of viable but criminal states ("rogue" states) and what I am calling "inept" states. See Robert S. Litwak, *Rogue States and US Foreign Policy* (Baltimore, MD: The Johns Hopkins University Press, 2000) for an analysis of the former. An inept or incompetent state is one which does a poor or incompetent job in any or several of these categories of essential human needs.

7 In Thomas Aquinas' discussion of the morality of war in *Summa Theologica*, legitimate authority is listed as the first criterion (ahead of "just cause") to be fulfilled. It is Hugo Grotius who first reverses this priority and gives pride of place to "just cause" (specifically eliminating religious wars as eligible categories). Johnson explores this history in *The Holy War Idea in Western and Islamic Traditions* (University Park, PA: Penn State University Press, 1998).

8 Martha Finnemore, "Constructing Norms of Humanitarian Intervention," *The Culture of National Security*, ed. Peter J. Katzenstein (NY: Columbia University Press, 1996), pp. 153–85. See also Paul Christopher's discussion of Grotius on the rationale for humanitarian military intervention as early as the seventeenth century, EWP, p. 192.

9 See *Perspectives on Humanitarian Military Intervention*, p. 10. See also Julia Driver, "The Ethics of Intervention," *Philosophy and Phenomenological Research* 57, no. 4 (December, 1997), 851–70; more recently John W. Lango, "Is Armed Humanitarian Intervention to Stop Mass Killing Morally Obligatory," *Public Affairs Quarterly* (July 2001), 173–92, who argue in favor of such an imperative. It is important to recognize that imperfect duties are no less stringent than

perfect duties. The term "imperfect" refers not to their stringency but their lack of specificity: such obligations do not precisely specify the nature of actions taken to fulfill the obligation ("what sort of good acts should I undertake?") nor do they always specify an obligee ("whom should I choose as beneficiary of my good actions?"). Assuming that interventionism is a species of "good Samaritanism," the obligees are specified, but the precise actions undertaken in their defense are not.

10 Lucas, *Perspectives*, pp. 20–25; see also Martin L. Cook, "The Moral Foundations of Military Service" in *Ethics for Military Leaders*, 4th edn., eds. G. R. Lucas, S. French, P. G. Roush (Boston: Pearson, 2001), pp. 35–43.

11 Cook suggests this possible alternative at the conclusion of the article cited above, and Gen. Henry H. Shelton, US Army, former head of the Joint Chiefs of Staff, made this proposal during his Senate confirmation hearings in 1997. Gen. Anthony C. Zinni, US Marine Corps (retired), however, offers a sharply contrasting perspective: see Lucas, *Perspectives*, p. 65.

12 Caspar W. Weinberger, *Report of Secretary of Defense Caspar W. Weinberger to the Congress*, 5 February 1986 (Washington, DC: US Government Printing Office, 1986), pp. 78f. See my discussion of the contrasts between the Weinberger Doctrine and the Albright Doctrine in "The Reluctant Interventionist" (1997/99), in Lucas, *Perspectives*, pp. 2–13.

13 In point of fact, I think it implausible in the extreme to compare the role of uniformed professionals operating with considerable training and under solemn oath to the nation that deploys them in this effort to that of random passers-by, with no strong obligations to incur risk or avoid unnecessary harm. While no analogy is exact, surely the role of intervening military forces engaged in a humanitarian mission is closer to that of the domestic police in the morally relevant respects than to that of a helpful though otherwise untrained and unobligated stranger who just happens upon an unfolding tragedy. I am grateful to an anonymous Cambridge Press reviewer and to the editors, especially to Don Scheid, for calling this problem to my attention.

14 *Virtual War: Kosovo and Beyond* (New York: Metropolitan Books, 2000).

15 See Martin L. Cook, "Immaculate War: Constraints on Humanitarian Intervention," *Ethics and International Affairs* 14 (2000), 55–66 and Don M. Snider, John A. Nagl, and Tony Pfaff, "Army Professionalism, the Military Ethic, and Officership in the 21st Century," United States Army War College Strategic Studies Institute, December, 1999.

16 He cites this in "The Moral Foundations of Military Service," p. 36.

17 Hoffman, EPHI, 15; see also "The Crisis of Liberal Internationalism," *Foreign Policy* 98 (Spring 1995), 159–77.

18 For a discussion of the legal status of "failed" states, see Anne Julie Semb, "The New Practice of UN-Authorized Interventions," *Journal of Peace Research* 37, no. 4 (July 2000), 469–88.

19 Samantha Power, "Bystanders to Genocide: Why the United States Let the Rwandan Tragedy Happen," *Atlantic Monthly* (September 2001), 84–108.

20 For a catalogue of these problems, see the comments on Somalia by Gen. Anthony C. Zinni (Lucas, *Perspectives*, 53–63), whose former position as CINC-CENT (Commander-in-Chief of the US Central Command) seems almost to have been gerrymandered to include the lion's share of the world's inept states.

21 Walzer, "The Moral Standing of States," *International Ethics*, eds. Beitz, Cohen, Scanlon and Simmons (Princeton, NJ: Princeton University Press, 1985), pp. 217–35.

22 EPHI, 23.

23 Paul Christopher appears to agree that suitable collective bodies should be able to authorize or otherwise post facto legitimate unilateral interventions with clear humanitarian intent: see EWP, 193, 198.

24 EWP, 199.

25 This proposal is suggested by James Turner Johnson (see Ficarrotta, *The Leader's Imperative*, p. 122), but given the extraordinary logistical difficulties of coalition operations to begin with, this additional provision might add an insuperable burden to interventions justifiable on other grounds.

26 EWP, 201.

27 Lucas, *Perspectives*, pp. 53–63; note that this is an eloquent defense and rejoinder to the charges of "mission creep" that were made against that operation initially as the putative cause of its failure.

28 See, for example, Gen. Wesley K. Clark, *Waging Modern War: Bosnia, Kosovo, and the Future of Combat* (New York: Public Affairs Press, 2001) for a discussion of the differences between US and European military and civilian leadership on these questions.

29 Douglas P. Lackey, *The Ethics of War and Peace* (Upper Saddle River, NJ: Prentice-Hall, 1989), pp. 58–97.

30 For a discussion of how this standard convention plays out in humanitarian intervention, see James Turner Johnson, "Maintaining the Protection of Noncombatants," *Journal of Peace Research* 37, no. 4 (July 2000), 421–48.

Chapter 6

Bombing to rescue?: NATO's 1999 bombing of Serbia

HENRY SHUE

Many of the targets of NATO's bombing of Serbia in 1999, as announced, were said to fall into a category relatively unfamiliar to people outside the military. I will first distinguish a possible bombing strategy aimed at these targets as officially described from the two more familiar kinds of bombing strategies conventionally referred to as "denial" and "punishment." Then I will turn to the vexing and important questions of whether the alleged third kind of strategy was actually implemented and whether what was in fact done ought to be permitted by law or morality.

A bombing campaign of classic "denial" directly confronts the military forces on the other side and attempts to destroy those forces to the extent necessary to coerce them. Traditionally, the targets are, for the most part, in the theatre of battle. Bombing with the purpose of "punishment," on the other hand, tries to win the war indirectly by "punishing" the society, thereby breaking its will, or destroying its morale, in the hope that the general populace will somehow make their government stop fighting, even while, in military terms, it is still capable of fighting. Thus punishment aims at surrender short of full coercion; its targets tend to be outside the field of battle. Bombing for the purpose of societal punishment was often called "strategic bombing," which appears to have been a bit of persuasive labelling designed to imply that it is cleverer than denial bombing that – the hint is – unimaginatively merely attacks the enemy force.

As most people who speak of the "Kosovo bombing" know, the majority of NATO's bombs and missiles struck Serbia proper and its infrastructure, not the Serbian military, paramilitary, and police in Kosovo. This bombing, then, physically fits the geographic pattern of strategic bombing for punishment purposes in that the targets are outside the military theatre, taking the theatre to have been Kosovo. NATO's bombing looks, then, like "punishment," or strategic bombing. Few, however, would any longer attempt to justify it morally, and its illegality was strongly re-affirmed after World War II in the 1949 *Geneva Conventions*. Further, strategic bombing has been devastatingly critiqued on military grounds in Robert A. Pape's book, *Bombing to Win*.[1] Pape maintains that strategic bombing for punishment has invariably failed. Bombing for punishment, according to Pape, has *never* been a decisive factor in *any* military victory. In every case, the bombs would have been better used, from a military point of view, against the military forces, at the front, for denial, however uncleverly obvious a thing to do that may appear to be. Strategic bombing is supposed to provide the smart indirect route to victory. Unfortunately, it is based on a merely wishful hypothesis that if the civilians are made to suffer enough, they will somehow be willing and able to stop the war. The German civilians in World War II were not willing, even if they had been able, to stop Hitler, while Iraqi civilians in the Gulf War were not able, even if they had been willing, to stop Saddam Hussein. In both wars (and, according to Pape, in every war in which punishment bombing has been attempted) victory was actually gained at the front by military forces, including air forces insofar as they directed their attacks in theatre.

One of Pape's most compelling specific theses is that the myth of strategic bombing rests on what I would call the missing mechanism. The basic idea of strategic bombing, starting with the prophet of airpower, Giulio Douhet, was that if (1) one could terrorize or de-moralize the general civilian population, then (2) the government would give up the war.[2] The missing mechanism is whatever political lever is supposed to connect (1) to (2). As is now well known, strategic bombing tends counter-productively to stiffen, not weaken, the target population's will to resist, in any case. But even if the partisans of strategic bombing had gotten that first step right, how is a de-moralized population supposed to make its (frequently authoritarian) government stop the war at a time when it is far more difficult, and dangerous, to oppose the government than in peacetime? Pape's basic conclusion is that the case for strategic bombing rests upon wishful thinking about political action that will obviate the need to prosecute the war militarily.

Bombing for punishment, strategic bombing, could be justified *only if* it were effective. Such high levels of destruction could not possibly satisfy even the requirement of proportionality unless they were productive of great effect, instead of being, as they are, ineffective or counter-productive. If Pape is correct, and strategic bombing does virtually no good from a military point of view, then nothing is achieved that could possibly outweigh the enormous civilian damage that is done. Therefore, any attempt to provide a moral justification by claiming that proportionality is satisfied even if non-combatant immunity, or discrimination, is violated, or ignored, cannot get started. For there is no military good against which the civilian harm could be weighed. What Pape establishes is that even those willing to flout the principle of non-combatant immunity still have no grounds for a possible justification! Strategic bombing undeniably violates one of the two fundamental principles for the conduct of war, discrimination, and cannot even begin to satisfy the other, proportionality. Given that both principles must separately be satisfied, strategic bombing is about as far from being defensible as military conduct can get.

"Classic" strategic bombing has, as a necessary element, a particular intention – the intention to break the will of the civilians in the hope that the suffering civilians will then find a way to make their own government stop the fighting, even while it is still capable of continued resistance. But "shock," which may seem cleverly brutal, does not in reality work. We do not have a single clear example – certainly, using conventional bombing – of a successful implementation of the punishment strategy, and Pape argues further that even Hiroshima and Nagasaki are not examples of a successful punishment strategy because the Japanese surrender resulted from the impending entry into the Asian conflict of Soviet ground-troops, not from the civilian slaughters wreaked by US attacks on those two cities.[3]

Now, as I mentioned, the 1999 bombing of Serbia fits the geographical profile of strategic bombing in the sense that the bombs and missiles, for the most part, struck, not forces on a battlefield in Kosovo, but installations on the home front. For example, Michael Ignatieff quotes a well-informed friend in Belgrade as saying of the NATO bombing: "It was vandalism whose main purpose was to intimidate the population."[4] The official rationale provided by NATO, however, was not the usual strategic-bombing story about destroying morale and about shock producing submission that American and British proponents of airpower have often been willing to offer. The stated rationale was not that if NATO made Serbian civilians suffer enough, they would overthrow Milosevic. The official rationale was rather that the bombing within Serbia was mostly aimed at infrastructure; and the infrastructure was conceived as neither purely military nor purely civilian, but as being in an intermediate category that constitutes legitimate military targets. Thus, the bombing of infrastructure is presented as a third category: extra-theatre denial. Its purpose is denial, military coercion; but unlike classic denial, and like punishment, its targets are outside the military theatre. While punishment's goal is to break the civilians' will, that is not the announced purpose of infrastructure bombing, or anyhow not the primary purpose. The main goal is, instead, said to be to thwart the military efforts of the adversary, not by confronting the military directly, but by, for example, depriving the military of energy: electricity and oil.

Thus, one might consider possible targets of bombing as coming in three crude categories. Troops, and tanks, and military ships and planes are clearly and purely military targets. Bombing them is bombing combatants. Hospitals and schools and residences, at the other extreme, are clearly and purely non-military. Bombing them is bombing non-combatants. It is pure punishment. In the middle lies infrastructure, which, as is now often said, is "dual-purpose." NATO appears usually to have been implying that its attacks upon infrastructure were aimed either exclusively or primarily at the infrastructure's military functions and thus that these attacks amounted to extra-theatre denial, a third kind of bombing strategy.

Of course, there have always been difficult borderline cases for the distinction between combatant and non-combatant. But the existence of gray cases does not disprove the existence of black cases and white cases. Infrastructure, however, is not so much straddling the fence as clearly being on both sides. If radar and missiles designed to bring down attacking aircraft cannot function without electricity, electricity-generating plants then serve a vital military role. But operating rooms in hospitals and water-purification plants also do not function without electricity, and they are both central for civilian life. Electricity-generating plants clearly have dual functions. Some functions are entirely military, and some functions are entirely civilian. This is dual-purpose in a deep sense. A "dual-purpose" missile can carry either a nuclear or a conventional warhead. Its dual purposes are "disjunctive"; that is, it can carry one or the other, but not both warheads simultaneously. Electricity-generating plants, by contrast, are dual purpose in a "conjunctive" sense; they provide energy to both operating theaters in hospitals and anti-aircraft radar simultaneously. So the question is: which, if any, conjunctively dual-purpose facilities are morally legitimate targets? To ask a somewhat different but closely related question: which dual-purpose targets could justifiably be included as targets in a bombing campaign with the purpose of denial, rather than punishment?

Unfortunately, the laws of war seem to be fairly clear. I say "unfortunately," because they seem to make virtually all dual-purpose facilities possible military objectives. Here is the first half of the standard definition of a military objective from the most authoritative source, 1977 *Protocol I*, Article 52:2: military objectives are "those objects which by their nature, location, purpose or use make an effective contribution to military action."[5] Thus, a facility that contributes to military action among other things, if the contribution is effective, can be a legitimate military target, irrespective of how much it may also contribute to civilian actions. The thesis of this chapter is that this is an extremely indulgent legal definition and ought on moral grounds to be tightened up.

Now it is important that the preceding quotation so far gives only one of two necessary conditions of an object's being a military objective. In addition to being an object which "makes an effective contribution to military action," as specified in the clause just quoted, it also must, as Article 52:2 immediately continues by saying, be an object "whose total or partial destruction, capture or neutralization, in the circumstances ruling at the time, offers a definite military advantage." This second requirement recognizes that, although a certain facility may indeed make a military contribution for the adverse party, the destruction of the object in the circumstances at hand may not contribute sufficiently to the military goals of the side that would destroy it to justify its destruction there and then. The jurisprudence has built up a fairly clear understanding of "definite military advantage," and this provides a significant further limitation on what may be attacked.[6] I do not mean to minimize this second necessary condition, but in this chapter I will focus exclusively on the first. That is, I will focus on the fact that making a military contribution is sufficient to bring an object into the arena of military objectives; I will not in future instances add that it might, even so, be the case that its destruction in the circumstances ruling at the time would still not offer an adequately "definite military advantage" fully to justify attacking it. Generally I will refer to a facility as a "possible military objective" if it satisfies the first clause requiring that a facility make an effective military contribution, and I will leave aside the further issue of whether it fully qualifies as a military objective in view of its destruction's offering a definite military advantage to its attacker. The latter is an important additional limitation on attacks; my concern here is simply the height of the first hurdle, not the height of the second.

On my understanding of the current laws of war, the electricity-generating plants and oil refineries and at least a lot of the other infrastructure of Serbia were possible military objectives, and the bombing of them by NATO may not have been in violation of international law, at least not of the legal definition of military objective in (the first half of) Article 52:2.[7] This particular legal understanding ought, on moral grounds, to be changed – at least, this is my thesis. The reason is basically that the definition is so liberal that it undermines the purpose that the combatant/non-combatant distinction was intended to serve. It undermines it, I believe, almost as completely as would permission for the now clearly impermissible strategic bombing strictly for the purpose of punishment.

Here is the fundamental reason for moral concern about the first part of the definition of military objectives in the *1977 Geneva Protocol I*, Article 52:2, which allows a facility's serving a military function to be sufficient for its being a possible military objective, irrespective of the civilian functions also served. The combatant/non-combatant distinction was supposed to prevent total war. It was supposed to allow some minimal form of human society to continue during war. Even while the young people fought each other on parts of the land, the sea, and the air, elsewhere babies were still to be born, and stroke victims nursed back to health, so that when the victory in battle came for one side or the other, the ordinary people in both societies could continue their lives. The state on one side might have been destroyed, but neither society would have been destroyed.

Perhaps, as the pacifists say, adherents to just-war theory (like me) are simply dreaming of neat, little compartmentalized wars that are, at best, rare and more likely illusory. In any case, if we grant that all the infrastructure of a modern society – especially its energy sources (electricity-generation and oil-refining) – that by its "nature, location, purpose or use make[s] an effective contribution to military action," irrespective of its simultaneous contribution to civilian life, can be a legitimate target – that anything that is partly military in function can be totally legitimate as a target – then we have effectively abandoned the principle of non-combatant immunity. We are left, at best, with some vague principle of proportionality, which we all think must be true, but none of us knows how to specify with meaningful precision.

What should be done? What I believe is essential is to find a way, conceptually and legally, to wall off the most vital infrastructure, the infrastructure that is indispensable for minimal decent human life. We should start exactly where, in the Gulf War in 1991 as well as in Serbia in 1999, the targeteers started – with the energy sources for the major concentrations of population.[8] One cannot deny that electricity generation and oil refining are highly useful for the military, but they are also absolutely indispensable for civilian use for minimal safety, minimal sanitation, and minimal health care. My suggestion involves following a kind of basic-rights logic.[9] The general thought is to consider conjunctively dual-purpose facilities and ask, not, as *Protocol I*, Article 52:2, would, "Do they make an effective contribution to military action?" – obviously they do – but to ask, instead, something like: "Can the most utterly uninvolved civilians maintain a minimally decent human life without this facility?" Will people have clean water to drink, or will the water be polluted by untreated sewage because of the lack of electricity? Can a potential mother whose baby can be delivered only by Caesarean section get the surgery, or will the baby, or mother, or both, be casualties of war for lack of hospital electricity?

Then the most vital portions of the infrastructure would go on a short list of illegitimate targets. In effect (the first half of) the current legal definition of military objectives should be reversed. A facility that is conjunctively dual-purpose, but makes an irreplaceable contribution to vital civilian needs, should be treated as if it were entirely civilian – just as it is now treated as if it were entirely military. Instead of asking, as is in effect done now, "Does this electricity plant contribute to the adversary's military capability?", we would ask: "Is the protection of this facility indispensable to the maintenance of a minimally decent life?" If so, the plant would be excluded from the list of possible military objectives; it would be on the short list of completely illegitimate targets.

A DOUBLE-EFFECT DEFENSE OF ARTICLE 52:2

A serious question about this proposal is whether attacks upon dual-purpose targets can be defended using a somewhat modified version of a double-effect analysis. Accordingly, I would next like to examine this theoretical possibility. Double-effect analysis was of course designed to deal with the ineliminable fact that much of what we do causes not only the effects we intend but also effects we do not intend. The actual effects of action are often double: the intended ones and the unintended ones. This is true at least as frequently during war as at any other time.[10]

The double-effect analysis is most importantly the juncture at which consideration of the two core principles for the conduct of war, discrimination (or non-combatant immunity) and proportionality, are brought together. Two necessary conditions must, therefore, be met simultaneously but independently: absolutely no civilian death or civilian destruction may be intended (discrimination); and the total civilian death and civilian destruction, even where unintended, must not be excessive compared to the good done (proportionality). In the simplest case, two objects are situated in close proximity; one is a legal military objective and one is not. It is physically impossible to destroy the military objective, for instance a tank, without destroying or damaging the object that is not a military objective, for instance a house by which the tank is passing. The proportionality assessment required by double-effect analysis mandates that one ask: how important is it to destroy this tank while it is near this house – can it wait until the house is safely left behind? Nevertheless, it is conceivable that a well-grounded answer is: no, it is urgent to destroy the tank before it can fire another round, so the tank and the house must both be destroyed if there is no other way to destroy the tank quickly enough. Thus, destruction of the tank is the intended and – in the context of war – good effect; and destruction of the house is the foreseeable but unintended bad effect. And destruction of the house is not the means to immobilization of the tank: the house is not being directly attacked so that it will collapse on the tank. If the tank could be destroyed without harming the house, that would be done – destruction of the house has no advantage, even as a means.

The obvious difficulty about applying double-effect to the case of bombing a dual-purpose target, by contrast, is that in this instance, unlike the simple case, only one object is involved. Rather than a tank that is a military objective and a house that is not, there is a single object, say, a bridge, that has both military functions and civilian functions. If one targets the bridge, one cannot claim that one did not intend to destroy the bridge that farmers use to go to market. For it is the same bridge that the army uses to move up tanks, which one did intend to destroy. There is only one bridge, and this bridge was intentionally bombed. Now, I would very much like to think that the moral defense of attacks on dual-purpose objects and facilities, such as bridges that have both military and civilian functions, faces insuperable problems. I would be pleased if it turned out that the best defense of bombing dual-purpose facilities turned out to be sophistical and, say, to involve hair-splitting of a morally objectionable kind. Unfortunately, although the moral defense does involve drawing a distinction, I cannot honestly maintain that this distinction reflects anything other than a substantial and relevant difference.

Yes, there is a sense in which the attack on the bridge was an intentional attack on an object with a civilian function – farmers used the bridge to take their produce to market – but it could be perfectly sensible to maintain that the bridge not only was not attacked because of its civilian function but was attacked in spite of its civilian function. This would be true if the bridge was attacked only because of its military function and would not have been attacked if it had not had the military function. Suppose some bridges are too narrow to admit, or too light to support, a tank; other bridges accommodate tanks nicely; and only the latter, and none of the former, bridges are bombed. This certainly does not prove, but it is perfectly compatible with, the claim that bridges are being bombed only because of their military functions. The intention is to destroy bridges with military functions, and there is no intention to destroy bridges with civilian functions. That some bridges with civilian functions are being destroyed is as unintentional as was the destruction of the house by the attack that destroyed the tank.[11]

It is important that once the bridge has been bombed it is as impossible for the farmers to bring produce to market as it is for the army to advance tanks to the front, but this fact should properly be handled by the proportionality assessment (will the farmers' potential customers starve? How important would more tanks have been to casualty levels in the battle?). One object – a bridge – has two descriptions, which is after all not unusual; under one description it is intentionally bombed, but under the other description it is bombed unintentionally. To maintain that this is tendentious hair-splitting would require maintaining that any police officer who arrests a subject against whom there is compelling evidence, but who happens also to belong to a certain ethnic group, is engaged in 'racial profiling' directed against the ethnic group in question. A second description can correctly apply to an object without being the primary description under which an agent acts toward the object. The applicability of the second description cannot simply be ignored – this is why in the bombing case the proportionality assessment must be conducted unless actual consequences are to be ignored – but it is impossible to insist that, because a description is correct, it must be the description of the object under which the action toward the object was judged to be desirable. Accordingly, it is impossible to maintain that because the person arrested was, say, an African-American, the officer intentionally arrested an African-American, or that because the bridge had a civilian function, the bombing intentionally targeted a civilian bridge. The arrest of an African-American and the bombing of a civilian bridge may each have been unintended, and even have been considered undesirable.

RESTRICTING ARTICLE 52:2 NONETHELESS

I can, then, see no compelling way to object to all cases of the application of the first half of the definition of military objective in Article 52:2 of *1977 Protocol I*. Sometimes, I believe, it can be justified to attack a dual-purpose facility, especially when the significance of its military function overwhelms the significance of its civilian function. The justification in these cases appears to be essentially the same as the justification provided by any double-effect analysis, although perhaps one degree more subtle because it involves one object with multiple descriptions rather than multiple objects. Since what I am conceding is that in some cases the bombing of a dual-purpose target will indeed pass a proportionality test, one might conclude that the matter can safely be left there, with proportionality standing as the main barrier against attacks on some dual-purpose facilities. We will next be able to see, however, that the definition of military objective in paragraph 2 needs to be narrowed. While it is not totally unacceptable, it is also not fully acceptable as it stands. Article 52:2 now has the effect of certifying that all dual-purpose facilities automatically satisfy the principle of discrimination, leaving all moral decisions to be based on whether the principle of proportionality is satisfied as well.[12] This is too quick and too permissive: that some dual-purpose facilities qualify as possible military objectives most certainly does not entail that all do.

There is absolutely no reason why all dual-purpose facilities must be treated alike, irrespective of the type and significance of civilian purpose they serve. The dual-purpose facilities that serve vital civilian functions ought to be distinguished from those that do not, by being classified as predominantly civilian objects that are immune to intentional attack. If the civilian function of a dual-purpose facility is not vital, the facility may continue to be treated as if it had no civilian function, as Article 52:2 now treats all dual-purpose facilities without exception. If the civilian function is genuinely indispensable, however, the facility ought in parity to be treated as if it had no military function, in the sense that it is not to count as a possible military objective that may be intentionally attacked. This requires re-writing Article 52:2, or at a minimum authoritatively re-interpreting it. Instead of all dual-purpose facilities automatically being treated as if they were exclusively military, whether they are treated as military or civilian would depend on the importance of their civilian function. Whether the civilian function can be eclipsed should depend strictly upon its importance.

As I indicated in the opening section, the fundamental purpose of the principle of discrimination, resting on the distinction between combatants and non-combatants, is to prevent total war – to preserve as much as possible of civilized social life even in the midst of armed conflict. Granting the admissibility of double-effect analysis already constitutes a giant concession to the fighting of wars: incursions into social life, even when they kill uninvolved persons and destroy ordinary property, are permitted provided that they are both unintentional and proportional to the distinct military advantage gained. Allowing the extent of military good to determine the extent of permissible unintentional civilian harm makes the concession especially great and makes military rationality the dominant consideration in proportional conduct of war. To do otherwise would be "unrealistic," that is, it would be to adopt a pacifist, not a just-war, approach, because it would demand limits on war that might be incompatible with the successful prosecution of warfare. If one's strategy is to attempt to limit, rather than to attempt to abolish, war, one must evidently grant the admissibility of double-effect. I want only to emphasize that this is already a great compromise in the protection of civilized social life and the protection of the most basic rights, including the right not to be killed arbitrarily.

Article 52:2 of 1977 *Protocol I* takes another huge bite out of the protection provided to civilians. Not only may civilians be killed proportionally (relative to militarily determined necessity) provided that their deaths are unintended – all permitted by traditional double-effect analysis – but now, thanks to 52:2, many facilities with civilian functions are to be treated as if they had purely military functions by being classified as possible military objectives. Indeed, every facility with a civilian function but a military function as well – that is, every dual-purpose facility – is to be classified as a possible military objective. This is an extreme measure, groundlessly encroaching upon basic rights and normal life far in excess of any reasonable military requirements.

If the question were: granted that something is partly *X* and partly *Y*, can it reasonably be treated as if it were entirely *Y*? Then the general, commonsense-based answer would be: if the thing is 99 percent *X*, then it would obviously be bizarre to treat it as if it were entirely *Y*.

In other words, even if there are instances in which something that is partly civilian and partly military may reasonably be treated as if it were entirely military, this treatment is not reasonable when the significance of its civilian function dwarfs the significance of its military function. At least at the extremes, one would need to ask: what is the relative significance of the two kinds of function? This is simply a matter of what comports minimally with commonsense, and it involves a broad comparative judgment.

The crucial judgment ought not, I suggest, to balance civilian function with military function, but to make a judgment about an absolute threshold for civilian functioning. The purpose of the principle of discrimination is to protect as much as possible – but certainly to protect an *adequate minimum* – of normal social life from the ravages of war. The performance of certain civilian functions is essential to the maintenance of normal life for children, the aged, and others who indisputably are non-combatants. Specifically which functions these are is an empirical matter and varies among societies and across times and places. Paradoxically, as is frequently noted, more advanced societies have usually become dependent upon functions that less advanced societies have never yet enjoyed and can therefore more readily survive without. For example, Afghanistan in 2001 may have been better able to survive without large-scale, centralized electrical grids than Serbia in 1999 (or Iraq in 1991) because Afghanistan had never enjoyed them, while Serbia was a modern, industrialized society dependent on electricity for essential services. The bombing of infrastructure is, then, not a central moral issue of the war in Afghanistan to remotely the same degree it was in Serbia, and in Iraq in 1991.

In a society like Serbia in which essential services cannot now be maintained without power from a central electrical grid, the electrical grid is providing a civilian function that is indispensable for social life at this time. Where the electrical grid is now serving a vital function, it ought to be immune to attack. This is irrespective, I suggest, of whether the grid is also performing military functions. Where the civilian function is vital to the minimal functioning of the society, the military function ought to be thwarted in some other manner that does not also thwart minimal civilian functioning. The reason is that the deprivation of civilian society of all electrical power will be fatal for non-combatants in such large numbers as to constitute a general failure in the protection that the principle of discrimination is fundamentally intended to provide. To be acceptable, a definition of possible military objectives must not actively frustrate the main purpose of the principle of discrimination. A definition of possible military objectives that permits the general undermining of civilian public health by paralyzing the provision of clean water, medical care, and basic sanitation – as destruction of the electricity grid would in many modern societies (including the US) – is a reduction to absurdity of the project of distinguishing acceptable from unacceptable targets. Such a definition produces the result that no amount of civilian harm is undeniably unacceptable. Article 52:2 has gone to such an indefensible extreme. It ought to be tightened.

NATO'S BOMBING OF SERBIA IN 1999

Pape's *Bombing to Win*, which made the powerful case that strategic bombing had always failed to be important in any military victory, appeared prior to NATO's bombing of Serbia. In a report on the bombing of Serbia produced for the US Air Force by RAND, Stephen T. Hosmer has argued that "the key reason Milosevic agreed to accept the terms presented to him on June 2 [1999] was his fear of the bombing that would follow if he refused."[13] As described by Hosmer, NATO's campaign is an example of successful coercion as distinguished from defeat. It was not that NATO had inflicted so much damage on the Serbian military that it had become unable to continue to fight, that is, had defeated it – quite the contrary, in fact – but that in spite of a substantial continuing capability for military action on the part of his forces, Milosevic felt compelled to cease military action in Kosovo and withdraw the forces. This sounds more like classic punishment than classic denial.

On the testimony of the Serbian leadership gathered by Hosmer, it was more the imagined future bombing than the actual past bombing that led to the acceptance of NATO's terms. But this is merely to restate the point that Serbian forces had not been defeated by actual past bombing – the Serbian military was not damaged to anywhere near the point of being incapable of further resistance – but the Serbian leadership chose to end the fighting in order to avoid losses that were yet to occur. The Serbian state was coerced, not defeated. If one can thus get one's way with a minimum of actual damage, why is this not the best possible outcome?

Some of the explanations for accepting the terms of June 2 quoted from top Serbian leaders by Hosmer are quite bizarre. An "official, described as 'close' to Milosevic and his wife, Mirjana Markovic" told the *New York Times* on June 5: "We knew that the carpet bombing of Belgrade would start the next day after we refused, so what was the choice?"[14] General Pavkovic, the commander of the Serbian Third Army, told Army reservists in July: "The Russians then came back and said we had to accept the Western plan, that we had to take it or leave it. We were told that if we refused the plan, every city in Serbia would be razed to the ground. The bridges in Belgrade would be destroyed. The crops would all be burned. Everyone would die."[15] In August, General Pavkovic, speaking of a "research facility near Belgrade, which housed a cache of some 60 kg of highly enriched uranium," said: "Can you imagine what would have happened had they struck Vinca, like they threatened?"[16] Foreign Minister Zivadin Jovanovic claimed: "It was a most inhumane war. They tried everything but nuclear weapons...I think they were getting out of their minds. NATO commanders were seeking excuses to burn the country and commit further massive killings. So the government...decided not to risk massive genocide by NATO against the whole population."[17]

Now I myself do not believe that the leadership of NATO had any intention of committing "massive genocide," attacking a nuclear research facility housing enriched uranium, carpet-bombing Belgrade, or razing to the ground every city in Serbia. And while I have not met any of the people quoted, I doubt seriously that they themselves believed the wild accusations they were making. These were, after all, defeated and disgraced leaders attempting to portray themselves as having been without any alternative to giving in. The NATO bombing campaign was far from faultless.[18] Yet it was also far from the maniacal genocide portrayed in the preceding quotes by leaders at least some of whom had themselves been conducting a vicious campaign of ethnic cleansing in Kosovo.

Nevertheless, there is enough here to worry about. Lieutenant General Michael Short, USAF, who was to become the commander of the air component of the NATO campaign against Serbia, claims to have said the following to the commander of the Serbian Air Force in the October (1998) preceding the campaign: "The speed and the violence and the lethality and the destruction that is going to occur is beyond anything that you can imagine. If, indeed, you're not going to accept my terms, we need to break this meeting right now. I suggest you go outside, get in your car and ride around the city of Belgrade. Remember it the way it is today. If you force me to go to war against you, Belgrade will never look that way again – never in your lifetime, or your children's lifetime. Belgrade and your country will be destroyed if you force me to go to war." Hosmer notes: "When asked by the VJ general if he 'really' meant what he said, General Short responded, 'Absolutely. This is past the point of bluffing, and professional soldiers don't bluff.' "[19] Fortunately, bluffing or not, General Short was subordinate during *Operation Allied Force* to General Wesley Clark, who refused to authorize any such bombing campaign as General Short would have liked, as General Short has loudly complained ever since.[20] But one possible source for wild expectations on the part of the Serbian leadership is certainly evident!

If tough talk can prevent, or shorten, actual war, it is, however unappetizing, probably to be welcomed. Better that generals should strut than that young people should die. Of course intelligent military leaders generally pay very little attention to rhetoric and instead focus on capability: what is to be feared is not what one individual or another threatens, but what the adversary is capable of doing to you. The genuine threat is capability. Nothing happens without "will" as well as capability, naturally, but when the capability is present, the will can change. It is perfectly clear that NATO, and specifically the US Air Force, is perfectly capable of "carpet-bombing" Belgrade – no matter who says that it will or will not do so. And the general willingness of the United States to use airpower, as distinct from ground troops, is not in doubt.

RAND's Hosmer does not believe, any more than I do, that NATO would in fact have done everything that quoted Serbian leaders claim to have feared. Nor, I would add, would the North Atlantic Council representing the nineteen Nations of NATO ever have dreamed of authorizing everything that General Short might have liked to do. So, as Hosmer notes, "the question naturally arises as to how Belgrade officials could have so badly misread NATO's intentions and freedom of action that they would give credence to future air attacks as indiscriminate and destructive as those described above" (in the quotations from Serbian leaders).[21] And Hosmer goes on to present six reasons, some accurate perceptions and some misperceptions, to explain Serbian fears of indiscriminate bombing to come if the terms presented on June 2 were not accepted.

I want to focus, however, on dual-purpose infrastructure that, as I understand the international law, can constitute possible military objectives under Article 52:2, and specifically the electricity grids that I have already been emphasizing. Under the sub-title, "Winter Would Magnify the Hardships of Bombing, Particularly Electricity Outages," Hosmer offers the following speculations about Milosevic's thought-processes: "Milosevic further knew that if there were no reconstitution or containment of the damage being inflicted on Serbia, the coming winter would greatly magnify the hardships of the Serbian people. In this respect, the prospect of a prolonged NATO denial of electric power was undoubtedly the most worrisome contingency, as it would severely affect the most basic needs of the citizenry."[22] Hosmer buttresses the hypotheses about Milosevic's reasoning with such facts as the following: "Widespread electricity outages could threaten the heating of 75 percent of the homes in the FRY [Former Republic of Yugoslavia]"; and "electricity outages would prevent the use of the deep freezers on which more than 50 percent of Yugoslavs typically depend for food storage."[23]

On the one hand, Hosmer offers no direct evidence that Milosevic thought specifically about deprivation of electricity. On the other hand, the objective situation would certainly have made electricity a sensible focus if Milosevic cared either (1) directly about the welfare of Serbian citizens or (2) about the effects of their misery on his own grip on political power by way of some mechanism by which suffering citizens could translate their misery into effective political opposition (and thus indirectly about their welfare). It is this crucial mechanism – the political mechanism for translating misery into effective political opposition – that Pape found has been consistently missing in the past, especially of course in authoritarian systems. Of course Milosevic might have feared that effective opposition would develop even if it would not in fact have; this is another respect in which it is the fear that is felt that matters to the choices made, not how well grounded the fear is.[24]

Suppose Hosmer's speculation about the psychological importance for Milosevic of the electrical grid is correct. If it is, then entirely without the war crimes supposedly promised by General Short (bombing Belgrade into unrecognizability for generations) or the war crimes supposedly expected by General Pavkovic (bombing of nuclear facility at Vinca, plus every city in Serbia), the prospect of NATO bombing that would have fully accorded with *1977 Protocol I* and that could have been reasonably expected to come after June 2 may well have coerced agreement from Milosevic. The good news, then, would be that airpower used in accord with current international law can coerce. The situation would be somewhat analogous to my fictional example in which, although I would never physically harm my students, they all turn in their work on time for fear that I will. Suppose that NATO would never intentionally strike a target that did not qualify in accord with international law as a military objective but could nevertheless inspire fears of such extremely indiscriminate attacks that its adversaries would accept its terms. Would this not be the best of everything?

The bad news, as I have already explained, however, would be that, because of the definition of military objective in Article 52:2, attacks are permitted on dual-purpose infrastructure – most notably, electricity supply – that, in Hosmer's words, "would severely affect the most basic needs of the citizenry." Further troubling is that what I consider "bad news" can be seen, from a political point of view, as good news: an obdurate adversary can be coerced by being made to fear attacks that would severely affect the most basic needs of ordinary people without those attacks needing actually to be conducted (and without its being the case that the misery caused by those attacks would in fact lead to effective political opposition to the regime, provided the regime fears that they would produce effective opposition, as Hosmer, among others, supposes happened in the case of Milosevic).

It is here that we must return to the question of the kind of bombing in fact conducted by NATO: specifically whether NATO was indeed engaged in a distinctly third kind of bombing, namely denial outside of theatre through the destruction or damage of infrastructure that is militarily vital apart from its civilian functions. The answer, if one accepts Hosmer's account, is perfectly clear: this was not a distinct third type of bombing the only purpose of which was denial but the targets of which were outside the military theatre. On the contrary, it was denial and punishment combined – not a distinct third type, but merely the two original types merged. Hosmer concludes: "The vast majority of these targets [in Serbia proper, as distinct from Kosovo] were of the 'dual use' variety in that they served a civilian as well as a military function, and ... part of the rationale for attacking these targets was to cause the civilian population to bring pressure on the Belgrade government to terminate the conflict."[25] And earlier, in more detail, Hosmer makes it clear that NATO not only hoped for and welcomed the civilian destruction, but intended it: "Attacks on Serbia's electric generating system caused particularly severe hardships, as the resulting power shutdowns often denied the public both electricity and running water. While contending that the strikes on infrastructure targets had legitimate military-related purposes, NATO officials also acknowledged that the attacks were *aimed* [emphasis added] in part at damaging the quality of life so that suffering citizens would start questioning the intransigence of their political leadership. Lieutenant General Short [USAF], the NATO air component commander, hoped that the distress of the Yugoslav public would undermine support for the authorities in Belgrade."[26] This raises questions of both morality and legality, which in conclusion I now take up in order.

In spite of the fact that double-effect analysis was designed precisely in order to provide some "wiggle room" for the military – in particular, to allow for (proportional) "collateral damage" – NATO's bombing of Serbia fails the moral test. A certain amount of civilian misery unavoidable in the process of denying enemy forces valuable military functions could have been justified. However, attacks upon the electrical grid that welcomed the civilian misery in fact caused cannot be morally justified employing double-effect analysis. If the civilian misery is *welcome*, then it is *part of the plan*: the civilian misery is the intended means of provoking the political opposition that is in turn the means of coercing the regime into accepting terms. But the principle of discrimination, taken into account in the second and third stages of double-effect analysis, prohibits intentional civilian destruction as either end (second stage) or means (third stage). NATO's bombing of Serbia flagrantly violated the principle of discrimination by intentionally causing civilian distress as a means to producing acceptance by Milosevic of NATO's terms (by way of his hypothesized worry about losing political power to an aroused public unwilling to endure further misery, especially perhaps loss of electricity during the winter to come). Hosmer concludes that the bombing strategy worked. I conclude that it violated the fundamental principle for the conduct of war: respect for the lives and property of non-combatants. Nothing prevents our both being correct.

What about legality? Since under Article 52:2 dual-purpose facilities can qualify as possible military objectives, NATO's target selection does not appear to violate the first half of 52:2 itself. Indeed, my central thesis is that precisely because Article 52:2 seems to allow – and arguably, even encourages – immorality in the serious form of violation of the principle of discrimination, the extreme permissiveness of 52:2, taken in itself, ought to be changed. I do not believe that it ought to be legal intentionally to deprive civilians of goods and services indispensable for their survival, irrespective of whether doing so is an intended end or an intended means.

I believe, then, that, insofar as the attacks on dual-purpose targets in Serbia were intended to cause civilian harm, they fail to survive a double-effect analysis and are therefore immoral. I am not certain whether they were also illegal, but if not, I take this as a reason to change the law so as to make them unambiguously illegal as well.[27]

NOTES

1 Robert A. Pape, *Bombing to Win: Air Power and Coercion in War* (Ithaca, NY and London: Cornell University Press, 1996).

2 See Giulio Douhet, *The Command of the Air* (New York: Coward-McCann, 1942). For the influence of Douhet's speculations on formative strategic thinking in the US Air Force, see Ronald Schaffer, *Wings of Judgment: American Bombing in World War II* (New York and Oxford: Oxford University Press, 1985), pp. 23–24.

3 On "nuclear punishment" see Pape, *Bombing to Win*, ch. 4, "Japan, 1944–1945." On the general question of whether "shock" is likely to produce submission, my undergraduates at Cornell noted that the US reaction to the shock of the attacks on civilians on 9/11 hardly supports the speculative hypothesis, which seems to have originated in the early theorizing of Douhet about airpower. The speculation that shock must somehow lead to submission dies hard, however, as we will later see. Fanatics for airpower always suggest that if a shock did not work, it simply was not big enough or sharp enough.

4 Michael Ignatieff, *Virtual War: Kosovo and Beyond* (New York: Henry Holt, 2000), p. 150.

5 *1977 Protocol I Additional to the Geneva Conventions of 1949*, Art. 52:2 [1125 U.N.T.S., adopted June 8, 1977].

6 See Robert K. Goldman, "The Legal Regime Governing the Conduct of Air Warfare," in *Needless Deaths in the Gulf War: Civilian Casualties During the Air Campaign and Violations of the Laws of War*, A Middle East Watch Report (New York and London: Human Rights Watch, 1991), pp. 27–64, esp. pp. 36–37.

7 I leave aside a number of dubious cases of target selection. See subsequent note citing the reports on the NATO bombing by Amnesty International and Human Rights Watch.

8 In the US war in Afghanistan, starting in 2001, the main issues about the protection of civilians may involve the acceptability of various tactics on the part of special operations forces, including the responsibility for avoiding reliance upon dated or false intelligence. See, for example, Craig S. Smith, "After Green Beret Operation, Townspeople Have Questions about Bound Bodies," *New York Times*, January 28, 2002, p. A6, cols. 1–6.

9 Demonstrating that I have had, at most, one idea – see Henry Shue, *Basic Rights*, 2nd edn. (Princeton: Princeton University Press, 1996).

10 The most convincing brief recent treatment of double effect for the case of war is, I believe, in A. J. Coates, *The Ethics of War* (Manchester: Manchester University Press, and New York: St. Martin's Press, 1997), pp. 239–72. I have also discussed double effect briefly in the context of just-war theory in general in Henry Shue, "War," in *Oxford Handbook of Practical Ethics*, ed. Hugh LaFollette (Oxford and New York: Oxford University Press, 2002).

11 I suppose someone might try to object that the destruction of the civilian bridge is a means to the destruction of the military bridge. Unfortunately, again, the sophistry and artificiality seem to lie with the objector who is trying to maintain that the destruction of an object is a means to the end of destroying that same object, which strikes me as incoherent.

12 I have discussed some general reasons for doubting the adequacy of the proportionality principle in "War," *Oxford Handbook of Practical Ethics*, ed. LaFollette (Oxford: Oxford University Press, 2003), pp. 734–61.

13 Stephen T. Hosmer, *The Conflict over Kosovo: Why Milosevic Decided to Settle When He Did*, MR–1351–AF [Project AIR FORCE] (Santa Monica, Calif., and Arlington, Va.: RAND, 2001), p. 91.

14 Hosmer, *The Conflict over Kosovo*, p. 94.

15 *Ibid.*

16 Hosmer, *The Conflict over Kosovo*, p. 95.

17 *Ibid.*, p. 96.

18 See Amnesty International, *"Collateral Damage" or Unlawful Killings? Violations of the Laws of War by NATO during Operation Allied Force* [NATO/Federal Republic of Yugoslavia], EUR 70/18/00 (London: Amnesty International, 2000); Human Rights Watch, *Civilian Deaths in the NATO Air Campaign* [NATO] (New York and London: Human Rights Watch, 2000); and *Final Report to the Prosecutor by the Committee Established to Review the NATO Bombing Campaign Against the Federal Republic of Yugoslavia* (The Hague: International Criminal Tribunal for Yugoslavia, 2001).

19 Hosmer, *The Conflict over Kosovo*, p. 100 and p. 100, n. 24.

20 See John A. Tirpak, "Washington Watch: Short's View of the Air Campaign," *Air Force Magazine*, vol. 82 (September 1999); I am grateful for this reference to Margarita Petrova. "Had he been free to structure the air effort as he wanted, Short would have arranged for the leaders in Belgrade to wake up 'after the first night . . . to a city that was smoking. No power to the refrigerator and . . . no way to get to work' " (p. 45). Compare Gen. Wesley K. Clark, *Waging Modern War: Bosnia, Kosovo, and the Future of Combat* (New York: PublicAffairs, 2001).

21 Hosmer, *The Conflict over Kosovo*, p. 97.

22 *Ibid.*, p. 104.

23 *Ibid.*

24 This also makes it difficult to say whether the bombing of Serbia does or does not depart from the past pattern delineated by Pape. It could be that the NATO strategy succeeded because Milosevic did not know that Pape is generally correct, that is, it could be that Pape's thesis about earlier bombing campaigns would be incorrect if applied to Serbia (but only given Milosevic's actual beliefs, which did not include the general truth of Pape's thesis). Fortunately, I do not need to take a position here on this explanatory question, although it is important and intriguing.

25 Hosmer, *The Conflict over Kosovo*, p. 66.

26 *Ibid.*, p. 54.

27 With the help of an international lawyer, I have explored the legal options in a companion article: Henry Shue and David Wippman, "Limiting Attacks on Dual-Use Facilities Performing Indispensable Civilian Functions," 35 *Cornell International Law Journal* (2002).

Chapter 7

The burdens of collective liability

ERIN KELLY

The notion of collective liability directs us to the moral significance of what we do, or fail to do, together with other people. Many grave and unjust harms follow from the action and inaction of groups of people: inequalities in wealth and access to basic resources, the fighting of unjust wars, racial discrimination, environmental damage. Narrowly focusing on individual action or inaction may obscure the moral significance of how a person's contribution interacts with the contributions of other people to produce a serious harm. This may make it too easy to assume that responding to a harm is someone else's business. Insofar as we are drawn to this perspective, exploring the nature of collective liability may lead us to reorient our sense of moral responsibility.

I

Accounts of collective responsibility, such as those developed by Peter French and Larry May, push us to recognize the moral importance of group membership. They examine the metaphysics of group identity and the significance of the concept of moral responsibility as it attaches to groups, and they urge us to understand the roles we play, however marginal, in groups that commit wrongs.[1] This represents an important contribution to ethics, especially for thinking about justice, in both its domestic and international applications. But these philosophers do not go far enough when it comes to thinking about morally permissible ways to distribute the costs of responding to injustice. In some important cases, these thinkers resist the idea that collective responsibility is distributive. Collective responsibility distributes to individual members of a group when they can be held responsible, if to varying degrees, for what the group does. This might mean that individual members can be blamed for the group's action, that they incur obligations to make reparations for the wrongs their group has committed, or that harms may legitimately be imposed upon them when others take action to remedy the injustice. Collective responsibility that is corporate, by contrast, attaches to a group but not to its individual members. This means that the relevant burdens of corporate responsibility cannot legitimately be imposed on individual group members. Those who resist the idea that collective responsibility distributes to individual group members maintain that although people together produce a certain result, individually they may not be responsible for it. If individuals are not responsible, then they do not deserve to be blamed or to bear the costs of rectifying the group's wrong, and imposing costs on them would be wrong.

The problem with this line of thinking is that it may unduly hinder us from acting to alleviate serious injustices. It is often not possible to contain and direct the costs of such efforts only to those persons, such as a group's leaders, who have freely and willfully caused an injustice. The individual members of a society may ultimately and directly bear the costs of foreign military intervention or domestic rebellion, for example. Theories that deny that costs could legitimately be imposed on more passive members of involved groups would appear disproportionately to represent the interests of persons who, while not having actively promoted injustice, may have indirectly supported and benefited from it. This potentially self-serving and obstructionist position comes at the price of failing to acknowledge the moral urgency of the claims of persons who suffer an injustice.

Surely it is reasonable to think that people generally have a right not to be harmed or seriously burdened for the sake of benefiting others. The moral urgency of responding to injustice, however, should lead us to examine the circumstances under which persons may lose this right. This paper develops a moral notion of collective liability that provides us with reasonable grounds for distributing the costs of alleviating serious injustices. It specifies conditions under which it is permissible to impose special burdens on members of groups that have caused harms. These burdens may include those commonly associated with the use of military force, such as loss of authority, wealth, property or life.

I have suggested that those who resist the notion that collective liability distributes to individual group members often do so based on judgments of what persons deserve. I submit, however, that we should distinguish between liability and desert. Persons may sometimes legitimately be forced to bear serious costs, even when those persons or the larger group cannot be said to deserve the costs that are imposed upon them.[2] Collective liability, as I will understand it, can be less metaphysically and morally exacting than the notion of moral desert. But although the criteria of collective liability fall short of establishing desert, they do not neglect our culpability as individuals altogether.

I will suppose that, generally speaking, when serious costs are imposed on a liable group for the sake of rectifying an injustice, all members of the group must be at fault in some respect, if not to the same degree. We should distinguish the moral concept of liability from the legal concept of strict liability. Strict liability describes a situation in which the requirement of contributory fault is relaxed.[3] At the limit, no one is judged to be at fault, morally speaking. Sometimes companies assume strict liability for defects in their products as part of the cost of doing business. The legal assignment of strict liability is simply a way of covering the costs of harms that result from defects. It does not reflect judgments of moral blameworthiness. The distribution of moral liability, by contrast, presupposes the fault of each member via an act or omission. There are some important exceptions to this presupposition. Nevertheless, a presupposition of contributory fault should generally be maintained, even though each person's responsibility may be merely partial, indirect, and inessential.

Utilitarians and other consequentialists may object that this presupposition places too much moral importance on individual agency. They might claim that even a weak conception of contributory fault should be given up as a condition of distributive collective liability in favor of more simply determining what would promote the greatest overall good. I maintain, however, that persons who have not caused harm to others nor had an opportunity to renounce unjust benefits or otherwise to dissociate themselves from a serious injustice have a right not to be harmed for the sake of the greater good. This idea is behind our moral interest in the protection of basic rights and serves to orient our common-sense understanding of justice. The account of collective liability defended in this essay thus requires more than is presupposed by the concept of strict liability but less than what may be needed to establish desert.

Section II of this essay further analyzes the significance of claiming that collective liability is distributive. Section III elaborates an account of the criteria of collective liability. Section IV brings the account directly to bear on the topic of military intervention.

II

A response that violates the basic rights of perfectly innocent persons may sometimes be required to halt an extreme crisis such as genocide or "ethnic cleansing." In these kinds of circumstances, such rights violations may be morally justified; rights are not absolute. The concept of collective liability I am concerned to develop, however, is not addressed to these cases. Rather, the notion of collective liability speaks to cases in which there are grounds for doubting that persons who would bear the costs of addressing an injustice have a right not to be harmed. An account of collective liability is designed to fit situations in which there is some discretion about which among several possibly effective strategies to take in combating an injustice. It looks to when the actions and allegiances of persons who will be affected are relevant for thinking about which strategy to embrace. This may help us to think about whether the use of violence in order to contain an unjust regime or to liberate an oppressed group could be permissible. The notion of collective liability may also help us to think about, for instance, the extent to which civilian casualties should be minimized at the cost of the lives of combatants. The question is whether reasons to avoid harming civilians are weakened by the role, perhaps indirect, that those civilians have played in an unjust scheme.

Further, the notion of collective liability can be used to resolve questions about who owes reparations for harms done. We may think of reparations, in a broad sense, as encompassing various forms of assistance – from money and supplies to military personnel and action. Considerable controversy surrounds the question of when we are morally obligated to help others in need and how strong our obligation may be. On the view I defend, when we are collectively liable for harms we have caused, we may be obligated to provide aid.[4] This might mean, for instance, that a state has an obligation to intervene on behalf of a group whose unjust suffering it has helped to cause. The fact that we have caused serious harms provides a clearer and more compelling basis for establishing our duty to help than simply examining the severity and urgency of people's needs. Surely the latter consideration also has moral force, but it is much harder to deny that one has a duty to respond to suffering one has helped to cause.

The costs we are considering in connection with collective liability are those that may result from the use of military action, the imposition of sanctions or the provision of non-military forms of aid. We are addressing the matter of how these costs should be distributed when they are required in order to address a serious injustice. I will not present a full account of how this matter should be settled or which sort of response to an injustice would be most appropriate. I aim only to present some modest guidelines and to argue that imposing costs of these kinds on liable groups need not be a matter of wronging group members for the sake of a greater good. Persons who are wronged have a moral basis for complaint. When a group is liable for bearing certain costs, however, its members may have no such basis for complaint. Specifically, when the fault of each member suffices to render collective liability distributive, members of a liable group may have no legitimate complaint to bearing the costs of furthering the cause of greater justice.

We should, however, acknowledge an important exception to the general presupposition of contributory fault. This concerns practical obstacles to implementing ideal moral concepts.[5] When dealing with large groups of people, we encounter some individuals who may not exemplify the features of group membership that warrant judgments of liability. These persons may reside in the same territory yet not be involved in a group's unjust activities. Practical pressures to choose a viable target, for instance, or to apply sanctions effectively may point toward a group of persons who are largely, but not entirely, collectively liable, strictly speaking. Action may urgently be called for to combat an injustice, yet it may not be possible to exempt all uninvolved persons from bearing the costs in question.

It is disturbing to think that persons who have done nothing wrong should ever be harmed for the sake of a greater good. This brings us back to the problem of when and whether some persons' rights may be infringed for the sake of greater justice. That is, as I have said, a problem that an account of collective liability will not enable us to solve. But we should acknowledge that insofar as we wish to implement a notion of collective liability in our thinking about justice, it might not always be possible to avoid permitting harm to some persons who are not liable. This is an unfortunate cost of the often blunt instruments of foreign policy and collective action. To be useful, the notion of collective liability must be a practical political notion. It has moral content, but cannot retain the precision of ideal moral theory. A practical moral philosophy must allow that a group that would otherwise be liable cannot necessarily shield itself from liability by pointing to the fact that it contains some members for whom we can identify no contributory fault. Those members are not liable, but sometimes we may treat them as though they are.

III

I will assume, for the remainder of our discussion, that the relevant notion of collective liability is distributive. Now let us take up the question: How can liability distribute across groups? Persons can sometimes be held liable, I argue, when their actions together bring about an injustice.[6] Some injustices could only have been produced collectively, through the coordination or interaction of a group of persons. This helps to give sense to the idea that liability must be collective. Difficulties for justifying a notion of distributive collective liability arise when we consider how direct or remote the causal contributions are that group members make to a harmful result. The more indirect people's causal contributions, the harder it becomes to make the case for distributive liability, especially when an individual's contribution is small. Also of concern are the conditions under which participation in a collective scheme takes place and whether those conditions can be said to be manipulative or coercive. Manipulation and coercion pose a serious challenge to an account of collective liability.

It may seem that persons can be held collectively liable only when they act together in a metaphysically strong sense, such as when individual members willfully participate and endorse the group's aims as their own. Some metaphysical accounts of joint action focus on a high degree of coordination and mutual responsiveness.[7] In cases that interest me, however, persons may act out of self-interest and with little concern for how their actions interact with those of other people. Although they may be fellow citizens, participants could lack shared goals or what is sometimes referred to as a "we-attitude."[8] Nevertheless, their interactions may be morally significant and could provide the basis for ascriptions of collective liability. I maintain that liability for an injustice may distribute to some extent to the group as a whole, even when the coordination among group members is weaker than what is required by most metaphysical accounts of collective action. Those accounts fail to illuminate the concept of collective liability most relevant to our topic.

This is not to deny that features of group membership may be needed to explain how people's actions causally interact in such a way as to bring about some harm. It may often be true that in order for persons together to perpetuate an injustice they must share goals or a decision-making structure, acknowledge a common authority, be mutually responsive or experience a sense of solidarity. But none of these explanatory factors is essential to the concept of collective liability. Different explanations will apply in different cases. What is relevant, morally speaking, is more simply that a person causally contributes to an injustice, when we consider that person's actions together with the actions of others.

Thus let us begin by considering the following principle of collective liability: *Persons are collectively liable for an injustice when what each person does causally contributes to an injustice produced by the group* (P1). The injustices with which we will be concerned are severe. They involve, for example, widespread human rights violations. We may think of P1 as a principle of distributive justice. To be distributed are the costs of working to address a crisis. When serious costs are inevitable if the crisis is to be addressed, this principle states that it is acceptable, generally speaking, to generate those costs and more appropriate to impose them on persons who are together causally responsible for the crisis than on persons who are not.

In evaluating this principle, we should allow for the fact that the causal relationship of some members to the result caused by the group may be remote. Members of a firing squad who, as it turns out, have no bullets in their rifles, contribute to the successful functioning of the squad even though their participation does not directly cause the death of the condemned person. Since their involvement helps to enable the collective scheme, I will count their participation as an indirect causal contribution to the death of the condemned. It does not present a counterexample to P1.

In other cases, however, the actions of some may be causally irrelevant because the result has already been produced by other members. For example, the participation of a California voter in a national election is causally inefficacious when voters elsewhere have already determined the result.[9] We should, however, still count the California voter as a full participant, morally speaking. Our principle should be revised in view of the possibility of causal preemption. One causal chain preempts another when it brings about an event that the other would have brought about had the first not already been completed.[10] The causal chain that was not completed would have been completed under relevant counterfactual conditions. Consider P2: *Persons are collectively liable for an injustice when what each person does causally contributes to an injustice, or would have contributed to it under relevant counterfactual conditions.*[11] In these ways, collective liability can legitimately distribute to non-essential members of a group.

It is important to note that the principle under consideration takes no account of how tightly organized a group is. Mobs and corporations may both be liable, and in a distributive sense, although the former has no discernable structure and the latter is highly structured. Here I position myself against some philosophers who take facts about the organizational structure of groups to bear directly on the question of whether a group's liability could be distributive.[12] They believe that when a group is highly structured, its structure tells against the idea that the group's liability distributes to individual members. French, for example, argues that collective liability can be distributive only when collectives are mere aggregates or collections of people and when, furthermore, the participating individuals have no valid excuse for their participation.[13] In contrast to the lack of structure in such groups, the intentional agency of a corporation, for example, is made possible by decision structures that allocate authority and orchestrate the intentions and actions of its members. The interests, decision, and actions expressed and taken within these structures are, therefore, those of the corporate entity as such and are not attributable to its individual members. For instance, individual members may not intend the outcome but, rather, merely to do their specific jobs, they may not contribute significantly to the total outcome, and the outcome may not advance their goals. Also, they may not be essential to the group in the sense that the identity of the corporate entity survives change of membership. Accordingly, French holds that individuals within corporate entities cannot be held liable for corporate decisions and actions, although the corporate entity itself may be liable.

I am not here interested in the metaphysics of groups and so will set aside questions about whether a collectivity should be counted as an entity that exists in and of itself. Let us focus instead on the moral conditions for attributing liability. French's understanding of the limits of distributive collective liability is too strict. His conditions for the assignment of liability appear to be designed for use in justifying, for example, the punishment of corporations for criminal wrongdoing. There we can draw a meaningful distinction between penalties imposed on a corporation, such as fines or negative advertising, and penalties imposed upon individuals connected with it.[14] But when dealing with the prospects of the use of sanctions or violence to achieve political aims, a non-distributive conception of collective liability has little relevance. This is because the costs to individuals cannot adequately be contained and separated from the costs to the collectivity. To harm the collectivity is directly to harm its individual members. But, in French's view, if the injustice being addressed is the result of highly organized collective action, then costs directly imposed upon individual members of that collectivity cannot be justified, since those individuals do not meet the relevant agency requirements.

The fact that the group in which I participated could continue to exist and act without me hardly seems to imply that I bear no liability for its actions when I do participate. I may have contributed causally even when my contribution is non-essential in the following sense: the outcome would still have occurred without my participation since someone else would have assumed my place in the larger scheme. This fact does not block the distributive attribution of liability. It is morally relevant that I was actually involved in the collective scheme. Even a group's leaders may be non-essential, in the sense just elaborated, but surely we often are right to hold them liable. A more compelling objection is the idea that if a person plays a circumscribed and relatively unimportant part in a larger scheme, perhaps for no other reason than to earn a living or to avoid trouble, that person should not have to bear any special burden for rectifying the wrongs produced by that scheme. She may not have intended or foreseen the harmful result, and her reasons for action may, in themselves, be unobjectionable. Holding her liable for the harmful result seems unfair.

This argument has some force, yet its claims are too strong. We have a responsibility as members of larger groups to explore the implications of our participation. Imagine that as citizens of a democratic society we cast our votes for a leader who implements an oppressive policy against some people. Perhaps we do not intend what the leader does and did not know about his plans. Certainly our contribution was small and the effect of our action indirect. The same could be said for paying taxes under an unjust regime. We might pay taxes because we support government spending on public works and education or simply because we do not wish to break the law by refusing to pay. Imagine that our government uses some of the tax money to support an unjust regime with which it is allied, a regime that is guilty of human rights violations. It turns out that what we have done is causally linked to the violation of human rights, although we do not intend it and some of us may be unaware of this connection. However small the contribution any one of us has made, it is morally relevant that we have in fact acted together to empower an unjust regime. The fact that we, as voting and tax-paying citizens, did not intend and are unaware of the harmful effects of our government's foreign policy should not serve to protect us from the costs of measures taken by others to address those harmful effects. The harms being suffered are not merely unfortunate, they are unjust. Since we together caused the injustice, it is more appropriate that we should bear the costs of repairing it than that those who have been harmed should continue to suffer or that some uninvolved third party should pay the costs.[15]

Nevertheless, we should qualify our principle in two ways. It is not necessary that members of a liable group should each have acted with the intention of causing the result that they together in fact caused. Nor is it required that they knew the result would ensue. But it is important that they could have foreseen the significant possibility that unjust harms would occur.[16] This does not mean that the actual result must have been foreseeable, but only that members of the liable group could have foreseen the significant possibility of some unjust result or other. For example, given the history of American foreign policy, it is surely foreseeable that a US administration might well support an unjust regime somewhere to serve our national interests. The burden of collective liability for such support is one we assume by participating in a political society in which the government's activities are accessible to public scrutiny.

The second qualification states that members of a liable group must have had an opportunity to refuse the indirect causal role that they in fact played. This qualification is important for the following reason. The plausibility of assigning collective liability to us depends on the idea that we ought to explore the implications of our participation in larger groups. This idea is important, from a practical point of view, because it may help to forestall the possibility of injustice. Accordingly, we assume that if members of a liable group had explored the implications of their participation and opted out, the harms their group caused might not have occurred. Thus, to be held liable persons must have had some opportunity not only to foresee the possibility of unjust harms, but also to opt out.

While persons who contribute directly or indirectly to an injustice do not always benefit from the unjust scheme, it is often the case that they do. For example, they often enjoy access to goods and resources that flow from group membership. The moral repugnance of benefiting from an injustice should lead us to interpret the "opting out" condition to be quite weak. The opportunity to opt out of participation in political society exists when persons have a right to protest or to emigrate. Perhaps it is even met when persons lack these rights, but could engage in these actions without incurring severe penalties, such as serious bodily harm, loss of life, substantial loss of liberty or impoverishment.

Of course, the fact that we may protest or emigrate does not make our participation in political society voluntary. We typically do not choose to be members of our political society, and the costs of leaving or engaging in serious political opposition may be high.[17] But possessing these opportunities may be enough to show that we have no rightful objection to bearing the costs of rectifying an injustice in which we are, albeit indirectly, implicated. Recall that we are supposing that the injustices caused by a liable group are severe. Accordingly, the fact that the costs of refusing to participate in the group's unjust scheme are high should not relieve participating members from sharing liability. We are morally responsible for doing what we can to see that how we lead our lives does not harm others, even when altering our conduct is costly to us. Our participation in a harmful scheme is morally significant even when it is not voluntary and willful.

We should revise our principle to include the following provisos: *Persons are collectively liable for an injustice when what each person does causally contributes to an injustice produced by the group* (P1), *or would have contributed to it under relevant counterfactual conditions* (P2), *provided that: (a) they could have foreseen the significant possibility that an injustice would occur and (b) they had an opportunity to opt out of participation.* Call this principle P3.

This principle can be understood to recognize the implications for collective liability of the existence of highly repressive regimes and other serious threats to people's political freedom, and we should understand it in this way. The existence of threats may raise the stakes of opting out to such a degree that it would not be reasonable to maintain that refusal to opt out implies liability. We should accept P4: *Persons are not collectively liable for an injustice when their contributions to an injustice are indirect and they could not have opted out of the collective scheme without incurring credible threats to life, basic liberty, or bodily integrity.* Political resistance in China or the former Soviet Union is and was dangerous enough that even if people's passive compliance with their government could be said to have provided indirect support for their government's human rights abuses (for example, in Tibet or Eastern Europe, as well as domestically), we should not hold them liable. Similarly, we should not hold the citizens of Afghanistan collectively liable for the Taliban's support of Al Qaeda.

The existence of highly repressive regimes subsumes these cases under P4. To protest or attempt to emigrate would be so dangerous that we may regard the subjects of such regimes as, for practical purposes, like hostages. We do not hold hostages liable for the wrongful actions of their captors. Hostages are not, in a meaningful sense, agents of their own destiny.

P1 has been significantly qualified. Still, one might worry that the emphasis on causal responsibility in P3 is too narrow. It might be that some members of a group are not even indirectly causally responsible for harms caused by the group, and that how they have acted is not part of a causal chain that would, counterfactually, have been effective. Familiar attributions of negligence imply that one can be liable for harms one has not caused.[18] Liability is established by virtue of one's failure to prevent the harms in question. Let us now consider P5: *Passive members of a group are distributively liable to the extent that they could each have played a role in preventing an injustice perpetuated by the larger group.*

May employs this sort of principle quite broadly. He argues that the responsibility of persons for a harm caused by their group can be traced to the role they could have played in averting it.[19] What May finds relevant is the relative power each individual member had to influence the outcome. Suppose it is the case that the case that non-opposition by a passive sub-group was a necessary condition for the larger group to achieve its injustice; if the sub-group had been organized or if a critical number of its members had voiced some opposition, the sub-group would have influenced key people in the larger group to stop the injustice. Perhaps members of the sub-group could have achieved this together through widespread protest. In that sense, each member of the passive group could have played a role in preventing the injustice perpetuated by the larger group. Still, this possibility does not necessarily suffice to establish that collective liability distributes to the passive sub-group, thinks May. The reason is that there may have been nothing a given individual could have done to stop the harms from occurring. This is because she could not have persuaded enough other members of the passive group to take action, and she could not alone have achieved the desired effect. May thinks that in cases such as these, in which we could not have influenced enough other people, we may turn out to be blameless, even though we may, in a weaker sense, be morally tainted by what the larger group has done.[20] Nevertheless, it may still be true, he maintains, that the group as a whole is to blame.

May's line of thinking is guided by the idea that blame is a desert-entailing notion;[21] it is appropriate only when certain strong metaphysical conditions on agency are satisfied. A group may deserve blame because it has acted freely and deliberately to cause some harm or it has failed to do what could have averted a harm. Yet this may not be true of individual group members. Thus collective responsibility may not reduce to aggregated individual responsibility.[22] Blame does not distribute to the individual members of the group when they do not deserve it.

I question the idea that liability presupposes a desert-entailing notion of moral blameworthiness. The metaphysical presuppositions of liability may be weaker than what is required to establish moral blameworthiness.[23] Individual members of a group may rightly be held liable for a harm even when, as we have seen, their actions are not fully voluntary, they do not intend the harmful result, and their behavior is causally influenced by their culture and political environment. It is no less plausible to think that members of a sub-group are liable when it is true that members of the larger group have caused a harm that the sub-group could together have acted to avert.[24] We are liable if we fail to try to stop harms from occurring, when those harms are caused by our associates and we could have acted to prevent them. This is true even when the success of our efforts as individuals depends to some extent on what other people do; the requirements of justice may require collective action. This means that we may have no moral grounds for complaint when we are forced to bear the costs of repairing or responding to damage our group has caused. Consider P6: *The collective liability of a group distributes to its passive members when the passive sub-group could have acted together to prevent the injustice caused by the larger group.*

Still, even those who reject a desert-entailing notion of blameworthiness may dig in their heels. They may doubt the moral relevance of the fact that persons belong to a group that causes an injustice when those persons themselves have not have contributed, even indirectly, to the injustice and could not individually have done much to prevent it.[25] Why should we think that liability for harms should fall on passive and relatively powerless members of a causally responsible group, but not on third parties (that is, non-members), who may actually be in a better position to act?

The following line of reasoning addresses this objection. It is morally significant that other people can in effect act on our behalf. They may act as our political representatives, whether or not we endorse their actions.

They may, for instance, set up institutions or pursue policies intended to benefit people who are, in the relevant way (for example, by race, gender, ethnicity, nationality, or religion) like us. Benefits may flow to us as a result of those institutions or policies. The moral repugnance of profiting from an injustice that is perpetuated by a group to which we belong is sufficient to render us liable for that injustice when we could together have helped to prevent it. It is more appropriate that we bear the costs of remedying the injustice than that these costs should fall on some uninvolved third party. Thus let us replace P6 with P7: *Persons are collectively liable for an injustice when they either contribute causally to an injustice or benefit from an injustice, perpetuated by other members of their group, that the passive sub-group could together have played a role in preventing.*

Our topic concerns the permissibility of imposing special burdens on particular groups. This leaves us only to consider the case of passive members who live at a significant remove from a larger group that commits an injustice, as do, for instance, the Kurds in Iraq. Such persons are members of their larger society not by virtue of their participation or because they enjoy its benefits; they are members perhaps only insofar as they inhabit the same territory and possess the same nationality as persons who together have caused unjust harms. These passive members are not liable and imposing special burdens on them would violate their rights. Harming them could be justified only when a case can be made that infringing upon their rights is necessary in order to redress a greater harm. I will not attempt to outline what such a case might look like, although I acknowledge that in practice the need to do so could arise.

IV

The account I have proposed holds the following. Collective agents are liable for an injustice when:

(1) The group or some of its members are causally responsible for an injustice via the political and social arrangements they impose or perpetuate.
(2) Passive members of the group, that is, members who do not actively promote the offending result, benefit from the injustice and could together have played a role in preventing it.
(3) Members of the group could have foreseen the possibility that some injustice or other could result.

(4) Members of the group have had an opportunity, weakly construed, to exit the group, to take political action to combat the injustice, or to refuse the benefits that accrue to them as a result of the injustice.

Let us now address the question of which further moral conditions must be met in order to justify humanitarian intervention. I assume that the target of intervention is a group that is liable for a serious injustice. The group in question could be liable for abuses within the borders of its own state or in some other state. Thus the liable group could be a subset of a larger society, or it may be the society at large. We want to know whether and when we are permitted to interfere with a group's unjust activities, possibly through military force. Below I elaborate several conditions that it is reasonable to think permissible interventions must meet. The broader question of whether and when we could be justified in harming members of a non-liable group, if only as a side-effect of aiming at some other target, is not one that I take up here.

Implicit in my discussion of collective liability is a claim about the moral limits of sovereignty. To be explicit, those who are liable for a serious injustice should not be protected by a principle of state sovereignty. We should regard only just or decent states as sovereign and thus as morally immune to intervention by outsiders.[26] Sovereignty is compelling from a moral point of view only for states that protect the basic human rights of their members and comply with the terms of international justice. When a government violates the fundamental interests of some of its subjects or acts aggressively against another state, a principle of sovereignty could come to function as a protective device for the perpetuation of an injustice. This is unacceptable within a decent international society of societies. We should assume that respect for a state's sovereignty is conditional on that state's decency or minimal justice.

Turning now more directly to the question of intervention, I submit that when an injustice is severe, we are permitted to intervene with a group that is liable for it, provided that our action would help to alleviate the injustice and doesn't run afoul of other relevant moral constraints (specified below). I have argued that the liability of perpetrators allows us to focus primarily on the needs of victims, even at serious cost to the perpetrators. Establishing collective liability means that we may shift costs toward the perpetrators and away from the victims, as we act to address an injustice. But doing this is justified only when it helps to alleviate the injustice. Punishing perpetrators while leaving them fully in power, for instance, would not be warranted. We should stipulate that:

(5) The proposed intervention would (with significant likelihood) improve the cause of justice, and the alternatives are inadequate or more costly for the victims.

This principle is especially important since liability is not a matter of dealing out desert but, rather, concerns how to determine a fair distribution of the costs of alleviating serious injustice.[27] The prospects for improving the justice of a situation cannot, of course, be guaranteed, while the costs of using violence may be very great. Some think this a reason sharply to restrict the use of violence.[28] But we should be careful to avoid being overly restrictive. The ongoing violation of human rights itself involves great suffering, and it is hard to understand how states that form a global society through their complex interrelations could together affirm a conception of global justice that does not treat the systematic violation of human rights as morally urgent enough to warrant intervention.[29] The account of liability I have presented offers grounds for loosening moral prohibitions on the use of violence in response to injustice, even against non-combatants. The moral prohibitions loosen when non-combatants are members of a liable group. In this respect, my account deviates from standard liberal just war theory, which strictly prohibits the intentional harming of non-combatants.[30]

At the same time, a principle of restraint will be an important aspect of any plausible account of permissible intervention. Restraint is important in order to contain the overall costs of using force and in recognition of its dangers. Hence we introduce the following principle:

(6) The costs imposed on the liable group should not exceed what can reasonably be thought to be necessary in order to achieve the goal of rectifying an injustice.

Some serious injustices may be entrenched enough that only violence will stop them (for example, South African apartheid, the "ethnic cleansing" campaign in Kosovo). Yet the use of violence is so dangerous that it must be a last resort. We assume, again, that the targeted or significantly affected group meets the above stated criteria of liability for injustice. Our focus is on alleviating serious injustice, and in so doing, shifting the costs away from those who have already unjustly suffered.[31] The idea is that when injustice is grave enough and violence is required to stop it, it is permissible to use violence, provided that only the minimum necessary force is used and that those who will absorb its costs are liable for the injustice.

Disagreement will surface around the question of how to determine when a particular military strategy is necessary and whether, in making that determination, we ought to take into account existing political realities. Bombing campaigns conducted at high altitude are a case in point. Such campaigns are less risky for pilots but they reduce accuracy, putting civilians on the ground at greater risk. It may be that conducting an intervention is not politically feasible unless the risks to the intervening nation are minimal. Thus a bombing campaign conducted at high altitude may appear to be necessary. Here we should be cautious. I have claimed that harming civilians is not always objectionable when political realities require it and those civilians are liable for grave injustice. Even so, the intervening group must assume the burden of justifying the strategy it embraces, in full view of the consequences in human terms for those who are harmed. The range of politically feasible options may not be fixed. It is the task of political leadership to argue for the moral urgency of the cause without dehumanizing the enemy. Harming persons always comes at some moral cost, even when those persons are collectively liable. Responsible leaders will make the case for public support of intervention so that risking more than the most minimal casualties on their own side in order to reduce casualties and damage on the other side is politically feasible. The reality of suffering casualties should be accepted by the intervening agent as a risk of the business it is in.

Furthermore, what counts as necessary must be worked out in conjunction with a reasonable requirement of proportionality. This is so despite the relevance of determining who is liable and what the political constraints are. We should affirm the following principle:

(7) The morally relevant costs of the means employed, in terms of the number and severity of resulting harms, do not threaten to surpass the moral importance of the goal achieved.

This principle is not a strict proportionality requirement that would allow, at most, as many casualties as are prevented overall. Inflicting greater casualties on a liable group may be permissible in order to protect the lives of persons who have already unjustly suffered and to promote just political institutions. The liability of the target group allows us to reject a moral limit of strict proportionality. Nevertheless, the moral urgency of alleviating an injustice must be measured against the number and severity of casualties likely to result from intervening. Some constraint is affirmed. Serious attention to this matter is especially important, as the criteria of liability do not imply desert. It is doubtful, however, that a more concrete principle or formula is available to provide reasonable guidance; judgments will have to be rendered on a case by case basis. Longer-term costs (regarding health, poverty, the environment) as well as immediate consequences must be estimated. Surely these costs have too often been underestimated. Appreciating their relevance may well make the use of violence only rarely justifiable.

Further limiting the conduct of military intervention is the following:

(8) Certain moral prohibitions on the conduct of intervention must be respected. For example, crimes of war may not be committed (torture, rape, the execution of prisoners of war, and so on).

And finally:

(9) Safeguards against self-serving actions by the intervening agent must be established, for example, by requiring that proposed interventions be approved by fairly constituted international bodies.[32]

In sum, an implication of the account of collective liability I have offered is that harming civilians, perhaps even deliberately, is not necessarily prohibited. Non-combatants could be liable for serious costs of alleviating injustice by virtue of their involvement with a group that has caused the injustice. They may be liable even though they are not directly responsible for the wrongs committed on their behalf. Perhaps they merely paid their taxes, obeyed the law and enjoyed the goods and services their society makes available to them. Which costs exactly it could be reasonable to impose upon them in order to alleviate an injustice requires serious discussion in recognition of principles 5–9. But the door is open to the use of violence.

I have claimed that it is commonly thought that an agent can deserve treatment of one sort or another only when she has acted freely or could have prevented some result. In the case of collective agency, an agent's responsibility may be thought to be a function of the features of the collective's organization that enable it to reflect, to deliberate and to make relatively autonomous decisions. Or collective responsibility may be understood as a function of the contributions its members make; for example, one might think that a collective agent deserves costs imposed upon it only when its members have all freely engaged in the objectionable behavior that produced a harmful outcome, when they could individually have acted to stop it, or when harmful action constitutes the self-conscious endorsement by individuals of a group's collective identity.

These are strong conditions and I have been concerned to argue that members of a group may be liable even when conditions such as these are not satisfied. Liability depends on the exercise or, at least, the possibility of agency on the part of the group's members, but that agency need not exhibit the freedom, power, self-awareness or self-control that is characteristically presupposed by the notion of desert. It should be admitted that not all costs that morality requires us to bear for the sake of addressing an injustice or promoting a greater good are costs we deserve. Perhaps we sometimes have the bad luck of finding ourselves implicated in an unjust scheme that is not of our own design. But however bad this luck may be, other people's lot might be worse, for they bear the brunt of the injustice, until action is taken to alleviate it.

To have a sense of justice is to recognize that our liability as members of a group is the product of the role we play as individuals in a collective scheme. Our participation in a broader scheme means that other people's wrongdoing raises the stakes of our own individual action or inaction. As a result, we may legitimately be asked to pay a price for the indirect or possibly unexpected consequences of what we do. Moreover, benefits that we may not have sought out may confer upon us a special responsibility to bear the costs of confronting injustice.

NOTES

For discussion and helpful comments on an earlier draft, I am grateful to Lionel McPherson, Don Scheid, Lukas Meyer, David Estlund, Arthur Applbaum, and Andreas Follesdal.

1 See Peter French, *Collective and Corporate Responsibility* (New York: Columbia University Press, 1984); Larry May, *The Morality of Groups: Collective Responsibility, Group-Based Harm, and Corporate Rights* (Notre Dame, IN: University of Notre Dame Press, 1987); and Larry May, *Sharing Responsibility* (Chicago: University of Chicago Press, 1992).
2 For related discussion, see Erin Kelly, "Doing without Desert," *Pacific Philosophical Quarterly* 83 (2002), 180–205.
3 For elaboration of the notions of strict and vicarious liability, see Joel Feinberg, "Collective Responsibility," in *Collective Responsibility*, ed. Larry May and Stacey Hoffman (Savage, MD: Rowman and Littlefield, 1991), pp. 53–76.
4 As Wesley Hohfeld understands liability, a liability is not a duty, "it is a liability to have a duty created." Wesley Hohfeld, *Fundamental Legal Conceptions*, ed. Walter Wheeler Cook (New Haven: Yale University Press, 1923), p. 59.

5 There is another possible exception. This concerns cases in which it makes sense to maintain that collective liability can be inherited. Those who mature after an injustice has already occurred obviously should not be blamed for it. Nevertheless, we may want to hold them liable for rectifying, or in some way redressing, the wrongs of their predecessors. Perhaps we may rightly do this when such persons bear a close political, cultural, or historical relationship to those who committed the injustice and when they have inherited the latter's resources. These cases are most compelling, however, when liability is limited to monetary reparations. I shall set them aside for present purposes. For further discussion see Jürgen Habermas, "What Does 'Working Off the Past' Mean Today?" in *A Berlin Republic: Writings on Germany*, trans. Steven Rendall, introduction by Peter Uwe Hohendahl (Lincoln: University of Nebraska Press, 1997), especially pp. 17–21.

6 Each partially causes the injustice. For a discussion of partial causation, see Alvin I. Goldman, "Why Citizens Should Vote: A Causal Responsibility Approach," *Social Philosophy and Policy* 16, no. 2 (Summer 1999), 201–17.

7 See Michael Bratman, "Shared Cooperative Activity," in *Faces of Intention: Selected Essays on Intention and Agency* (Cambridge: Cambridge University Press, 1999); John Searle, "Collective Intentions and Actions," in *Intentions in Communication*, ed. Philip R. Cohen, Jerry Morgan, and Martha E. Pollack (Cambridge, MA: The MIT Press, 1983); and Raimo Tuomela and Kaarlo Miller, "We-Intentions," *Philosophical Studies* 53 (1991), 115–37. Christopher Kutz argues for a minimalist account of collective action, appealing to the idea of "overlapping participatory intentions." See his "Acting Together," *Philosophy and Phenomenological Research* 61, no. 1 (July 2000), 1–31. This account is elaborated in Christopher Kutz, *Complicity: Ethics and Law for a Collective Age* (Cambridge: Cambridge University Press, 2000). Even this account, I maintain, is too demanding. Persons who act together may not each foster collective ends in the way Kutz supposes.

8 See Searle, "Collective Intentions"; and Toumela and Miller, "We-Intentions."

9 This is true unless we treat voting as a conventional causal system in which the system abstracts from the fact that voters cast their votes at different times and counts them all together. See Goldman, "Why Citizens Should Vote," 212–13.

10 For discussion of causal preemption and how it differs from causal overdetermination, see Martin Bunzl, "Causal Overdetermination," *The Journal of Philosophy* 67 (1979), 134–50. I set aside the controversial subject of causal overdetermination.

11 A person's actions are, thus, less counterfactually removed than in certain cases of moral luck. For example, Thomas Nagel describes the good moral luck of an individual who led a quiet and harmless life in Argentina, yet might have become an officer in a concentration camp if he had not left Germany for business reasons in 1930. See "Moral Luck," *Free Will*, ed.

Gary Watson (Oxford: Oxford University Press, 1982), p. 175. I am stressing, by contrast, the moral relevance of persons' actual participation in an unjust scheme, although that person's participation may have been causally inefficacious.

12 See Feinberg; Virginia Held, "Can a Random Collection of Individuals be Held Morally Responsible?" *Collective Responsibility*, ed. Larry May and Stacey Hoffman (Savage, MD: Rowman and Littlefield, 1991); and French, *Collective and Corporate Responsibility*.

13 *Ibid.*, p. 9. French does not deny that crowds, for example, act together. Rather, he stresses the difference between responsibility attributes of crowds and corporations. The former are distributive while the latter are not. See also Held, "Can a Random Collection of Individuals be Morally Responsible?", pp. 97–98.

14 Corporate punishment has a trickle-down effect on persons such as stockholders, but French argues that this trickle-down effect is not morally troublesome, pp. 188–89.

15 There is a similarity between this argument and the reasoning that Daniel Farrell thinks justifies self-defense. See Daniel M. Farrell, "The Justification of General Deterrence," *The Philosophical Review* 94, no. 3 (July 1985), 373.

16 This implies that some cases in which leaders violate their mandate may not support claims of collective liability.

17 See John Rawls, *Justice as Fairness: A Restatement*, ed. Erin Kelly (Cambridge, MA: Harvard University Press, 2001), p. 93.

18 I recognize that we sometimes describe harms as caused by neglect or negligence. I am using "cause" in a narrower sense.

19 May, *Sharing Responsibility*, p. 106.

20 See *Ibid.*, ch. 8.

21 I borrow this phrase from T. M. Scanlon, *What We Owe to Each Other* (Cambridge, MA: Harvard University Press, 1999), pp. 274–77. Scanlon's use of this phrase, however, is a bit different from mine. He uses it to mean that it would be a good thing for a blameworthy person in some way to suffer. I mean that a blameworthy person has acted freely and is responsible for what she is like.

22 See May, *The Morality of Groups*, p. 76.

23 A distinction between political liability and moral guilt can be found in Karl Jaspers, although his account of political liability differs from mine in some major respects. *The Question of German Guilt*, trans. E. B. Ashton (1947; New York: Capricorn Books, 1961), pp. 31–38, 75–79.

24 This interpretation weakens the principle, making it easier to satisfy.

25 The membership of these persons in the larger group obviously cannot be established by pointing to their causal contribution to the resulting injustice. But membership could be established by the fact that their interests were politically represented by people who bore causal responsibility.

26 On this point I follow the work of Charles Beitz, *Political Theory and International Relations* (Princeton: Princeton University Press, 1979), part 2. See also John Rawls, *The Law of Peoples* (Cambridge, MA: Harvard University Press, 1999), pp. 81, 93; and Erin Kelly, "Human Rights as Foreign Policy Imperatives," in *The Ethics of Assistance: Morality and the Distant Needy*, ed. Deen Chatterjee, forthcoming from Cambridge University Press. Cf. Michael Walzer, "The Moral Standing of States," *Philosophy and Public Affairs* 9, no. 3 (Spring 1980), 209–29; and Gerard Elfstrom, "Dilemmas of Intervention," *Ethics* 93 (July 1983), 709–25.

27 I assume that a conception of justice as fairness contrasts with a conception of justice as desert. See Rawls, *Justice as Fairness*, pp. 72–79.

28 See, for example, Charles Beitz, "Nonintervention and Communal Integrity," *Philosophy and Public Affairs* 9, no. 4 (Summer 1980), 390–91; also Beitz, *Political Theory and International Relations*, pp. 89–92.

29 This claim is most plausible on a narrow understanding of human rights. See Kelly, "Human Rights as Foreign Policy Imperatives."

30 See Michel Walzer, *Just and Unjust Wars* (New York: Basic Books, 1977), ch. 9; Thomas Nagel, "War and Massacre," in *Mortal Questions* (New York: Cambridge University Press, 1979); and G. E. M. Anscombe, "War and Murder," *The Collected Philosophical Papers of G. E. M. Anscombe, Volume Three* (University of Minnesota Press, 1981).

31 Cf. Virginia Held, "Terrorism, Rights, and Political Goals," in *Justice, Law, and Violence*, ed. James B. Brady and Newton Garver (Philadelphia: Temple University Press, 1991), p. 238.

32 I follow Beitz in formulating this principle. See *Political Theory and International Relations*, p. 90.

PART III

Secession and international law

Chapter 8

The ethics of intervention in self-determination struggles

TOM J. FARER

Should interventions which advance a claimed right to self-determination ever be deemed "humanitarian" on that ground alone? Lexically, "intervention" comprehends a wide range of coercive means for shaping political institutions, policies, and outcomes in other countries. In this chapter I am concerned primarily with cases of *military* intervention, because this particular means normally cannot achieve a humane end without causing some collateral damage to social goods, including those generally regarded as human rights. Therefore, in order to meet their ethical obligations, advocates of military measures must reasonably believe that the intervention they propose will not entail the violation of fundamental individual rights and will do more than other means or sheer inaction to enhance the well-being of affected peoples.

HUMANITARIAN INTERVENTION

For most of the last two centuries, it has subsisted on the shadowy periphery of international law, episodically invoked, with varying degrees of hypocrisy, more as a political/ethical than a legal justification for usually short-term military operations across frontiers. Its legal significance was hazy originally because nineteenth-century treaties and legal practices employed by the community of states (then dominated and largely constituted by the United States and the European great powers) did not prohibit governments from using force to advance their various political, economic, and other interests. In the absence of a general legal prohibition, governments had no need to hunt for categorical exceptions. Like the Athenians addressing the leaders of Melos in Thucydides' history of the Peloponnesian War, they needed to say no more than "the powerful do what they will and the weak accept what they must."[1]

Nevertheless, governments did tend to rationalize and in a sense to justify military interventions.[2] For their rationalizations, all had at least two and some had three relevant audiences. One was other great powers. Labeling an intervention "humanitarian" was a short-hand statement of intent to vindicate alleged rights, usually of the intervening state's own subjects, and to chastise the allegedly delinquent government, but not to replace it with a puppet or a colonial administrator and thereby acquire effective use of additional population and resources. In signaling limited ends, ends with which other powerful governments might sympathize, the intervenor could reasonably hope to discourage its peers from launching counter-interventions or interventions with annexationist ends in some other weakly governed territory.

A second possible audience for the signal was the government whose acts and omissions had sparked the decision to intervene. In effect it was being told that it held the key to its fate. If it did not resist and demonstrated a willingness to alter its objectionable behavior (and perhaps pay compensation for injuries already done), it might survive. The electorates, however limited, of those intervenors that bore some of the trappings of democracy were a third audience for explanations and justifications.

In a social system lacking any central legislative authority, the actions and explanations of its members inevitably create expectations and associated reciprocal reliances that over time tend to acquire a normative aura. So what may begin as a prudential or ethical rule of action comes gradually to appear obligatory among the system's members with their shifting admixture of cooperative and competitive relationships.

Humanitarian intervention is simply one example of this phenomenon. As bourgeois liberal values gradually acquired ascendancy over military-aristocratic ones in the West, entailing among other things the view that peace is normal and resort to war properly exceptional, humanitarian intervention acquired a penumbral legal existence by inclusion in standard international law texts as one of a number of "forceful measures short of war."[3] What gradually gave measures like "humanitarian intervention," "pacific blockade" and "reprisal" a normative rather than merely descriptive quality was their gradual crystalization in diplomatic discourse as actions complying with reasonably clear criteria. As the referential substance of these terms became generally accepted, states could no longer employ them effectively without accepting their definitional limits which, of course, had operational consequences.

As they subtly metamorphosed into de facto restraints on the use of force, these descriptive categories both expressed and advanced the movement to prohibit war as a normal instrument of statecraft. That movement and the values animating it culminated at the close of World War II in two phenomena. One was the Judgment of Nuremberg imposed for "crimes against the peace."[4] The other was the United Nations Charter, specifically Articles 2(4) and 51: The former banning the threat or use of force "against the political independence and territorial integrity of any state or for any other purposes inconsistent with the principles and purposes of the Charter," while the latter (without reference to the former) conceding only a "right of self defense against an armed attack." In the years immediately thereafter, most scholars adopted the view that self-defense against an armed attack was a unique exception and that all other uses of force (other than those authorized by the Security Council under Chapter VII of the Charter) were now outlawed. In short, they appeared to leave no legal space for "humanitarian intervention."[5]

For many decades before the adoption of the United Nations Charter, states characterized interventions as humanitarian regardless of whether their beneficiaries were nationals of the intervening state, of the target state, or of a third party. But gradually, defense of nationals began to be seen as a distinct and separate justification, perhaps akin to self defense in that a state was deemed to consist of a territory and its population.[6] Conversely, governments and writers began using humanitarian intervention only to describe the protection of non-nationals, usually the nationals of the state where intervention was occurring. During and perhaps in part because of the bipolar character of international relations during the Cold War, until its conclusion relatively few interventions satisfied this conception.[7]

India's invasion of East Pakistan in 1971 was one exception. Coming as it did in response to a massive campaign of rape and murder carried out in Pakistan's eastern half by armed forces directed by an ethnically distinct elite in the country's western half, the intervention appealed to the moral sentiments of liberal scholars even as they worried about possible erosion of Charter restraints on the use of force if India's actions were deemed legal. In order to reconcile the appeal and the concern, some scholars argued for treating humanitarian intervention like euthanasia in national legal systems, that is as an act formally illegal but in rare instances so ethically compelling that the illegality is condoned whether by prosecutorial restraint or a jury's refusal to convict.[8]

145

The dissolution of the Soviet Empire and the Soviet Union itself appeared to open vast new space for the material expression of the human rights norms that had been developing all through the Cold War era. But the coincident deterioration of political and social order particularly in the Balkans, the Caucasus, and much of Africa quickly exposed grim challenges to those norms, challenges which seemed resistant to methods short of force. Of course, pitiless civil conflicts over power, wealth and ideology were hardly new and neither was intervention in them. While keeping the war between them cold, the superpowers had regularly backed clients in brutal hot ones. What has distinguished the new era, arguably, is not so much the number of these conflicts or their brutality. Rather it is both the relative absence of those constraints on international action previously immanent in the polarized environment of intense superpower competition and the maturation of a global human rights network with unprecedented influence over public and elite opinion, particularly in Western nations.

These circumstances have catalyzed a series of international interventions, undertaken at least in part for humanitarian ends, while intensifying and broadening debate about their legality and morality. As far as legality is concerned, for present purposes it is sufficient to say that the jury remains divided except, perhaps, where the Security Council authorizes intervention pursuant to its powers under Chapter VII of the Charter to take or authorize action in order to avert or terminate a threat to the peace.[9] My concern here is with the moral or ethical basis (not wholly unconnected to the legal one) for intervention.

In the discourse of ethicists about the criteria for just humanitarian intervention, a central issue has been the threshold condition. What has emerged, it seems to me, is something like a consensus to define that condition as constituted by massive violations of personal security rights – killing, mutilating and raping – and the overlapping phenomenon of ethnic cleansing, overlapping in that it is usually accomplished through terrorization of the target population. Striking by their absence to date from this consensus are violations of the right to self-determination.

SELF-DETERMINATION

In some respects, its absence is paradoxical. After all, self-determination is the only right that appears in both of the two core statements of international human rights, the Covenant on Political and Civil Rights and its counterpart statement of economic, social, and cultural ones.[10]

Moreover, when international action to defend human rights was still highly controversial, opposed indeed by a strong majority of UN members (an alliance of the third World and the Communist Bloc), that same majority, with a considerable degree of support from Western nations, advocated pressure on states prominently resisting self-determination claims and assistance to the claimants then called and idealized as "National Liberation Movements."

Nevertheless, the appearance of paradox is superficial. By definition human rights are supposed to be timeless and universal, as ubiquitous as death. The right to self-determination championed by the Soviet bloc and third-world states was neither. For while, on the one hand, they were notionally eager to liberate peoples and territories involuntarily attached to various Western states during the centuries of colonial expansion, they were, on the other, determined to repress groups within their own territories who aspired to an independent national existence. And since, particularly in the case of the Soviet Union, heir to the Russian Empire, the potential claimants to liberation had been incorporated during the same epoch and by the same ruthless means as those employed by Britain, France, and the other West European states, and since the allegedly "inviolate" boundaries of the already decolonized states swarming with potentially restless ethnic communities were a direct legacy of the abominated colonial past, these champions of self-determination had to define it so narrowly as, in logic, to problematize its very existence on the list of human rights.

In the actual practice of the United Nations organs that concerned themselves with self-determination claims – primarily the General Assembly, the Human Rights Commission and the De-Colonization Committee – self-determination was definitionally restricted to territories (rather than people as such) with culturally and racially distinct populations that had been acquired by Western states during the previous three centuries *and* were separated from them by salt water.[11] While those criteria served peculiarly well the purposes of non-Western states, the West could be said to have authored them, since it dominated all of the UN's organs at the institution's inception when it adopted the list of "non-self-governing territories"[12] which thereafter, with two important exceptions,[13] set the metes and bounds of UN action. That list contained most of the West's existing colonies. It did not include the Soviet Union's Caspian Republics or the Baltic states or any of the other territories seized by the Russian state or its Bolshevik successor.

As Western de-colonization proceeded, one territory after another left the list until today almost none remains.[14]

But if the list is now a relic, the values it partially expressed are not. The idea that bounded onto the historical stage at the end of the eighteenth century retains the capacity to express, incite, and concentrate emotions of enormous power. Even its anti-colonial champions at the United Nations could not entirely cage it within the narrow normative confines that reconciled their interest in fostering the liberation of other peoples with their more imperative interest in repressing their own. For the pure decolonizing conception of self-determination did not quite cover the two claimants who came to engage the widest global circle of sympathizers: South African blacks and Palestinians living in Gaza and the land west of the Jordan River occupied by Israel during its 1967 war with neighboring Arab states.

Still, both of those cases were at least connected to the colonial era and so it was not a great stretch to support national liberation for people of color in South Africa and for Palestinians while husbanding a temporally and geographically limited idea of self-determination. What these constraints could not survive, however, was the collapse of will in Moscow to dominate Eastern Europe or even to enforce the territorial integrity of the Union of Soviet Social Republics. The mushrooming of independent states in the Baltic, the Caspian, and Central Asia, the consensual split of the Czechs and Slovaks and the vertiginous collapse of central authority in Yugoslavia could be read as auguries of a tsunami of national self-assertion unseen, outside the West's colonies, since the fragmentation of Ottoman and Austro-Hungarian authority in the course of World War I.

Hitherto muted self-determination claims quickly found voice and sometimes the form of violent action in the last decade of the twentieth century. Divorce could be consensual, as in the Czechoslovak case and, remarkably, within the former Soviet Union. Or it could be furiously contested as in the former Yugoslavia. Even where consensual, it could awaken within one or both of the divorced parties new claimants to independent peoplehood, the phenomenon underscoring the heterogeneity of populations in most of the world. Groups willing to subsist as one among many minorities in a larger entity sometimes resisted being a principal minority in a smaller one. So, for instance, Abkhazians, finding themselves in an independent Georgia, fought (not without help from some of their Russian friends) to escape and form their own little state.

Armed conflicts stemming in part or whole from self-determination claims have in some instances, like the one in Northern Ireland, been largely internal matters although never without some external ties and effects. Others, like Kashmir, are integrated into the simmering hostilities of neighboring states. And some, of course, like the Sudan, fall in between. Still others, like the Tamil rebellion in Sri Lanka, shift over time from one category to another. Most have been obdurately resistant to efforts, including those of the United Nations and other intergovernmental actors, to promote peaceful settlement. And many have served as great killing machines. Of the fourteen wars raging in 1999, eight of them involved claims by one group or another for some degree of self-determination.[15]

The sanguinary history of self-determination conflicts might by itself create for humanitarians a reasoned basis for discouraging secessionist claims. Proposals to regard foreign assistance to self-determination movements as legal or at least morally justified and hence in some sense "legitimate" would seem designed to have the opposite effect. Aside from its tendency to trigger armed conflict and the ensuing drama of death and devastation, secessionist moves would seem to cut against the grain of cosmopolitan values and identities that facilitate peaceful relations among groups of people who imagine themselves different from each other in affectively significant ways.

My polar case, exemplified by the Basques in Spain, is one where an effective state has offered to all of its citizens, regardless of their ethnicity, a fair chance to compete for power, wealth, and all other social goods and also has respected the secessionists' cultural rights as defined in various international declarations and conventions on minority rights. To demand secession under those conditions, one might fairly argue, is to opt for the warm, intensely insular, and implicitly exclusionary togetherness of tribal life as against one marked by the sharing of space in an open community of multiple loyalties and identities. Moreover, secession by itself is unlikely to produce that congruence of territory and "nationality" the militants demand. For in this era peoples are so intermixed that almost no substantial territory is occupied only by one. So as they tear themselves loose from the state that had hitherto contained them, the secessionists may drag along one or more other peoples whose felt differentness is a threat to the values for which secession seemed an answer. Thus the logic of secessionist values points toward ethnic cleansing, or forced assimilation. As long as minorities quietly accommodate themselves to their new situation, that terrible logic may not insinuate itself into the quotidian politics of the new state. But if they in turn begin demanding either equality of opportunity or, more provocatively, the autonomy the present majority exalted in its previous life as a minority, the latter's reserves of tolerance are likely to empty rapidly.

Nevertheless, intervention on behalf of self-determination has certainly had its defenders, from John Stuart Mill in the nineteenth century to the political theorist Michael Walzer in the second half of the twentieth. "[S]tates," Walzer wrote in *Just and Unjust Wars*, "can be invaded and wars justly begun to assist secessionist movements (once they have demonstrated their representative capacity)."[16] Not only were such interventions just, he seemed to say, they were privileged as against interventions to assist persons rebelling to overthrow a tyrannical government in order to establish a democratic one. Rebellion for that end, he conceded, also might be deemed an exercise in self-determination, but it was of a different kind, a kind that made foreign intervention incongruent with its purpose of fostering liberty. Following Mill, he argued that the

members of a political community must seek their own freedoms, just as the individual must cultivate his own virtue. They cannot be set free, as he cannot be made virtuous, by any external force. Indeed, political freedom depends on the existence of individual virtue, and this the armed forces of another state are most unlikely to produce . . . "It is during an arduous struggle to become free by their own efforts that these virtues have the best chance of springing up."

(quoting Mill)[17]

Beyond this rosy, ahistorical view of the capacity to overthrow tyranny and of the personal qualities an insurrectionist movement fosters, beyond as well the reductionist notion of the conditions for a viable democracy, lay a more arresting argument. Freedom for the individual can only be realized within the framework of a democratic state which means, among other things, a defined space where democratic institutions can operate. Merely putting them in place is one thing. That could be done through one violent exertion in which foreign intervention plays a major role. But then they must be animated and sustained by a community committed to colonizing these institutions lest they remain empty or develop a life and interests of their own. A brief foreign intervention will not create such a community and an extended one replaces one authoritarian government with another, however initially benign. "[T]he recognition of sovereignty," Walzer writes, "is the only way we have of establishing an arena within which freedom can be fought for and (sometimes) won. It is this arena and the activities that go on within it that we want to protect, and we protect them...by marking out boundaries that cannot be crossed..."[18]

The liberal value driving Walzer's thought is communal autonomy.[19] It follows, he believes, that "when a particular set of boundaries clearly contains two or more political communities"[20] and one is struggling to acquire its own space, the moral barrier to foreign intervention lifts. For Walzer's purposes, it was necessary neither to define precisely and differentiate among "political communities" nor to investigate their origins, but only to observe that some sovereign states enclose one or more substantial groups that feel alien in their political setting and aspire to create one that is uniquely their own. Consistent with the deep liberal value of free association, that shared aspiration enjoins moral respect. Moreover, he implicitly argued, liberty cannot thrive and liberal values flourish in a space containing alienated peoples. For all the elegance of their statement, Walzer's arguments in this work have a certain airy quality,[21] particularly because they do not consider in detail the dark side of communal self-determination. For more searching analysis one turns to works dedicated to illuminating the nationalist phenomenon.

NATIONS AND NATIONALISM

If, as Ernest Gellner has proposed, nationalism is a political movement designed to achieve symmetry between a nation or "people" (to use the UN's idiom) and its frontiers,[22] that is to make the people's space coterminous with the territory of a sovereign state or at least a political entity enjoying internal self-government, what is it that bonds the individuals who constitute the movement? What, in other words, is a "nation." "Two men are of the same nation," Gellner writes, "if and only if they share the same culture, where culture in turn means a system of ideas and signs and associations and ways of behaving and communicating."

Culture is, however an insufficient condition, since it also is necessary that "they *recognize each other* as belonging to the same nation"[23] [emphasis added]. While also emphasizing the centrality of a shared *perception* of common nationality, another leading scholar, Yael Tamir, suggests that it is necessarily accompanied by the shared *belief* that members of the nation have certain features in common, the most important of them being ancestors, however remote, and a continuous genealogy.[24] What most writers agree on, the ones cited being typical, is that at its core, the nation is an inter-subjective phenomenon, what Benedict Anderson described in his memorable phrase as "an imagined community."[25] The community may in fact share various objective features: language, religion, culture, skin tone, long residence of a determinate territory, and so on. And these common features may help explain why the sense of collective identity arose. But while they may be a source, they should not be identified as integral to the phenomenon itself, because even where several of these features are present, it may not arise.

The essence of the phenomenon being subjective, it might seem dependent to some extent on free individual choice. However, as Margaret Canovan has perceptively noted,

That choice is . . . experienced as a destiny transcending individuality; it turns political institutions into a kind of extended family inheritance, although the kinship ties in question are highly metaphorical; it is a contingent historical product that feels like part of the order of nature; it links individual and community, past and present; it gives to cold impersonal structures an aura of warm, intimate togetherness.[26]

This imagined community, what I would call "the community of blood," can be contrasted with what some writers call the "constitutional nation," exemplified by the United States. The constitutional nation is, to be sure, a sovereign state, but, unlike many of its kind, it is not felt by its members to be a mere contingent cluster of institutions and legal norms, at most a temporarily useful contrivance, an impersonal thing that is better than anarchy and the Hobbesian state of nature, but unimaginable as an object of devotion. The constitutional nation both in perception and fact is a community of choice. It has an identifiable historical beginning, often heroic, associated with a voluntary pact that is either the extant constitution or the core of principles on which the present one is based. The historical specificity of this nation's origins discourages notions about common genealogy. Members know that their ancestry predates the community, that their ancestors once were part of other political arrangements possibly in remote geographic space. Nevertheless the constitutional nation distinguishes itself from mere sovereign states by having acquired that "aura of warm, intimate togetherness" shrewdly evoked by Canovan in reference to the community of blood.

In the ideal case, though its members may differ in religion, race, domestic practices and even language (consider Switzerland, for instance), they participate in a common political culture, call it "the constitutional culture," and it evokes that same passionate loyalty, that sense of belonging to a bounded, distinctive, and admirable community which characterizes the imagined nation, the community of destiny with its myth of common origin. In the real world, however, a sovereign state may be a constitutional nation for only a portion of its citizens. Others, like many Basques in Spain, may identify with a community of blood and feel in varying degrees alienated from the constitutional system. In other words, constitutional nations are not immune to self-determination challenges.

Imagined nations by their nature *are* immune. They are like billiard balls, all of a piece, unitary actors glued together by the sensation of membership in an extended family. Where the imagined nation is coterminous with a sovereign state, of course it controls the material means – the media, schools, patriotic rites, language of power, and opportunity – for the glue's perpetual renewal. Perhaps even more important, its members automatically experience a quotidian sensation of separate and distinct existence from other unitary actors. So if we think of the imagined community as an organic thing and if we assume that the primal impulse of organic things is to survive, it seems natural that it should aspire to sovereignty. For where it shares political space with other communities, it cannot monopolize the means of cultural reinforcement. Moreover, its members may easily acquire cross-communal ties of friendship, family, love, and instrumental interest that progressively erode the primal communal identity. This risk is greatest within a liberal constitutional state, since in opening place and power to members of all its communities, that state creates conditions inimical to willed ghettoization.

Aspiration to sovereignty, to the undisputed mastery of a determinate space, is only one consequence of the imagined community's primal instincts and to the self-conscious interests of its political entrepreneurs. Why struggle for the power to govern – to prescribe rights and duties; to monopolize the use of force; to tax and spend; to construct and defend collective memory; to protect the community from all the cosmopolitan forces at work in the wider world – if, having attained it, you cannot use it single mindedly to maintain and enrich the tribe?

NATIONALISM AND LIBERALISM

Suppose the world were divided into a neat checkerboard of sovereign imagined communities. Would this be a moral utopia? Would liberalism's respect for associational autonomy then be reconciled with all other liberal values? Or, to put the issue in a slightly different form, would nationalism and liberalism be thus made compatible? Surely, even then, the answer is "no".

It is "no" in this world where unparalleled ease of communication and movement and the global division of labor foster fraternity and identity across national lines and offer a smorgasbord of "histories" in place of a single myth. But it would have been "no" even before there was liberalism much less globalism. When men traveled no faster than a ship could sail or an ass be made to trot, there was apostasy. And not just by the remarkable aberrant individual, because aberrancy is more than a matter of genius. It is encouraged by the contradictions between expectation and its fulfillment, by the failure of prophecy and the parsimony of justice, by the particularities of place, each with its layered history of successive myths. Aberrant individuals give passionate voice to doubt and disillusionment or to unsanctioned sources of hope. They challenge the tribal myths. They can be the offspring of merely endogenous contradictions, needs and inspirations. In the Middle Ages, before there were nations, the Albigensian Christian heresy flourished less than a thousand land miles from Rome and alongside areas unswerving in their conventional faith. The Albigensians constituted an internal challenge to the imagined community of Catholic Christianity which, in self-defense, extinguished them by fire and sword.

The short of the matter, then, is that globalization has simply accelerated (to be sure, greatly) the tendency toward instability endemic to national communities (as defined by Gellner) except, perhaps, where they are very small or exist in conditions of extreme isolation. Unifying narratives being vulnerable to replacement or schismatic interpretation, defenders of the status quo have repeatedly employed coercion in an effort to maintain them. They have been willing to employ the power of the collective to discipline the imagination of the individual (one community imagined once).

If, as I suggest, nationalism has an impulse toward cultural monopoly and, correspondingly, to ferocious intolerance susceptible to cultivation by political adventurers, why would anyone who resonates to the liberal tradition in political philosophy find anything positive about it, much less propose the legitimacy of interventions on its behalf when it pursues sovereignty at the expense of an established state? Nationalism's virtue is the other side of its vice. It sustains a sense of fraternity among a sometimes vast host of strangers. It is arguably the main emotional adhesive which allows this host to enjoy domestic peace and, by clothing governmental institutions in an aura normally associated with the warm intimacy of kinship ties, it encourages these strangers to do justice to each other and to cooperate in the production of public goods.

Without some feeling of fraternity, what will foster generosity among the "haves" and soften resentment among the "have nots"? National feeling helps greatly to fill the gap left when Divine Sanction for inequality and compassion loses its authority. In a secular, consumerist age, the imagined community may sometimes seem the only affective basis for consensual government. To the extent it facilitates government by consent, national feeling actually serves liberal values, according to this line of argument. Pure constitutionalism, where it takes root, is a happier alternative to the same end. But up to now it has only occasionally found nourishing soil.

Community-of-blood nationalism can thus be seen from the perspective of a human-rights advocate, that is someone who stands philosophically within the broad liberal tradition, to possess two kinds of virtues. One is intrinsic: nationalism is an exercise, hugely important to its practitioners, of the individual human right of free association along with the collective human right to cultural preservation. The other cluster of virtues is instrumental: facilitating government by consent and encouraging recognition of economic rights by sympathetically connecting the advantaged and the miserable.

The great problem, then, for contemporary liberal moralists is how to reconcile nationalism with its inherently bounded interests and liberalism with its universal ones implicit in the conviction that all human beings, regardless of their circumstances, possess a great constellation of rights. The dilemma is dangerously edged precisely because the instrumental virtues of blood nationalism appear to be a function of its exclusionary devotion. It seems futile to ask the devoted not to favor their own and expect to be reciprocally favored. So where one community of blood shares space with others, the logic of fraternal feeling as well as group survival dictates both communal bias in the recognition of individual merit and inter-communal struggle for power. In the right circumstances, a balance of communal power may maintain an uneasy peace and the sharing of public goods, but it would not logically entail the concomitant recognition of an individual's right to be judged on his or her secular merits.

The liberal's philosophical response to this dilemma assumes two analytically distinct albeit related forms. One is to take blood nationalism as an organism anti-liberal at its core, not without virtues, to be sure, and useful in its way, but a perpetual threat to humanitarian values, demanding anxious vigilance and close restraint by human rights norms. To the extent a community of blood accepts those constraints, it deserves acceptance. The other intellectual strategy is to insinuate liberal values into the nationalist core and to insist that the only good nationalism is a liberal one.

How can "liberal nationalism" avoid being an oxymoron? Liberalism emphasizes the essential moral identity of all peoples. Nationalism celebrates their differences. For liberals boundaries are contingent and instrumental. For nationalists they are destined and essential. At the same time, liberalism is no enemy of groups. It values all free association. It respects difference and prohibits coerced assimilation. Rights are universal, but one of those rights is to act collectively. Nationalism is liberal when it respects the rights of all other national communities to flourish. Being liberal does not prevent it from being national in the sense of acting to promote the interests of its members in competition with other groups. But it remains liberal only if in the course of that competition it respects the rights necessarily shared by all human beings if life is to be anything other than a war of all against all.

To put it in Rawlesian terms, liberal nationalists acknowledge as universal those forms of respect they would propose behind a veil of ignorance which prevented them from knowing to which group they would belong. Richard Miller's homely analogy suggestively distinguishes between the rights liberal nationalists concede to all and the benefits they would husband for their own communities. "I have an obligation," Miller writes, "to rescue the daughter of my neighbor if I see her drowning, because I respect her equal right to life. But I don't have an obligation to buy her a present every time I buy one for my own daughter."[27]

The liberal nationalist distinction between goods that must be shared and those available for competitive appropriation works up to a point with respect both to the relations between sovereign states and those among national communities within a state. In interstate relations it commands mutual respect for political independence and territorial integrity. These are the basic shared goods. It does not enjoin agreement on mechanisms for transferring wealth to poorer nation-states or for assuring that equal benefits flow from every treaty regime. Within states, it arguably requires consultation with all communities in matters requiring collective action and it clearly prohibits ethnic cleansing and forced assimilation. The extent to which it correspondingly commands public assistance to every community's projects for cultural self-defense is rather less clear.

Liberal nationalism envisions competition between communities and respects up to a point the unequal outcomes implicit in competition. Success in political competition equals control over state institutions. Consistent with the restraints of liberal nationalism, to what extent can a victorious community insinuate its distinctive cultural traits, language for instance, into the public realm? Does the "liberal" dimension of liberal nationalism require that there be as many languages of public business as there are communities within the envelope of the sovereign state? What does liberal nationalism imply for favoritism in the distribution of public goods and the state's obligations, if any, to combat private discrimination in favor of ethnic kin? The more forms and degrees of communal preference liberal nationalism is construed to preclude, the less it appears as a coherent form of nationalism.

LIBERAL NATIONALISM, SECESSION, AND HUMANITARIAN INTERVENTION

As I have already argued, liberal nationalism would be a morally arduous stance even in a uni-communal state. For it would still have to arbitrate questions of apostasy and sacrilege, still have to weigh the expressional right of the communal dissidents and the deracinated cosmopolitans to challenge the community's core beliefs, practices, and taboos. But at least it would be relieved of the challenging moral issues stemming from the co-location of national groups. And since communities seem most intolerant, most apt to demand internal conformity, when they apprehend threats from other communities to their independence and physical space, inhabitants of the uni-communal state should in theory be relatively tolerant of doubt and dissent, as well as more mutually generous and more inclined to feel like stakeholders in the structures of the state.

That is the essence of the case for the Walzerian injunction to assist in the birth of uni-communal states by intervening on behalf of secessionist movements. What are the moral limits of that injunction, limits imposed by the logic of liberal premises and the constellation of human rights and law-of-war norms to which liberals are constitutionally committed? One, prominent in Walzer's moral calculus, is to act only after the existence of a separatist blood community committed to the terrible rigors of armed struggle is indisputably clear. For liberalism war is unnatural, awful: a last resort. Those who beg for outside aid must first demonstrate that they actually speak for the greater part of a community committed to independence. Normally, Walzer seems to say, the proof of the claim is the actual launching of a substantial and tenacious war to achieve it. Not necessarily one calculated to succeed without external assistance: Intervention is not limited to facilitation of an already certain birth, just to reducing its pain and duration, although such reduction is, along with the intrinsic merits of self-determination, a part of intervention's ethical justification.[28]

But what is to be done in the case where a national group's aspiration to independence, its unity of purpose and its resolution are indisputable but its human and material resources too meager in relation to those of the enveloping state to sustain armed resistance? One possible answer is to treat the hypothesized case as implausible, even internally contradictory; to insist, in other words, that where a group is sufficiently united and determined, it will necessarily succeed either in negotiating its independence or creating the threshold conditions laid down by Walzer.

Much depends on how one construes the threshold test for a just pro-secessionist intervention. If its satisfaction requires a people to seize and hold a substantial part of the territory in which they propose to locate their new state, my case is highly plausible and Walzer's answer correspondingly evasive. Virtually no one, for instance, doubts the collective aspirations and resolution of the Palestinian people or doubts their inability to hold territory in the face of the enormous power of the Israeli state. Even the Chechins, operating in much more favorable conditions against a weaker state, can't hold much territory. If, on the other hand, it is sufficient for a people to demonstrate a sustained willingness to die in hopeless confrontations with superior force, episodically drawing a little blood from the perceived occupier's exposed parts, then the test becomes a fairer index of a people's resolution. But at an aching moral cost.

In a classical civil war, one fought between large organized units with identifiable markings, it is possible to maintain the distinction between combatants and non-combatants which lies at the heart of humanitarian law. Where, however, the occupier enjoys overwhelming superiority, armed resistance, if it is to make any impact at all, will have to be against poorly or unprotected non-combatants. So here we seem to have another dilemma for the Walzerian liberal interventionist: Choose a threshold test that will frequently fail to measure accurately the unity and resolve of a people or choose one which rewards terrorism.

Walzer implies strategies for escaping this dilemma. One is to distinguish between discriminating attacks on civilian officials (including police) arguably part of the apparatus of domination and indiscriminate attacks on the civilian population. While the former may be legitimately punishable by death, only the latter should be seen and condemned as "terrorist." The other strategy is to endorse intervention "to rescue peoples threatened with massacre" whatever the basis of the threat.[29] So secessionists opposed by overwhelming force can nevertheless make themselves subjects of a morally legitimate intervention by first setting themselves up to be massacred. Mass passive resistance in the spirit of Gandhi may not do, since it can be repressed by such means short of massacre as large-scale internment under horrific but not generally fatal conditions, combined with systematic torture, confiscation of property, dispersal of families, and organized rape, just to name some of the familiar tactics short of massacre.

Repression on so grand a scale may well be unnecessary. If a regime fears foreign intervention, should it cross the Walzer threshold and anticipate that wide-spread passive resistance might spiral into deadly confrontations with the potential to become telegenic massacres, it will presumably preempt in part by detaining potential organizers and, more generally, by a closer repression of organized activity within the potentially secessionist community. There is a third escape from the dilemma, which is simply to circumvent it by insisting on the legitimacy of intervention only in the case of open war between organized military formations. To do so would be to admit that neither the unity of a people nor its intense alienation from the state in which it is held nor its passionate aspiration to independent national existence collectively suffice to justify foreign intervention. For as I have noted, we can see before us cases where, although all those elements exist, an irreducible asymmetry of power – which can, as in the case of Israel and the Palestinians, result from a concatenation of factors including relative numbers, terrain inhospitable to guerrilla war, intimidated or unsympathetic neighbors, foreign assistance to the recognized government, technological inferiority – prevents the repressed community from launching an armed struggle.

Walzer's threshold is, in short, problematic because it fails to offer an ethically appealing test for determining whether sovereign political space contains two "peoples" and whether, where two exist, they are able to coexist in a condition of mutual respect. If it is defensible it must be by means of other morally engaging reasons. One such reason for insisting on an armed conflict as a precondition for intervention, a reason arguably buried in Walzer's concern for maintaining determinate space in which a people can struggle to achieve and maintain freedom, is to provide a test, not of the unity and commitment of the repressed community and of the representative character of secessionist advocates, but rather of the bona fides of the intervenor.[30] The armed-struggle condition makes it more difficult for another state to conceal aggressive intent – for example, by carving off a satellite from the body of an existing state – behind a humanitarian rhetoric.

It is hardly a foolproof test of the intervenor's bona fides. A state with aggressive intent may facilitate the condition by conspiring with and arming ambitious members of some minority group in another country in the hope of ultimately arousing popular support for secession. To that end, the foreign state's local agents may undertake operatically violent acts designed to provoke the government of the target state into an indiscriminate, broadly alienating response. But however dubious its roots, once the aspiration to independence takes feverish hold, once a people has acquired a nationalist elan and has established itself, it may prove as intractable a partner for its erstwhile benefactor as it was an opponent of the previous constitutional order. So however poisoned the intention, the objective outcome may be a genuinely independent nation-state.

Another reason which could be adduced to support the high threshold proposed by Walzer is the sheer awfulness of war. The only thing certain about its conduct and outcome is that it will destroy things. The rest is speculation. Where, however, war has already begun, intervention may hasten its outcome and so reduce the scale of devastation as well as helping in what Walzer argues is the morally salutary achievement of a new authentic political community. Where there is no war, the moral gains from prospective self-determination must be weighed at the outset against the losses certain to be generated by a conflict which may in fact be avoidable.[31]

Yet another arguable basis for Walzer's high threshold is the extent to which the initiation and conduct of a considerable armed conflict demonstrates leadership with the organizational skills and political coherence required to administer an independent state. A conventional world-order-based objection to secession has been the potential proliferation of "unviable" states. Until recently, those invoking the criterion of "viability" have usually had in mind mini-states deficient in natural resources, particularly food. Global integration has cut the ground out from under that concern. Well-organized micro-states can import capital investment and knowhow, export the resulting products and then use export revenues to pay for essential and, for that matter, a stunning array of non-essential goods and services, as anyone who has lived and shopped in Singapore can attest. In the contemporary world, viability is a function of stable and rational administration sufficiently consensual to allow the openness essential for effective integration into the global economy.

CONCLUSION

Until the 9/11 destruction of New York's World Trade Center turned the world upside down, Humanitarian Intervention had seemingly become the issue *de jour* on the international relations menu. Seminars, symposia, conferences, articles, reports, and whole volumes were dedicated to defining its limits, categorizing its forms, and assessing its precedents, while proposing and predicting its future. For present purposes what is most striking about this vast essay in collective cerebration is the almost total absence of secessionist struggles from the short list of conditions justifying humanitarian intervention.

Quite typical in this respect were the conclusions of a multi-national group of scholars convened in the Fall of 2000 to explore the prospects for great power consensus on international action to prevent, mitigate or terminate conflicts with a self-determination dimension. They came from almost a dozen countries – including China, Japan, Russia, Germany, France, Canada, Australia, and the United States. They represented a considerable diversity of political and ideological views. They disagreed on some key issues, particularly whether humanitarian intervention should be codified by treaty or UN Declaration. But essentially without exception they agreed that if international action without the consent of the target state is ever justified (and most participants believed it is under the right conditions), the justifying condition is mass killing and other gross violations of personal security rights, not the denial of secessionist demands. In addition, they agreed, again essentially without dissent, that self-determination claims by groups in established states should generally be processed within the normative framework of minority rights.

Not surprisingly, governments are at one with the broad scholarly consensus that the right to self-determination does not imply a right to secede. The key UN resolutions proclaiming the self-determination right during the era of decolonization carefully disclaimed any intention to authorize action threatening the territorial integrity of existing states.[32] Nothing that has happened since the end of the Cold War suggests any erosion of this intergovernmental consensus. Any intergovernmental legal consensus has, as such, a certain moral weight even though many of the regimes participating in it lack democratic legitimacy. It does so particularly where, as here, it relates to the primary interest of state elites in political independence and territorial integrity. There is moral weight because challenges to the norm are likely catalysts of international conflict with all of its attendant human costs. How much weight depends in significant measure on the relative movement of the legal norm and associated moral convictions. Changes in the trajectory and velocity of moral convictions can augur withdrawal of support for a long-established legal rule. With respect to secession, change is not visible and cannot be anticipated because the moral case for encouraging secession is weak.[33]

Secession has two possible roles in the moral universe of human rights. One is as a means for protecting a people from serious and sustained violation of political, civil, and cultural rights. Let us assume that the Tutsi minority had predominated in a part of Rwanda and that the genocide of 1994 had been aborted by foreign intervention which expelled Hutu forces from the Tutsi-populated region and provisionally sealed it off. At that point, the deadly vulnerability of the Tutsis demonstrated by the attempted genocide would have justified international support for secession as a last resort remedial measure. This unfortunately hypothetical case closely approximates the real one of Kosovo, although, like all real cases, it is more complicated. The second role, which strategically precedes the first, is as a negative incentive encouraging respect for minority rights. Secession becomes the remedy of choice when the threat of internationally backed secession fails to deter persecution.

A third (we might call it the Walzerian) role, that of giving full expression to the passionate aspirations of an intersubjective community, is one barred, I believe, by the humanitarian calculus except where it is the outcome of a genuinely consensual divorce proceedings.[34] There is, admittedly, a human-rights dimension to the secessionist claim: free association is an indisputable human right. But as Mill argued in his seminal elaboration of the liberal ethical paradigm from which the human-rights regime stems, the liberty of one reaches its moral frontier when it impinges on the liberty of another. Clearly the core individual rights are capable of broad exercise by some individuals (or groups) without jeopardizing the rights of others. That is true at least in part because, while we are accustomed to stating them in positive terms (for example, freedom to speak), their original and still primary thrust is the negative one of restraining state action to limit their exercise. In its most common manifestations, freedom of association is like the other individual rights. Formation of a cycling club by one circle of friends in Perugia does not prevent another circle from forming one of its own.

Association by blood nationalists to carve out an independent state from the body of an existing one is different both in theory and practice. It differs not because it is bounded and hence exclusionary; that is, after all, true of many private associations. And it is lexically susceptible to description as a negative right, that is a restraint on the executive power of the state from which the nationalists wish to secede. But its essential character is not to evade, it is rather to capture and then employ state power. Admittedly, other rights like freedom of speech can be exercised in order to secure control of the state. Elections could be defined as competitive speech activities. But that is not the general essence of free speech. Seizure of state power *is* the essence of nationalist association.

Be that as it may, what really constrains the moral appeal of blood nationalism to practical moralists is its likely consequences for human rights. For the ineluctable purpose of seizure is to privilege the association to some degree at the expense of the individual and collective interests of non-members. While not necessarily heinous, the purpose is certainly problematical.

How problematical depends on the extent of the privileges the secessionists choose or are able to claim and also on their openness to new members. In most heterogeneous societies, one culture enjoys some measure of preeminence. Where, as frequently occurs, one dimension of cultural differentiation is language, preeminence is particularly marked, because one language is likely to predominate in public and private arenas of power. Irrespective of the intentions of members of the dominant culture, this predominance encourages assimilation sometimes to the point of reducing minority cultural traits to the status of folk art. International law plainly restrains majorities from conscious suppression of minority languages and religions. It arguably requires some limited state action to help members of minority cultural groups maintain themselves. But I do not see it as requiring multi-lingualism in the realm of state, much less private jurisdiction. So secessionists can fairly claim that they seek only that degree of advantage the preponderant community in the existing state already possesses.

Even if one could easily evaluate the sincerity of that claim when first made, it would remain difficult to anticipate with confidence what the erstwhile minority would do once it actually found itself in possession of state power. Skepticism about the likely generosity of today's alienated minority *vis-à-vis* minorities in a state it eventually succeeds in forming is deserved, because moderation is not normally a distinguishing feature of militants pursuing secession from a democratic state which (a) allows assimilation, (b) enforces equality of opportunity and (c) while making competence in the dominant language a requirement for official position, allows the minority full use of its language in intracommunal matters.

Humanitarian intervention is an extraordinary means for the defense and promotion of human rights and so it should remain. By their nature, successful struggles to transform blood communities into sovereign states primarily to sustain or even to intensify the sense of community tend towards illiberal outcomes. The world is already divided comprehensively into sovereign states, each of them increasingly occupied by a plurality of imagined communities. There is no unclaimed space on Earth. In such a world, respect for sovereignty, *wherever the state reasonably accommodates the interests of diverse peoples*, is the optimal norm for maintaining areas where the human rights of individuals living in, bridging, or moving between communities can flourish.

NOTES

1 Thucydides, *The History of the Peloponnesian War*, book v para. 89, translated by Richard Crawley (1992).

2 On nineteenth-century rationalization of the use of force, see generally Tom Farer, "Law and War," ch. 2 in *The Future of the International Legal Order*, Cyril E. Black and Richard A. Falk, eds. (Princeton University Press, 1969).

3 Lassa Oppenheim, *International Law, a Treatise*, vol. I, ed. Hersch Lauterpacht (London, New York: Longmans Green, 1955, 8th edn.).

4 Article 6(a) of the Charter for the International Military Tribunal at Nuremberg gave the tribunal jurisdiction over: Crimes against peace: namely, planning, preparation, initiation or waging of a war of aggression, or a war in violation of international treaties, agreements or assurances, or participation in a common plan or conspiracy for the accomplishment of any of the foregoing.

5 For a discussion on the divergent views on what constituted legitimate intervention and the development of the concept through the first half of

the twentieth century, see Charles Fenwick, "Intervention: Individual and Collective," *American Journal of International Law* 39, Issue 4 (October 1945), 645–63.

6 A state is defined as "A people permanently occupying a fixed territory bound together by common law habits and custom into one body politic exercising, through the medium of an organized government, independent sovereignty and control over all persons and things within its boundaries capable of making war and peace and of entering into international relations with other communities of the globe." *Black's Law Dictionary*, abridged 5th edn., by Henry Cambell Black (1983).

7 Michael Waltzer argues that there are few clear examples of interventions for purely humanitarian purposes, and that most, if not all, interventions stem from mixed motives. Michael Waltzer, *Just and Unjust Wars* (1977), p. 101.

8 See, for example, Ian Brownlie, *Principles of Public International Law* (Clarendon Press, 1966), pp. 575ff.

9 The International Commission on Kosovo, established by the Government of Sweden, concluded in its report that the intervention probably was not legal in the sense of being compatible with UN Charter norms, but it was nevertheless "legitimate." *Kosovo Report*, Independent International Commission on Kosovo (Oxford University Press, 2000). See also, Richard A. Falk, *NATO's Kosovo Intervention, Kosovo, World Order and the Future of International Law*, 93 AJIL, 847 (1999), discussing the competing legal, political and moral debates surrounding NATO's intervention in Kosovo.

10 International Covenant on Economic and Social Rights, Art. 1.1. Adopted Dec. 19, 1966, entered into force Jan. 3, 1976, 999 UNTS 3; International Covenant on Civil an Political Rights, Art. 1.1. Adopted Dec. 19, 1966, entered into force March 23, 1976, 999 Dec. 19, 1966, 999 UNTS 171.

11 The two main General Assembly Resolutions addressing self-determination are the Colonial Declaration No. 1514 (or "Declaration 1514") and the Friendly Relations Declaration No. 2625 (or "Declaration 2625").

12 A list of territories that were subject to United Nations Trusteeship Agreements or were listed by the General Assembly as non-self-governing between 1945 and 1999 and the dates of independence or other change in status is available at http//www.un.org/Depts/dpi/decolonization/trust2.htm.

13 The cases of South Africa and Israel/Palestine do not quite fit the colonial paradigm.

14 Eighty nations whose peoples were formerly under colonial rule have joined the United Nations as sovereign independent states since the UN was founded in 1945. Additionally, many other Territories have achieved self-determination through political association with other independent States or through integration with other States. Today there are only seventeen non-self-governing territories remaining. These are: American Samoa, Anguilla, Bermuda, British Virgin Islands, Cayman Islands, Falkland Islands

(Malvinas), Gibraltar, Guam, Montserrat, New Caledonia, Pitcairn, St. Helena, Tokelau, Turks and Caicos Islands, United States Virgin Islands, and Western Sahara. The United Nations and Decolonization, Prepared for Internet by the Information Technology Section Department of Public Information © United Nations 2000–01, available at http://www.un.org/Depts/dpi/decolonization/main.htm.

15 Those wars were: Afghanistan, Democratic Republic of Congo, Indonesia (East Timor), India (Kashmir), Russia (Chechnya), Sri Lanka, Sudan, and Yugoslavia (Kosovo). (Wars in Angola, Algeria, Colombia, Congo, Sierra Leone, and between Eritrea and Ethiopia did not significantly feature current self-determination claims.) In 2000, the Israeli–Palestinian dispute re-erupted into significant violence, thus returning to a pattern of conflict reminiscent of the Intifada in the late 1980s.

16 Michael Walzer, *Just and Unjust Wars*, p. 108.

17 *Ibid.*, p. 87, quoting John Stuart Mill, *On Liberty* (1859).

18 Walzer, *Just and Unjust Wars*, p. 89.

19 Actually there are two albeit closely linked principles of liberal political thought that apply here. One is that everyone has a right to enter whatever associations he or she chooses. A state that seeks to impose an unwanted association infringes this right and thereby, according to the principle, lacks legitimacy in relation to the persons coerced. The other is the principle of voluntary obligation which holds that people acquire obligations only when they choose to incur them. See Paul Gilbert, "National Obligations: Political, Cultural or Societal," in Simon Caney, David George, and Peter Jones, eds., *National Rights, International Obligations* (Boulder: Westview Press, 1996), pp. 103–04.

20 Walzer, *Just and Unjust Wars*, p. 88.

21 Walzer's subsequent response to his critics – "The Moral Standing of States: A Response to Four Critics," *Philosophy and Public Affairs* 9, no. 3, 209–29 – leaves untouched his position on intervention in self-determination struggles.

22 Ernest Gellner, *Nations and Nationalism* (1983), p. 1.

23 *Ibid.*, p. 7.

24 Ernst Renan has written caustically that a nation consists of a group of people who share many things but have forgotten what they are. Ernst Renan, "Qu'est-ce qu une nation?" (Paris, 1882).

25 Benedict Anderson, *Imagined Communities* (1991).

26 Margaret Canovan, "The Skeleton in the Cupboard, Nationhood, Patriotism and Limited Loyalties," ch. 5, p. 60 in Carney, George and Jones, *National Rights, International Obligations* (1996).

27 Richard Miller, "Cosmopolitan Respect and Patriotic Concern," *Philosophy and Public Affairs* 27 (1998), 202–24, p. 207.

28 See Waltzer on Intervention, *Just and Unjust Wars*, ch. 6.

29 *Ibid.*, p. 108.
30 This reason is arguably implicit in Walzer's concern to demarcate and protect arenas where peoples can struggle to achieve and sustain free societies.
31 Waltzer, *Just and Unjust Wars*, p. 95.
32 For example, art. 6 of General Assembly resolution 1514 (xv). Declaration on the Granting of Independence to Colonial Countries and Peoples stated: "Any attempt aimed at the partial or total disruption of the national unity and the territorial integrity of a country is incompatible with the purposes and principles of the Charter of the United Nations," GA res/1514(xv) December 14, 1960.
33 The most systematic analysis of the morality of political divorce is Allen Buchanan's fine book *Secession* (Boulder: Westview Press, 1991).
34 The proceedings are not consensual when one party overcomes by brutal acts of terrorism, for instance, the resistance of other stakeholders, as militant Basque nationalists are attempting in Spain.

Chapter 9

Secession, humanitarian intervention, and the normative significance of political boundaries

CHRISTINE CHWASZCZA

Secession and foreign intervention are in many respects quite different things. But considered as topics of political philosophy, they pose similar theoretical problems in at least two respects: normative discussions of both topics focus on the legitimate grounds of political sovereignty and the significance of political boundaries. Both the concept of sovereignty and the normative significance of political boundaries, in turn, have two aspects: internal and external. They can be regarded from an internal perspective, the perspective within a sovereign state; and they can be regarded from an external perspective, the perspective of a sovereign state *vis-à-vis* other states.

My approach is theoretical rather than practical. I shall try to reconstruct a normative and conceptual framework for discussions of secession and humanitarian military intervention. Since any normative discussion has to begin with some substantive normative commitments, I will rely on a broad account of political liberalism.[1] The first section takes up the topic of secession in the restricted sense that it discusses theoretical claims for a "right to secede." The next section deals with humanitarian intervention under the special issue of whether there exists a "duty to intervene" and the final section summarizes the results in order to propose some general considerations about the normative significance of sovereignty and political boundaries in political theory and international ethics.

IS THERE A "RIGHT TO SECEDE"?

Delineation of the concept of secession

Secession involves a claim to political autonomy, but not every claim to political autonomy should be regarded as secessionist. In order to

discuss the legitimacy of a right to secede, we may exclude decolonization, the dissolution of a treaty-based federation, and the regaining of
political autonomy from illegitimate usurpation. The reason for excluding these three cases is that they do not pose problems for justification
under any reasonable ethical standards or under contemporary international law. The problem that colonial and usurpatory rule involves is,
rather, to judge where they exist, because almost every existing state has
at some point in its history been established by conquest, colonialism, or
usurpation. Because it is impossible to define *in abstracto* general moral
standards for which individual people constitute a political unity and
which claims for territory are legitimate, I suggest that we rely on the
practice of mutual recognition. The aim of normative theory cannot be
to eliminate every feature of contingency and to rectify every past act
of injustice; instead, it must be to develop norms of just behavior and
standards for just institutions that apply to people that live and act now.

Accordingly, "secession" in this restricted sense can be understood
as involving a claim to political autonomy by a group of citizens that
(i) was formerly united with others in a political *and* civil union on shared
territory, and (ii) aims at forming a politically sovereign state of its own.[2]

Exploration of the normative dimensions of secession

Given a concept of secession as delineated in Section 1, secession can
be understood as both the dissolution and the creation of sovereign
political unity. When a part of a state secedes, the citizens of the seceding
part reject the claims of the previous government to legitimate rule; and
they claim for themselves the right of self-determination in the sense
of political sovereignty. Thus, a discussion of a normative theory of
secession must deal with (i) the conditions of legitimate rule and (ii) the
value of sovereignty.

In contrast to conditions of legitimate rule, the value of sovereignty is
not such a familiar topic in political theory. It therefore seems appropriate to start by asking what there is about it that is not already covered by
questions of legitimate rule. From an international-law perspective, the
claim to territory seems central to the concept of sovereignty,[3] because
the claim to territory is one of four *definienda* of the international-law concept of sovereignty.[4] I want to suggest, however, that claims to territory
are not the most interesting aspect of the value of sovereignty, at least
from the perspective of political theory. Rather, what is crucial is that in
the course of the secession, mutual rights and obligations which existed

among citizens as members of a common political union are dissolved. Of these rights and obligations, the claim to the hitherto collectively used territory and the collective goods that are located in it is only the most obvious. Therefore, it is rather the definition of a political collective itself that is at stake in secessionist claims to sovereignty. Of course, every political union necessarily needs some territory to live upon; but, nevertheless, the normative emphasis is on defining a political unity or, if one prefers, political membership. Consequently, I take it as granted that claims of territory in a case of secession cannot be reduced simply to questions of property rights. For a "political union" is fundamentally different from an aggregation of property owners, although some libertarian thinkers come quite close to such a conception.[5] The conditions of (i) legitimate rule and (ii) the value of sovereignty, distinguished above, offer two fundamentally different justificatory arguments for a right to secede. The former justifies secession, or grants a right to secede, as a measure taken against unjust rule. The latter attempts to justify secession on the basis of a normative conception of political membership. Allen Buchanan distinguishes, in an analogous way, between "remedial right type" arguments and "primary right type" arguments.[6] I shall begin my discussion with arguments of the second type.

LEGITIMIZING POLITICAL MEMBERSHIP. Generally, one can say that liberal political philosophy, because of its commitment to ethical individualism, lacks the conceptual framework for normative discussions of social groups regarded as (normative) entities *sui generis*. It therefore takes up the concept of political unity in terms of individual membership in a democratically organized group, transforming "unity" into "individual membership" and "political" into "democratically enacted forms of government" or "democratic forms of collective self-determination."[7] Among the arguments for a right to secede that belong to the broader paradigm of liberal political theory, we can distinguish between a strictly individualistic version, which I shall call "libertarian," and a more holistically oriented version, which I shall call "communitarian."

The libertarian argument for secession. If one interprets the right of a people to self-determination in a radically democratic and strictly individualistic way, then it is natural to construe the right of citizens to self-determination broadly so that even political membership requires a citizen's consent. Even within the framework of a liberal contract theory, political membership not only guarantees the protection of individual rights and essential collective goods, but also generates political duties *vis-à-vis* fellow citizens and the state as an institution (which itself requires legitimation).

According to Harry Beran, for instance, these duties *vis-à-vis* other citizens and the state can be justified only insofar as they are subject to a procedure of individual consent.[8] This procedure is interpreted by Beran as factual, not hypothetical. According to him, it must be possible to cancel political membership, not only by "opting out," as in the case of emigration, but also by seceding when a large group of people (i) desire to cancel membership, *and* (ii) have a simultaneous interest in forming their own political unit and (iii) possess a territory that is to some extent self-contained.[9] The crucial point here is that, according to Beran, this right to secession is to be guaranteed (under certain qualifications) even against the will of a majority of citizens of the entire existing state. He takes it that, as a matter of the theory of legitimacy, the only decisive factor is the mere unwillingness of the individual citizens (aggregated in this case) to maintain the existing political membership. Accordingly, he suggests making the question whether to secede or not depend only on the will of the majority of the population in the relevant (seceding) area.

Fundamentally, the same form of argument is defended by David Gauthier, though his justification derives less from the theory of democracy than does Beran's.[10] It derives, instead, from a radical contractualist constructivism that emphasizes voluntary cooperation. Taking cooperation as a basic notion, Gauthier also considers the breaking up of cooperative enterprises in cases of secession but adds the restriction that the citizens of the remaining state may not be disadvantaged – for example, by dividing former collective goods to the one-sided advantage of the citizens who secede.

Both Beran and Gauthier take into account certain duties of justice between the two new states that result from a secession. Thus, the advantages and costs of undertakings and investments that have heretofore been supported collectively must be justly distributed to both of the new states or their citizens. Moreover, external security and resources necessary for existence must not be massively damaged.[11] Here, two criteria should also be adverted to: the seceding state should neither suppress fundamental individual rights (of the whole citizenry or of minorities) nor suppress further efforts toward secession within its own territory.

The libertarian argument amounts to a radicalization of ethical individualism. As with the liberal contract theories of the seventeenth and eighteenth centuries, it mostly neglects the problem of determining who the citizens of the state are.[12] For one thing, the universalistic and hypothetical character of the contractualist approach prevents it from taking into account the actual, historical establishment of a particular state. For another, the question of personal political identity and the meaning of what it is to belong to a specific political community recedes into the background. The state, in modern libertarian terms, is essentially reduced to being merely a necessary means to the pursuit of individual happiness.

The libertarian argument seems to be merely a consistent development of a weak, instrumentalist conception of the institution of the "state" in that it reduces the conditions of its establishment to the individual interests or the expressions of will on the part of its members. After all, if one is not inclined toward a statist conception of the state, one will ask why the "people of a state" should be forcibly welded together. Furthermore, the libertarian line of argument gives up the concept of "political" relations altogether. On closer examination, we can see that the libertarian argument for secession not only fails to address the conditions and problems of the constitution of a political union, but also is based on a problematic concept of democratic legitimacy.

We should be clear at the outset that, from a theoretical standpoint, the existence of actual consent does not yield a sufficient criterion for the legitimacy of political institutions, no matter how important it doubtless is empirically for their functioning. Actual consent alone cannot distinguish between just and unjust grounds or interests on which this consent is based. Actual or empirical interests are never sufficient in the framework of a contractualist justification of state institutions. They always require a normative, justice-related filter, such as, for instance, the equality of persons, impartiality, or the ignoring of differences of power. Hence, one sees the hypothetical and idealized character of contractualist argumentation and the artificial distinction between *status naturalis* and *status civilis*.

Similarly with the right to secession, a distinction is properly made between just (or justified) and unjust (or unjustified) grounds. In the form espoused by Beran and Gauthier, the libertarian argument would, for instance, permit the secession of the economically prosperous part of a country from the less prosperous part when it is the will of the citizens of the former to unload their "poor relatives." Moreover, the grounds for secession need not even be of a political or economic sort; they could, for example, have a purely aesthetic character. An interest in forming a nuclear-free zone or a rejection of any given law would, on this view, yield no better grounds than, for instance, an interest in keeping other people from the enjoyment of particular natural beauties or a desire to be rid of a population with a peculiar dialect. Although all liberal theories of justification are more or less consensus theories, the paradigm is quite clearly overextended by the requirement that everything is justified if and only if someone wishes it.

It might be replied that the libertarian theory's ignoring of justice-relevant specifications of grounds and/or circumstances does not weigh as heavily as it might on other theories. This is because a libertarian theory reduces the tasks of the state and the sphere of its regulation to a minimum that merely guarantees security, and it interprets "society" as a voluntary association of free individuals. The libertarian argument construes political membership by analogy to membership in a club, and the pro-secessionist argument trades on the obvious thought that we normally can decide which club we want to belong to.

This reply, however, does not deprive the objection of its force. The reason is that a political society is entirely different from a club because of its theoretical and practical existential necessity. Even when we pre-suppose a weak concept of the state, state institutions fulfill fundamental functions of coordination and security that are absolute preconditions for the establishment of rights and the pursuit of individual aims. The institutions of the state also regulate private social coexistence in a way that provides a basic degree of predictability and reliability in interpersonal interaction, as well as the peaceful settlement of conflicts.

Insofar as such relations of cooperation are not to be maintained by direct, coercive sanctions, they presuppose a sufficiently strong basis in *trust* or *solidarity*. But neither trust nor solidarity is to be established and maintained in a purely "contractualist society" (as Gauthier would call it). A right to secession that is as open and unrestricted as Beran and Gauthier demand would be completely unproductive for the functions of society that I have cited.

Moreover, even when it is considered in a less theoretical and more pragmatic way, such an unrestricted right to secession would be functionally much like an unrestricted right to a veto (whose defects for democracy are obvious).[13] Any group of persons could oppose any law by threatening to secede. Further, it could have the effect that, because of the uncertainty that would prevail, long-term and/or interregional collective investments would simply not be undertaken.

The libertarian argument not only underestimates the institutional significance of the state for the pursuit of private life-plans, but it also wins an increase in political autonomy for individual citizens only at the cost of the depoliticization of social conditions. These social conditions are viewed, especially in Gauthier's version, as a network of voluntary bilateral associations – that is, as mainly discrete links between coincident interests. This is not the place to criticize this atomistic concept of society, but it seems to me clear that any viable conception of a pluralist deliberative public and of a just social order presupposes a stronger conception of society than the libertarian perspective allows.[14]

The communitarian argument for secession. In contrast to the libertarian conception, there is another way of construing the right of a people to self-determination, namely, as a collective right that attaches to certain kinds of groups. I shall call this the communitarian argument. It is espoused most clearly by Avishai Margalit and Joseph Raz.[15] In contrast to the libertarian argument, which minimizes the significance and function of a society, the communitarian argument rests on a strong concept of society. "Society" is here understood primarily as "community." Factors that constitute a community, such as belonging to an ethnic group or agreement in cultural or normative attitudes, are regarded as necessary conditions for the constitution of either an actual or an ideal "political community." "Shaping" or "building" political communities in this strong sense can be taken as providing a basis for the justification of secession.[16]

According to Charles Taylor,[17] the communitarian argument derives from two traditions: the particularism of classical republicanism, and the ideal of identity-cum-authenticity of post-Enlightenment Romanticism.[18] The thesis of republicanism that is of interest here asserts that political virtue and interest in the *bonum commune* is the same as, or at least enhanced by, a collective feeling of identity or "belonging-together" by members of the political community. However, no pro-secessionist argument can be derived merely from emphatically asserting that thesis, because it does not imply any specification of the political community. The republican argument can be used for pro-secessionist purposes only if it is combined with what Taylor calls the "ideal of identity-cum-authenticity," that is, a concept of cultural identity that regards cultural identity and political agency as co-extensive. This amounts to saying either that cultural identity requires sovereign political self-determination of a cultural group or that democratic political agency requires cultural closeness. This second claim is a rather unconvincing empirical claim. The first claim is also partly empirical, but it has a normative core that can possibly create a derivative argument for secession for polycultural societies. This is because it regards political sovereignty as a means to realizing the good of cultural identity. To shorten the argument, I will not take up the question whether cultural identity possesses sufficiently great intrinsic value to override moral considerations against secession. Instead, I will stress the fact that the first claim conflicts with the liberal distinction between morality and politics and with the separation of private and public spheres of social interaction.[19]

Even if one regards cultural identity as an important value, it could be protected equally well by democratic measures that do not call the unity of the state into question. This fact raises obstacles to the use of these cultural considerations in the case for a right to secession; and it suggests types of solution that are, as Taylor himself says,[20] more appropriate to liberalism: minority rights, bilingualism, a federalist structure, and special formulas for representation, to mention the most common.

In actual cases where conflicts between different cultural groups within a society exist, an attempt at a liberal solution will always recommend attempts at conflict-resolution and mediation, thus presupposing a readiness on all sides to tolerance, compromise, and cooperation. To be sure, this readiness is often absent, and a political movement can develop its own dynamic so as to make a political compromise impossible. Moreover, in political reality, an appeal to cultural identity hardly ever appears in a pure form but, instead, is mixed with broader political and/or economic concerns or struggles. Nevertheless, practical difficulties concerning the implementation of a liberal solution are not sufficient to establish an outright justification for a primary right to secede.

To summarize: arguments for a right to secede cannot convincingly be developed within either a libertarian or a communitarian framework. This result is unsurprising because philosophical liberalism's main interest is not to spell out the conditions for the genesis or development of a political union, but the legitimacy of political rule.

SECESSION AS A MEASURE AGAINST THE UNJUST EXERCISE OF AUTHORITY. Although I have argued against the justification of secession as a basic right in the case of "just rule," I think there is good reason for regarding secession as justified in the case of "unjust rule." Dealing with the case of unjust rule, however, creates difficult problems for normative theory for two reasons. First, normative theory often employs certain idealizations, presupposing that people are willing and able to behave justly. It would be unreasonable to say that such ideal normative requirements are obligatory in circumstances of injustice; but what is morally allowed under such circumstances is difficult to define apart from vague principles like appropriateness, suitability for the aims of justice, and so on. Second, dealing with injustice cannot take only moral considerations into account. It usually involves the weighing of normative and pragmatic considerations, ideal and feasible options, and legitimate interests and norms that resist standardization. One must rely on prudence and judgment. Further, if one does not view political philosophy as solely an application of "pure" legal or moral theory, and if one acknowledges that politics also has legitimate extra-moral aspects, one must accept that rigorous normative theory faces serious limits in dealing with political injustice. The following remarks, therefore, will not present a comprehensive treatment of the subject, but only suggest some minimal lines of thought that have to be further developed throughout the discussion of concrete cases.

Ideally, the justification of secession as a measure against injustice might well imply that the seceding state itself satisfy normative conditions of justice.[21] In contrast to Lea Brillmayer (and also in part to Buchanan), however, I would not insist that in cases of unjust rule, the seceding part also has to demonstrate that it has a legitimate claim to territory. My reason is that it is not a claim to territory that is at stake here, but it is the fact that the existing state fails to fulfill a fundamental normative condition that legitimizes its existence and power. From this perspective, secession can be understood as a special form of the right of resistance.

Ideally, (a) resistance comes under consideration only in case of really massive injustice. Also, it seems reasonable to insist that (b) secession is an option only if other measures of reestablishing justice or overcoming intra-civil conflicts have been seriously undertaken and either have shown themselves to be ineffective or else cannot be undertaken at all because of substantive inequalities in political power. Third, (c) even under these conditions, one must still take certain pragmatic considerations into account.

As to (a): uncontroversial cases of massive injustice occur when fundamental human rights of a group in society fail to be respected or are not sufficiently protected. In these cases, the state institutions will not, or cannot, live up to their basic function of preserving security. Such things happen, for example, in the following sorts of cases:

– when physical, psychological, or mental integrity is threatened,

– when particular groups within society are systematically exploited or debased, or the security of the political and economic foundations is not guaranteed,

– when the possibility of participation in public affairs or fundamental rights of citizens are systematically violated,

– when cultural or religious minorities are massively discriminated against.

As to (b): if other measures prove to be ineffective, it is not a right to secede, but rather a right to defend oneself against injustice that provides the normative grounds for secession. In practice, the main problem seems to be that efforts to overcome injustice or intra-civil conflict are rarely undertaken wholeheartedly.

As to (c): despite the assumption that unjust rule can, under certain conditions, justify secession, a few pragmatic reflections are in order.

The justification of secession on grounds of massive injustice comes up for serious consideration when sharp conflicts exist within a society. Secession raises the hope of removing the basis of the conflict through a separation of the parties. This strategy, however, presupposes that a geographical separation and a division of collective goods is possible, and that it will equip the resulting states sufficiently to assure their existence with natural, economic, and technical resources (that is, infrastructure) that guarantee political self-reliance, at least after a period of time. Here, it is certainly an advantage for the seceding party to inhabit a self-contained area, which does not cut through the remaining state, does not form an enclave within it, and so on.[22] It is hardly possible, however, to develop general criteria for the sharing of natural resources, economic links, and technical resources. Instead, judgments concerning individual cases will always have to be made.

Realistically, one should not have unrestricted confidence in the possibility of settling conflicts by secession. In the first place, the possibility or intention of carrying out such a separation sometimes even intensifies the conflict (as the case of the former Yugoslavia illustrates), since there is an incentive for each party to strengthen its position. Secondly, a political separation by no means guarantees that the conflict will disappear. Thirdly, there is also the danger, which Buchanan especially adverts, of a continuation or intensification of the unjust practices directed against other groups in society besides the one that has successfully seceded.

Here, it is important to keep the following point in mind. The abolition of an unjust government and the reestablishment of just rule are, in principle, more desirable outcomes than a secession that leaves these conditions otherwise untouched. In view of the fact that massive injustices usually are carried out by massive means of repression by the stronger party, the requirement that other measures be taken first may seem somewhat cynical. However, this cynicism will seem less pronounced when possible measures of inter-state intervention are taken into account; and the next section will argue for this possibility by arguing for a weakening of the principle of non-intervention in international law.

IS THERE A DUTY OF HUMANITARIAN INTERVENTION?

Theorists of international law tend to define the concept of humanitarian intervention along the following lines.

The concept of "humanitarian intervention" in a proper legal sense has traditionally been ... understood as referring only to coercive action taken by states, at their initiative, and involving the use of armed force, for the purpose of preventing or putting a halt to serious and wide-scale violations of human rights, in particular the right to life, inside the territory of another state.[23]

I shall not dispute this definition, which stresses the coercive and military character of humanitarian intervention. Instead, I shall outline an argument as to why and under what conditions humanitarian intervention in this strong sense is not only normatively allowed but is also a duty. I shall then ask whether it is a stringent duty. My arguments will be based on philosophical grounds, although the discussion will touch certain aspects of international law. My focus will be on the normative status of individuals and sovereign states in international relations; and, as before, my basic normative framework will be philosophical liberalism.

Sketching the normative dimension

There seems to be widespread agreement that humanitarian intervention is, by present standards of international law, permitted if either: (1) the UN Security Council (in reference to chap. VII, art. 39 of the UN Charter), or (2) the UN General Assembly (in reference to GA Res. 337, "Uniting for Peace") declares that massive violation of basic human rights provides a challenge to peace, and (1a/2a) either initiates an intervention, or (1b/2b) authorizes an intervention initiated by an individual state or a collective of states. Cases (1a) and (1b) are rather theoretical, because the UN was never provided with the armed forces which chapter VII foresees. The main dispute, therefore, is whether humanitarian intervention can also be justified if it is initiated by an individual or collective of states without being authorized by either the Security Council or the General Assembly. I will come back to this question.

First, I want to stress the fact that, formally, it is not a massive violation of human rights in itself, but rather a challenge to world peace that is supposed to follow that provides the legal basis for humanitarian intervention. The indirect character of the legal justification is due to three aspects of international law: (1) the recognition of states only, in contrast to individual persons, as subjects of international law; (2) the restriction of the *jus ad bellum* to cases of individual and collective state self-defense; and (3) the commitment to the principle of non-intervention as part of the *jus cogens* of international law.

Theorists of international law might dispute about how far the human-rights regime, developed under the umbrella of the United Nations, challenges (1) above. From the perspective of philosophical liberalism, the acknowledgment of human rights is hardly compatible with granting states an inviolable moral status in international law. The commitment to ethical individualism intuitively counts against treating states as moral subjects in their own right. But this moral intuition has to be spelled out more concretely. I shall try to make some rather sketchy proposals in this direction, and I will concentrate on two aspects: the value of sovereignty and the concept of human rights.[24]

The normative status of states. The existence of constitutional government and contemporary international law show that Hobbes and Kant were wrong when they thought that 'sovereignty' could not be restricted without either collapsing or losing its meaning. Therefore, the right of self-determination and the principle of non-intervention need a normative justification for the role they play in international law. This is not too difficult a task, because both norms are conducive to international peace and serve to guarantee peoples' right of political autonomy. But almost every norm allows for exceptions. Regarding the principle of non-intervention as an absolute norm, therefore, would require showing either: (a) that the internal dimension of sovereignty constitutes an overriding value, regardless of whether legitimate constraints like respect for human rights are fulfilled or not; or (b) that the internal and external aspects of sovereignty are completely independent of a normative point of view (that is, the internal affairs constitute a closed moral realm); or (c) that sovereign states constitute entities with a moral status that is *sui generis*.

None of these options seems particularly convincing from the standpoint of political liberalism. The first is not, because the internal dimension of sovereignty is regarded as merely a means of guaranteeing social peace, cooperation and justice, which are, therefore, conditions of legitimacy.[25] As the discussion of a right to secede has shown, political liberalism does not emphasize sovereignty as an intrinsic value. The second option is unconvincing, because, as will be argued below, the concept of human rights links the domestic and international normative domains together. The third option is not convincing, because even though states play a special role in international-relations theory and international law, they are institutions which are ontologically dependent upon their citizens and, therefore, also depend on the moral status of their citizens for their own moral status.

There can hardly be any doubt that states and international organizations are the main actors in international relations. Therefore, it seems reasonable that they are the primary legal subjects of international law. Of course, there are migrants, refuges, prisoners of war, tourists, private businessmen, non-governmental organizations (NGOs), and transnational cultural or professional unions of individual persons; but the most significant international actors are states and international organizations. It is difficult to imagine how it could be otherwise. The peaceful and cooperative organization of interpersonal relations needs institutions that are manageable, effective, and – from the standpoint of philosophical liberalism – apt for democracy. Further, it seems desirable that there be states, because they allow for plurality and diversity of ideals of society and political self-organization to be realized. Nevertheless, neither the necessity nor the desirability of states is sufficient to grant states either an ontological status *sui generis* or a special moral status that is independent of the moral status of the people that constitute them.

Although states do not deserve a special moral and ontological status from the perspective of ethical individualism, the fact that states are the primary form of political organization on the world stage has some consequences for the normative relation between citizens of different states. This is especially the case if one regards justice as having to do with interpersonal relations – in contrast, say, to a conception of justice as a means of overcoming natural differences among individuals. One consequence is that relations between members of a common political institution are broader and deeper than those between individuals of different political institutions. This is not to say that there are no normative relations at all between members of different states, but that they are not as full-bodied as the normative relations among members of one and the same political institution. Social and political interaction between citizens, abstract as it may be, establish special relations that do not hold between members of different political institutions. In other words, the range of issues of domestic or municipal justice is wider than that of global or cosmopolitan justice and partly different, because fields of interaction between citizens and between states are different. Furthermore, even from the perspective of a modest universalist conception of justice like that of John Rawls, the requirements of domestic justice can be regarded as underdetermined, since they need to be adapted to particular cultural and social circumstances, and open to discretion in solving conflicts between goods and values.[26] For these reasons, there are overwhelming grounds for granting peoples the right of collective self-determination and non-interference – as long as self-determination does not violate reasonable norms of transnational justice and purely universal moral requirements.

The concept of human rights. I would maintain that human rights are moral requirements of a morally universal kind. The idea of universal human rights has been opposed mainly, but not exclusively, by communitarians. Nevertheless, I will not try to argue against communitarianism here. I would concede to the communitarian that the concept of human rights has a liberal core, because it is committed to ethical individualism inasmuch as it regards individual persons as of equal moral worth and expresses a secular and anthropocentric concept of normativity. I take that, however, to be less a Eurocentric position than *rather* a distinctively modern account of normativity. In addition, I should note that employing the normative language of "rights" is not equivalent to promoting a particular or unique ideal of society. Rather, it is a way of articulating moral ideas within a normative and institutional framework that is practically appropriate for modern societies.

The concept of a right is a triadic relation. To talk about rights is to say that (i) a person or a group of persons *holds* a right (ii) of specific *content* (iii) against an *addressee* or group of addressees. Philosophers tend to view human rights as moral and universal rights. In this sense, human rights are rights every person has against every other person, regardless of whether or not these rights are codified and transformed into positive law. In international law, by contrast, states represented by governments are regarded as the addressees of human rights. Importantly, the philosophical conception of human rights implies a universal duty to protect human rights, while the international-law conception does not.[27]

Because it would be too far-reaching for present purposes to unfold all the arguments for the philosophical account of human rights, I will mention only two features that support it. First, when we talk of violations of human rights, we hardly refer to acts done by individual persons as private actors. If we did, every murder would have to count as a human-rights violation.[28] I take this linguistic feature to indicate (in the terminology given above) that states or governments are not so much addressees of human rights as elements of their content. Human rights can be interpreted as rights that formulate restrictions on legitimate structures of political, legal, and social institutions and constrain the activities that representatives of these institutions may engage in. On this interpretation, human rights are not rights concerning interpersonal interaction, but the structures of institutions. It is because institutions act through individual persons that one can regard persons who represent these institutions as primarily *responsible* for the protection of human rights. That fact, however, does not imply that they are the only addressees of human rights. A second feature that supports the philosophical account of human rights is the fact that human-rights declarations have a traditional place in constitutions that define a state's basic political and legal structures. As such, they show themselves to be pre-political in character; that is, they do not depend on any political status (as citizenship does), but are prior to it.

If human rights can be interpreted as rights whose content refers to political, legal, and social institutions, then the universality of human rights seems to imply the requirement that every political, legal, and social institution (but perhaps not every voluntary association) is subject to their normative constraints. International law is also subject to the constraints of human rights. What kind of constraints these are depends on the content of human rights. That is a highly contested topic, especially with regard to economic and cultural human rights. Nevertheless, rather substantial agreement prevails that human rights grant individual persons basic physical and psychological integrity, basic legal protection (under the principle of Rechtsstaatlichkeit or rule of law), and an equal legal status in political and social institutions (the principle of non-discrimination). If one interprets human rights as both universal and as referring to institutions, it seems absolutely counter-intuitive that these core values should not be incorporated into and guaranteed by international law. What this argument amounts to is not a recognition of individual persons as overall subjects of international law, but rather an acknowledgment of their moral status. An appropriate form for doing this seems to be a qualification of the principle of non-intervention in cases of human-rights violations.

If individual persons cannot be denied moral status in international law, the question is not so much whether humanitarian intervention is permissible, but whether there exists a *duty* of humanitarian intervention in cases of massive human-rights violations and, if so, whether this duty is a stringent one. Although the content of human rights consists of the design and activity of institutions, the addressee of human rights is "mankind." Therefore, their protection is a common duty. One can argue that it is in every case the representatives of the actual institutions who are primarily responsible for guaranteeing human rights. One reason is that actual institutions are constituted and represented by particular persons. If those representatives resist their duty or fail in carrying it out, however, secondary responsibilities arise. To determine what these secondary responsibilities amount to, one has to consider that they arise because primary responsibilities were disregarded. Although failing to fulfill one's responsibility is not in every case identical with acting unjustly, human-rights violations are usually voluntary and intended actions that have to be regarded as acts of injustice. In taking up their secondary responsibility, parties who intervene in order to stop human-rights violations do not just step in to take over responsibility; they usually have to counteract the injustice as well. This has to be taken into account when one discusses the question of international duties concerning massive human-rights violations.

Counteracting injustice, as I have said, is a difficult topic for normative theory. However, it seems that when fulfilling one's duty involves counteracting injustice, it can only be regarded as obligatory when (i) it is feasible, (ii) it does not too seriously conflict with other legitimate rights of the counter-acting party, (iii) it can be done without imposing serious detriments to that party, and (iv) it is likely to be successful.[29] As military humanitarian interventions usually require that the members of the intervening forces risk their lives, humanitarian intervention can hardly ever be regarded as a perfect or stringent duty, but only as an imperfect one.[30]

It is sometimes said that no humanitarian intervention was ever undertaken for the sole purpose of combating human-rights violations; and this fact is regarded as morally cheap or wrong. But this point of view is too simple. First, having several reasons for doing something does not deprive a given moral reason of its moral worth. Second, considering the very significant burdens and costs that humanitarian intervention implies, it seems perfectly legitimate also to take non-moral considerations into account. Nevertheless, to avoid abuses and to assure that humanitarian interventions are really undertaken for the protection of human rights and not merely pretexts for other goals, it seems reasonable to require that intervention be authorized by one of the organs of the United Nations or a regional organization designed for and committed to the protection of human rights.[31]

Another reason for United Nations authorization is that although the group of primarily responsible persons is more or less defined, the group of secondarily responsible persons is not. In order to avoid the problem of diffusion of responsibility, collective procedures for identifying human-rights violations and for designating who should counteract them seem appropriate; and the existing procedures involving organs of the United Nations appear apt. It might be argued that, given the universalist conception of human rights, the approval of the United Nations for humanitarian intervention is not necessary as a normative matter. Nevertheless, the protection of human rights is not the exclusive aim of international law; and duties to protect human rights should be implemented in a way that is compatible with existing legal structures and the aims of the Charter of the United Nations. Therefore, it seems more reasonable to continue the existing practice (and maybe to enhance it) than to give over the task of protecting human rights to the discretion of every particular state.

TO SUM UP

Since philosophical liberalism claims that legitimate sovereignty is subject to moral constraints, it seems incoherent to regard sovereignty, either in its internal or external dimension, as of intrinsic normative value. The discussion at the beginning of this essay has shown that philosophical liberalism provides no normative criteria for the self-definition of a group of individuals as a sovereign people. Also, since a universalist conception of human rights clearly implies moral duties across borders, even if they turn out to be imperfect duties only, political borders can have only limited moral significance. But it would not be convincing to say either that sovereignty is of no value at all, or that political boundaries are of no moral significance.

It is obvious that human rights do not exhaust the moral realm, but leave room for special moral relations that are not universal but particularist. The moral significance of political borders connects with these particular moral relations. I would claim that a large part of political and social justice is particularist in that it deals with special political, economic and social relations that hold among an actual group of persons who are institutionally related in a particular way.[32] As for the value of sovereignty, I am inclined to regard it as intrinsically political. To be sure, sovereignty is subject to moral constraints; but its value lies in the fact that existing sovereign states provide the institutional framework for the political and social agency of their members. Perhaps other institutional frameworks that can play this role will come into existence one day. But they have not yet done so.

NOTES

1 That is: a methodological commitment to ethical individualism, a substantive commitment to basic human rights, the recognition of pluralist conceptions of the good and the ideal of democracy.
2 This "definition" is still rather loose, because it does not specify a fixed degree of political and civil cohesiveness within the formerly united group. But again I think that no such standards can be developed in abstracto. One has to rely on "considered judgments" to decide whether anarchy, civil war, or a political union prevails.
3 See Lea Brillmayer, "Consent, Contract, and Territory," *Minnesota Law Review* 74 (1989), 1–35; and "Secession and Self-Determination", *Yale Journal of International Law* 74 (1991), 177–202.
4 Cf. Lassa Oppenheim and Hersch Lauterpacht, *International Law: A Treatise*, vol. I, ch. I (London, 1952).
5 See Hillel Steiner, "Liberalism and Nationalism", *Analyse und Kritik* 17 (1995), 12–40: "(...) precisely because a nation's territory is legitimately composed of the real estate of its members, the decision of any of them to resign membership and, as it were, to take their real estate with them, is a decision which must be respected." Since libertarians tend to view society as an aggegration of persons interconnected by purely private relations, secession is like the dissolution of private contracts and raises only judicial questions but no political problems.
6 Allen Buchanan, "Theories of Secession," *Philosophy and Public Affairs* 26, (1997), 31–61.

7 Commitment to ethical individualism is compatible with the acknowledgment of group rights as long as group rights are either regarded as individual rights that only can be enacted collectively or else as rights of groups that are based on the normative status of the members of the group.

8 See "A Liberal Theory of Secession," *Political Studies* 32 (1984), 21–31; and "More Theory of Secession: A Response to Birch," *Political Studies* 36 (1988), 316–23.

9 In addition, the seceding part may not divide the remaining state in two unconnected halves, and secession may not generate enclaves. While it is theoretically rather radical, practically almost no secessionist movement might be able to fulfill Beran's geographic conditions.

10 David Gauthier, "Breaking Up: An Essay on Secession," *Canadian Journal of Philosophy* 24 (1994), 357–72.

11 Beran, "A Liberal Theory of Secession."

12 Hobbes and Locke are not concerned to define the group of contractors, but only to justify the transition from unanimity to majority rule. In contrast, thinkers belonging to a more republican tradition that is concerned about political virtue or the problem of how to constitute a nation, as were Madison and Hamilton, are interested in questions about how to establish or strengthen what might be called national feeling or identity, but, again, do not open discussion about how to choose one's fellow-citizens. Cf. Bhikhu Parekh, "Discourses on National Identity," *Political Studies* 42 (1994), 492–504, for an overview. Cf. also Brian Barry, "Self-Government Revisited," in Brian Barry, *Democracy, Power and Justice. Essays in Political Theory* (Oxford, 1989), pp. 156–86.

13 This reason is also mentioned by Cass Sunstein, "Approaching Democracy: A New Legal Order for Eastern Europe – Constitutionalism and Secession," in Chris Brown (ed.), *Political Restructuring Europe: Ethical Perspectives* (London, 1994), pp. 11–49, against a constitutional right to secede.

14 Hirschmann's result seems to apply here: if exit is too easy, incentives to voice criticism are very low; cf. Albert O. Hirschmann, *Exit, Voice and Loyalty* (Cambridge, Mass, 1970).

15 Avishai Margalit and Joseph Raz, "National Self-Determination," *Journal of Philosophy* 86 (1990), 439–61.

16 Taking into account the Rousseauistic roots of this conception of democracy, it is tempting to speculate that it is based on a mistaken analogy between personal and political agency: analogously to conceiving personal agency as presupposing an individual will to define its aim, political agency is conceived as presupposing a kind of at least basically homogeneous collective will to define a community's political goals.

17 "Die Politik der Anerkennung," in Jürgen Habermas (ed.), *Multikulturalismus und die Politik der Anerkennung* (Frankfurt/Main, 1992); and "Why Do Nations

Have To Become States?" in Charles Taylor, *Reconciling the Solitudes: Essays on Canadian Federalism and Nationalism* (Montreal, 1993), pp. 40–58.

18 In contrast to political liberalism, which stresses universalism, personal freedom and individual rights, republicanism is concerned with the ethical and action-theoretic foundations of a democratic commonweal. Accordingly the latter is more concerned with questions of political psychology, ethics, and cultural anthropology than most liberal theories are. By insisting that democracy is not only upheld by democratic institutions, but also (if it is not to decay) requires democratically minded citizens, republicanism emphasizes the need of political virtue and an interest in the *bonum commune*. Therefore it is more open to particularist values and attitudes, and also to special duties that exist between citizens. It should thus be no surprise that the renaissance of republicanism has not only enriched the debate over the foundations and value basis of liberal democracy, but has also brought with it a revitalization of the political concept of a nation and community.

19 For good reasons Pierre Birnbaum, "From Multiculturalism to Nationalism," *Political Theory* 24 (1996), 33–45, raises the question whether such a concept of cultural identity is still compatible with the idea of individual self-determination.

20 Taylor, "Why Do Nations Have to Become States?"

21 Allen Buchanan spells out these conditions in *Secession: The Morality of Political Divorce from Fort Sumter to Lithuania and Quebec* (Boulder/San Francisco/Oxford, 1991).

22 See Allen Buchanan, *Secession*, and "Toward a Theory of Secession," *Ethics* 101 (1991), 322–342; Beran, "A Liberal Theory of Secession;" Anthony H. Birch, "Another Liberal Theory of Secession," *Political Studies* 32 (1984), 596–602, and others for an extensive discussion of geographical aspects.

23 Wil D. Verwey, "Humanitarian Intervention in the 1990s and Beyond: An International Law Perspective," in Jan Nederveen Pieterse, *World Makings in the Order: Humanitarian Intervention and Beyond* (Basingstoke, London, New York, 1998), pp. 180–210.

24 In recent years the literature on these topics has exploded. See Jim Dunne and Nicholas J. Wheeler (eds.), *Human Rights in Global Politics* (Cambridge, 1999), for an overview of recent discussions of this topic. Since it is impossible to give attention to the different positions in a short article like this, inasmuch as almost every issue is contested, I will not try to respond to the literature but shall outline my own point of view.

25 This argument is stressed by Bhikhu Parekh "Rethinking Humanitarian Intervention," in Jan Nederveen Pieterse: *World Makings in the Order: Humanitarian Intervention and Beyond* (Basingstoke, London, New York, 1998), pp. 138–69; also John Rawls, *The Law of Peoples* (Cambridge, Mass., London, 1999), para. 10, who in other respects strongly defends the principle of

non-intervention, regards respect for human rights as a normative constraint to its applicability.

26 The values of social security or national economic development, on the one hand, and the respect for private property or individual liberty, on the other hand, come readily to mind as examples of cases in which a plurality of mediating schemes is thinkable.

27 The International Pacts on Human Rights require the signatory states to "promote" human rights domestically and internationally, but do not imply transnational duties to protect them. Further, because these pacts are international pacts, from the perspective of International Law a government that signed these pacts, but violates human rights does not committ a crime against its citizens, but does not fulfill an obligation it owes to the other signatory states.

28 Or when persons act who demand to be regarded as political representatives, like a guerilla faction or "liberation army" or something of that kind.

29 In practice this certainly is the most difficult part.

30 Non-military forms of intervention, e.g. diplomatic and/or political pressure, might, however, be appropriate in cases of less severe human-rights violations.

31 Of course, the United Nations are not a holy congregation of moral saints. Its members follow interests of their own that do not always coincide with justice. Therefore, I would not regard an authorization by the United Nations as an absolutely necessary condition for the legitimacy of an intervention. But it is surely desirable that United Nations or a regional multi-state organization be involved.

32 I have no space to argue for this position, but can only refer to Rawls' *Law of Peoples* for a similar account.

Chapter 10

Secession, state breakdown, and humanitarian intervention

ALLEN BUCHANAN

THE NEED FOR REFORM IN THE INTERNATIONAL LAW OF SECESSION AND INTERVENTION

The past decade has seen a remarkable increase in secessions, many of which have been marked by large-scale violations of human rights. There is a growing awareness that existing international law is ill-equipped to cope with secessionist crises.

Existing international law is inadequate in two distinct respects. First, it fails to provide a coherent, morally defensible account of when secession is justified and when it is not. Second, as Kofi Annan observed at the time of NATO's action in Kosovo, international legal constraints on humanitarian intervention are so stringent that humane responses to the violence of secessionist conflicts will usually be ruled out as illegal.

Without an adequate account of when secession is justified and when it is not, members of the international community will not know whether they should support the state in its attempt to crush secession, support the secessionists against the state, or remain neutral. Therefore the first step in developing a principled theory of intervention in secessionist conflicts is to work out a theory of the right to secede.

Once one appreciates the inadequacy of the existing international law of secession, the need for developing such a theory and changing international law to conform to it becomes quite apparent. Existing international law only recognizes a right to secede in two narrowly defined circumstances: cases of "classic" de-colonization, in which a colony liberates itself from a metropolitan colonial power, and liberation from military occupation by a foreign power.

The difficulty is that some cases in which secession seems morally justifiable do not fit either of these conditions. For example, the Kurds have a strong case for secession from Iraq because that country has systematically persecuted them and even committed acts of genocide against them. But most international lawyers would hold that the Kurds are not a colonized people who have a right to secede under international law. And since the Kurds have never had their own state, they cannot justify their secession as the attempt to liberate themselves from foreign military occupation.

Similarly, both because they were subject to systematic persecution by Serbian forces and because their constitutional right to autonomy had been unilaterally extinguished by Milosevic, the Kosovar Albanians had a strong case for secession, as a remedy of last resort against serious injustices. But here too international law provided no support for their independence.

Existing international law on humanitarian intervention is equally defective. Humanitarian intervention may be defined as the use of force across state borders by a state (or group of states) aimed at preventing or ending widespread and grave violations of fundamental human rights of individuals other than its own citizens, without permission from the state within whose territory the intervention occurs.

At present international law requires UN Security Council authorization if humanitarian intervention is to be legally permissible. As the recent case of Kosovo illustrates, it will often, perhaps almost always, be impossible to secure Security Council authorization, even in cases of massive violations of human rights, because authorization will not be forthcoming if only one permanent member of the Council votes against it.

This extremely constraining international law of humanitarian intervention compounds the deficiency of the international law of secession. Because international law does not recognize a right to secede except in the cases of classic colonization and military occupation by a foreign power, it provides no support for minority groups, such as the Kosovar Albanians and the Kurds in Iraq, who suffer systematic oppression by their own governments. When such groups take the desperate step of seceding without international support, they are likely to feel the full wrath of the state; yet at the same time international law prohibits other states from intervening to protect them and instead allows them to aid the state in its efforts to crush the secessionists.

Reforms in international law regarding humanitarian intervention and secession could be mutually reinforcing. A more permissive law regarding humanitarian intervention could provide international support for persecuted minorities early enough to avoid the need for secession; while an international legal right to secede as a remedy of last resort against oppression might deter states from engaging in the massive violations of rights that call for intervention.

The problem is not simply that international law fails to acknowledge a right to secede for those who have a strong moral case for seceding. In addition, two of the principles of international law that are relevant to secession seem to yield the wrong answer when applied to the question of how the international community should respond to secessionist crises. At least as they are ordinarily interpreted, the principles of *uti possidetis* and effectivity seem to pose serious barriers to the development of a more adequate international legal response to secession.

TWO PROBLEMATIC PRINCIPLES: *UTI POSSIDETIS* AND EFFECTIVITY

The problem of whether to intervene when states break apart is not novel. The international community faced it on a vast scale during the period of de-colonization in the 1960s and 1970s. Then as in the more recent wave of secessions, attempts were made to constrain the disintegration of political orders by appeal to principles of international law. Two principles were especially important: *uti possidetis*, according to which existing boundaries are to be respected (unless changed by consent), and *effectivity*, the principle that a secessionist entity becomes entitled to recognition as an independent state if and only if it secures effective control over the territory it claims. Both principles have been invoked in response to secessionist conflicts in the former Yugoslavia and the former Soviet Union. Whether these principles are applicable, and if so, how they are to be interpreted, makes a great deal of difference as to the legality of intervention in secessionist conflicts.

The rationale for both principles is said to be stability and, ultimately, the preservation of peace. *Uti possidetis* is supposed to contribute to stability by limiting the process of fragmentation.[1] In the case of decolonization, this means allowing the separation of colonial units from the metropolitan power, but prohibiting any further fragmentation within the colonial boundaries. In the break-ups of Yugoslavia and the Soviet Union, *uti possidetis* was invoked to limit the number of new states to the number of former federal units (Republics). In both cases the idea was that some constraint on fragmentation was needed to avoid a situation of extreme and continuing instability, and that appeal to existing boundaries provided a somewhat less than arbitrary limitation. Although *uti possidetis* originally applied to boundaries of colonial states (first in Latin American, later in Africa), in the Soviet and Yugoslav cases "boundaries" was interpreted to include the internal boundaries of federal units.

The principle of effectivity is said to contribute to stability by allowing the international community to accommodate changes in the political order in a realistic way.[2] According to the traditional view that dates back to the Peace of Westphalia in 1648, international law governs the relationships of states. Hence, what is of fundamental importance is that the members of the club of states know who are members and who are not, and that every bit of territory belongs to one state or another. From the standpoint of international law understood in this traditional way, to be a state is simply to exercise sufficient control over a territory as to be able to engage in relations with other states. In this sense, the principle of effectivity simply reminds states to recognize reality, to recognize that a new state has already come into existence when an entity gains control over a territory, and to act accordingly toward it.

By recognizing such an entity as a state, the international system contributes to the maintenance of that entity's control over the territory. And this in turn helps to ensure that the world continues to conform to the traditional international legal paradigm: a world in which every territory is governed by a single state and hence in which states can address all their external concerns by dealing exclusively with other states, while being left free to manage their own internal affairs. The principle of effectivity is understood in this way to contribute to the stability of the state system.

Both in classic decolonization and in the breakdown of the Soviet Union and Yugoslavia, the principle of effectivity did not play as prominent a role as that of *uti possidetis*. Effectivity was at least tacitly invoked, however, from time to time during the Yugoslav crises, in particular to support recognizing the conquests of the Serbs, first (and only temporarily) in Croatia, and later in Bosnia, as well as Croat conquests of Bosnian territory.

More recently, effectivity has been invoked in support of Quebec's secession from Canada. An *amicus curiae* brief submitted to the Canadian Supreme Court in its recent Reference Ruling on Quebec secession argued that if Quebec unilaterally secedes and is able to exert effective control over the territory of the present Province of Quebec, there will be a sovereign Quebec, a full-fledged member of the international community, and entitled to international recognition as such.[3]

The Yugoslav case demonstrates that the two principles can clash. Apparently relying on *uti possidetis* (understood as applying to the internal boundaries of a federation), the major European powers recognized the independence of Bosnia at a time when it did not control all or even most of the territory it claimed, thereby acting contrary to the principle of effectivity. The fact that these two principles can point in opposite directions in the same case, should prompt skepticism about the claim that each is justified in any straightforward way on grounds of its contribution to stability.

Neither principle has lacked for critics. The most familiar criticism of *uti possidetis* is that by refusing to consider revisions of what are in many cases highly arbitrary boundaries, it precludes more constructive solutions to problems of ethno-national conflict, and encourages "nation-building" projects by which one group seeks to destroy, displace, or at least dominate all others. In the de-colonization context, Sudan, with its North–South ethnic and religious division, is often cited as a case in point. Similarly, some have argued that less rigid adherence to *uti possidetis* in the early stages of the Yugoslav conflict would have allowed a redrawing of boundaries that would have left fewer minorities in a vulnerable position and would have reduced the incentives for conquest and ethnic cleansing of territory to "liberate" fellow Serbs.

There is a second, less obvious objection to *uti possidetis*. This objection recognizes that acknowledging the principle not only serves to limit fragmentation along the lines of existing boundaries but to *legitimize* it as well. Strictly construed, *uti possidetis* only says that *if* there is to be secession there should be no change of existing boundaries (without consent of all parties). But there is a tendency to slide from this assertion to the quite different claim that existing units of a federation have a kind of presumptive *right* to secede, or at least a right of self-determination that can under some circumstances be exercised by way of secession. Thus, Quebecois secessionists have pointed to the break-up of Yugoslavia, under the principle of *uti possidetis*, as a precedent for Quebec secession.[4]

This tendency to regard *uti possidetis* as creating a presumptive right of federal units to secede has a very unfortunate implication so far as incentives are concerned. Governments of highly centralized states will be even less likely to agree to devolution to various forms of federalism if they fear that in doing so they will have conferred a right of self-determination on regions within the state and that this right in turn may be invoked to support secession. Yet in some cases such decentralized arrangements may be the most promising solution to problems of ethno-national conflict within existing states.

It is true of course that the principle that if secession occurs it should follow existing boundaries does not logically imply any presumption of a right to secede for existing units. However, once the principle of *uti possidetis* is applied to the boundaries of federal units, as in the case of Yugoslavia, the tendency to slip toward a presumptive right to secede is understandable. For unless one assumes that the federal units have some sort of basis for independence – something like a right of self-determination – it is hard to see why the principle of *uti possidetis* should apply to federal units in the first place. In other words, it is hard to see why a principle originally designed to protect existing *state* boundaries could be said to apply to the protection of the boundaries of federal units *within* states, unless it is assumed that federal units are, as it were, quasi states, or nascent states, inherently possessing rights of self-determination than can issue in independent statehood. Unless some such assumption is made, the statement that the principle of *uti possidetis* supports the break-up of Yugoslavia or the USSR along federal lines because it requires the preservation of existing "boundaries" seems to be a bald equivocation on the term "boundaries" – a slide from "state boundaries" to "boundaries of jurisdictional units within states."

But if this is so – if the application of *uti possidetis* to secession of federal units makes sense only on the assumption that federal units have a rather strong right of self-determination – then the second objection to *uti possidetis* is unavoidable. If applied to the boundaries of federal units, the principle will carry the implicit assumption that federal units have a presumptive right to secede, and this will mean that acknowledgement of the principle will inhibit what might be very beneficial efforts at state-decentralization.

Later I will argue that there is another way of understanding the extension of *uti possidetis* from the colonial state case to the case of units of a federation that does *not* assume any right of self-determination on the part of federal units. I will also argue that this way of interpreting the principle imposes substantial limits on its application – limits that make for a much more plausible principle.

If anything, the principle of effectivity is even more vulnerable to criticism. Put most simply, effectivity appears to be nothing more than a thinly veiled assertion of the maxim that might makes right. Until very recently, states as the international legal system regarded them were in fact little more than "gunmen writ large" – effective enforcers of rules within territories. Legitimacy under international law was reduced to effective control. Given this normatively undemanding conception of state legitimacy, the principle of effectivity makes sense: it simply applies the criterion for existing states as a condition for recognition of new states.

However, in the last fifty years or so, international law has made halting steps toward a more normatively demanding conception of state legitimacy. Under international legal doctrine – though not yet always in practice – states are required to respect the human rights of their own citizens. Some have even gone so far as to argue that a more normatively rich conception of legitimacy is beginning to emerge, according to which legitimacy requires democratic governance.[5]

Given a more normatively demanding conception of legitimate statehood, the practice of international recognition of states can serve as a valuable instrument for improving the behavior of new claimants to the status of statehood by requiring them to meet certain conditions, including protection of human and minority rights. From this perspective, the principle of effectivity seems far too undemanding as a criterion of recognition. This line of thinking presumably underlay the attempt by the Badinter Commission to require respect for minority rights as a condition for the recognition of new states emerging from the dissolution of Yugoslavia.[6]

There are also non-instrumental reasons for requiring the respect for basic rights of all citizens as a condition for international recognition. In particular, it can be argued that only entities that respect basic human rights are *justified* in doing what claimants to the status of statehood attempt to do, namely, exercise a monopoly on the enforcement of rules within a territory. If a state that does not respect its citizens' human rights is not justified in exercising a monopoly on coercive power within the territory, then those who recognize and thereby support it become accomplices in its injustices. To summarize: Both as a means of inducing new aspirants to statehood to respect minority and individual rights by rewarding them with recognition only if they do, and for deeper reasons having to do with what justifies states as coercive entities in the first place, there is much to be said for requiring more than effectivity if a seceding group is to be recognized as a state, a member in good standing of the international community.[7]

Given these criticisms, it is tempting simply to say that *uti possidetis* and effectivity ought to be rejected altogether – that they should somehow simply be expunged from international legal doctrine and practice. However, because these principles are deeply entrenched norms of customary international law, expunging them would presumably require a protracted process of changing state behavior and attitudes over time or forging treaties that explicitly repudiate the two principles. If this is so, then the fact that these principles are presently included in international law would seem to pose a serious obstacle to establishing a more morally defensible international law of secession. Because of the difficulty of making fairly rapid changes in international customary law, proposals for reforming the law of secession that run afoul of these two principles may appear to be utopian in the worst sense.

However, it is a mistake to think that reforming the international law of secession requires eliminating the principles of *uti possidetis* and effectivity. Such radical surgery is unnecessary. I will argue that a deeper understanding of the normative structure of secession provides a key to rehabilitating both principles by demonstrating the proper limits of their application. A reconstruction of the rationale for effectivity and *uti possidetis* that can achieve this rehabilitation satisfies an important desideratum for a normative theory of international law: achieving progress without radical disruption of the fabric of the existing system.

Essential to my strategy will be a distinction between two quite different situations in which entities attempt to form new states out of old ones. I will distinguish between secession from *functioning states* and the attempt to form new states in a situation of *state breakdown*. And I will argue that *uti possidetis* and effectivity only have application in the latter case, not the former. In order to do this it will be necessary to locate these principles and the distinction between the two different situations in which secession occurs within the framework of a normative theory of secession for which I have argued in some detail elsewhere, and which I can only summarize here.

THE NORMATIVE THEORY OF SECESSION

A normative theory of secession attempts to articulate morally defensible principles for international responses to secession, in part by specifying the conditions under which a secessionist entity ought to be recognized in international law as having a right to secede. At minimum, if a group has the right to secede under international law, then others, including the state from which the group is attempting to secede, are legally prohibited from interfering with the group's effort to become independent. But legal recognition of a group's right to secede could also provide a justification for states to come to the aid of the secessionists if the state from which they are seceding attempts to block their secession by force. Forging a more extensive international legal right to secede, one that would, for example, recognize the right of Kurds or Kosovar Albanians to secede as a remedy for persistent injustices committed against them, would in that sense broaden the scope of justified intervention.

However, unspecified talk of a "right to secede" is dangerously ambiguous. It may refer to (a) a consensual right or (b) a unilateral right. A consensual right to secede may be of either of three sorts: first, one that is generated by an explicit constitutional provision for secession (as contained in the former Soviet Constitution and the present Constitution of Ethiopia); second, one that can be exercised through a process of constitutional amendment (as the Canadian Supreme Court indicated regarding Quebec secession); or third, one that is created by negotiations in the absence of explicit constitutional provisions (as in the case of the secession of Norway from Sweden). With some simplification, we can say that what these three rights have in common, and what distinguishes them from a unilateral right to secede, is the idea that secession is in some sense consensual – it proceeds by agreement, either having been agreed on as permissible in the ratification of a Constitution including a secession clause or an amendment process that permits secession, or agreed on at some later point, through negotiations between the state and the secessionists.

In contrast, a unilateral right to secede is non-consensual. If a group has a unilateral right to secede, then it is permissible for it to secede in the absence of any agreement on the part of the state that it may secede and in the absence of any constitutional process for secession.

Neither international law nor political theory seem to provide any obstacles of deep principle to consensual secession (though of course there can be serious disputes about what the just terms of secession ought to be, how they ought to be negotiated, and whether there is a legitimate role for international bodies in facilitating a peaceful secession process). The real controversy is over the nature of the unilateral right to secede.

Normative theories of the unilateral right to secede can be divided into two basic types: remedial right only theories and primary right theories. According to remedial right only theories, the unilateral right to secede is closely related to the right to revolution, as the latter is typically understood in the liberal tradition dating back at least to Locke. The right to revolution in this tradition is understood as a right to remedy serious injustices, usually understood in terms of the violations of basic individual rights, by overthrowing the government that perpetrates them. The right to revolution is thus a remedial right only, not a primary right: It is a right that only comes into being when other, more basic rights are violated, and revolution is the remedy of last resort for those violations.[8]

Similarly, in remedial right only theories of the unilateral right to secede, there is no primary unilateral right to secede. In the absence of a negotiation or constitutional provision, the right to secede comes to exist only when the group in question has suffered serious injustices and breaking off a portion of the state is the remedy of last resort. Both the right to revolution and the right to secede are remedial rights only; the chief difference between the two is that the exercise of the former is an attempt to overthrow the government, to deprive it of control over all the state's territory, while in the case of secession the attempt is to sever only a part of the territory from control by the state.

Primary right theories generally agree with remedial right only theories that there is a unilateral right to secede in cases of serious, persisting injustices. But, unlike remedial right *only* theories, they deny that such grievances are *necessary* for justified secession. Rather, they contend that groups can also have a unilateral right to secede from a state that is perfectly just and in which no one's basic rights are endangered.[9]

Primary right theories can be divided into two types: (a) ascriptive-group theories and (b) associative-group, or plebiscitary, theories. The former hold that it is only groups unified by certain ascriptive characteristics, for example "nations" or "distinct peoples", that have the primary right to secede. Associative-group or plebiscitary theories hold that in order to have a primary right to secede a group need not be an ascriptive group; all that is necessary is that a majority in the territory chooses to secede. Whether that majority consists of one "nation" or many, and whether it is one "people" is irrelevant.

Though I cannot hope to repeat all the rather complex arguments and counterarguments that I have examined elsewhere, I believe that a strong case can be made in favor of a remedial right only theory of secession – at least if the goal is to settle on a theory that can provide useful guidance for morally evaluating and improving international legal institutions.[10] A remedial right only theory has three signal virtues.

First, if implemented in international legal practice, it would get the incentives right: Just states would be rewarded with protection for their territorial integrity because unilateral secession from a rights-respecting state would be regarded as illegal, and unjust states would therefore be unable to invoke the right of territorial integrity to justify their opposition to secession and to claim assistance from other states in opposing it. In this way, the international implementation of a primary right theory of secession would encourage morally progressive behavior on the part of states and penalize bad behavior.

Second, a remedial right only theory also avoids what seem to be intractable problems to which both types of primary right theories are liable. Ascriptive-group theories face the objection that the principle that every "nation" or "people" has a right to its own state is a recipe for radical instability and ethnic cleansing if not outright genocide, due to the fact that the same territory is claimed as its rightful homeland by more than one such group. In addition, associative group theories face the objection that there is no non-arbitrary way of drawing the boundaries of the plebiscite by which state boundaries are to be determined.

Third, and perhaps most important, remedial right only theories provide the most cogent account of how a group can come to have the right to break off a portion of the state's territory. Secession, after all, entails not only the formation of a new political union among the members of a group, but the appropriation of territory that is claimed by a state. When combined with a justice-based theory of what gives states valid claims to territory in the first place, a remedial right only theory of the unilateral right to secede can explain how secessionists come to have a right to the territory they seek to separate from the state. In simplest terms, a justice-based theory of the state's claim to territory holds that the state can forfeit its claim if it fails to protect all its citizens' basic human rights. In other words, when a state persistently violates the fundamental rights of some of its citizens, it loses the legitimacy on which its claim to territory is based, and the way is clear for the persecuted group to take control of part of the state's territory, if this is necessary to remedy the injustices they are suffering.

In contrast, neither plebiscitary theories nor ascriptive-group theories of the unilateral right to secede provide a convincing account of how the state comes to lose its claim to the territory and how the secessionists come to have a valid claim. Plebiscitary theories cannot explain how the mere fact that a majority of persons who happen to reside in a portion of the state's territory come to have the right to sever that territory from the state. And given the doctrine of popular sovereignty – which entails that the whole territory of the state belongs to the people of the state as a whole – it is mistaken to assume that only a portion of the people can decide to remove part of the people's territory. If a state is legitimate – if it is providing protection of basic rights for all its citizens – it is hard to see why the mere fact that a majority *wants* to take part of the state's territory gives them a valid claim to it.

The difficulty for ascriptive-group theories of the unilateral right to secede is that they assert that various ascriptive groups (nations, distinct peoples, etc.) as such have a claim to territory, but provide no way of sorting out the conflicting claims that such groups have to the same territory. In addition, ascriptive-group theories typically fail to show why the groups in question must have their own states, rather than limited self-government or institutions providing special cultural rights for them within the state.

For these and other reasons I conclude that a remedial right only theory is more promising. Accordingly, in the remainder of this paper, I will assume that a morally progressive international legal system would view the unilateral right to secede as a remedial right only.

I now want to complicate the remedial right only view by introducing a distinction that I and others have tended to neglect: the distinction between separation from a functioning state and the attempt to form a new state in a situation of state-breakdown, where there is no functioning state. This distinction, I shall argue, is normatively significant in its own right, and is also crucial for determining the proper scope and limits of *uti possidetis* and effectivity. My objective is to show that if properly interpreted the principles of *uti possidetis* and effectivity do not pose a barrier to reforming the international law of secession and intervention by adopting a morally defensible theory of the right to secede. Properly understood, the two principles can contribute to, rather than impede, the development of an international law of secession that provides coherent, morally defensible guidance on the question of intervention in secessionist conflicts.

The contrast between the secession of Slovenia and Croatia from Yugoslavia and the possible secession of Quebec from Canada nicely illustrates the distinction between secession from a functioning state and secession under conditions of state-breakdown. At the time Slovenia and Croatia declared their independence, the constitutional order in Yugoslavia had already dissolved: Yugoslavia broke-down before it broke up. Key constitutional processes, including the rotation of the

Federal Presidency, had ceased to function. (In fact it has been argued persuasively that the process of breakdown, which accelerated greatly in the mid-1980s, had already begun before Tito's death.)[11] Increasingly, there was every reason to believe that the delicate system of checks and balances to reduce the threat of discrimination against minorities was no longer reliable.

In short, the breakdown of the constitutional order created a situation of radical insecurity in which people understandably feared that their most basic rights, as individuals and as members of groups, were imperiled. In these circumstances, secession by Slovenia and Croatia can be seen as an act of self-defense – what I shall call *sauve qui peut* separatism.

If the examples of Croatia and Slovenia seem less than fully persuasive, consider the current state breakdown in Congo. *Sauve qui peut* separation may well prove to be a reasonable last resort exercise of the right of self-defense for any of several regions in this crumbling state.

I choose the term 'separatism' here to signal that the attempt to form a new political entity capable of protecting one's rights under conditions in which one can no longer rely on the previous political order is quite different – normatively speaking – from what ordinarily goes under the heading of 'secession'. In an international system in which no third party can be relied on to shore up the disintegrating state in a way that gives credible assurance that basic rights will be protected, attempting to form a new state in a portion of the territory may be the most reasonable strategy.

In contrast consider the possible secession of Quebec. Canada is a functioning state, and one that does an exemplary job, comparatively speaking, in protecting individual and minority rights. Here, unlike the Yugoslav case, it would be most implausible to appeal to self-defense as a justification for secession.

With only minor modification, a remedial right only theory can properly recognize the normative force of the distinction between secession from a functioning state and *sauve qui peut* separation under conditions of state breakdown. According to the remedial right only theory, secession from a basic rights-protecting state is not justified (absent agreement or constitutional process), but unilateral secession is justified as a remedy of last resort for violations of basic rights. Such a theory can be extended to justify *sauve qui peut* separation by adding the principle that where there is no functioning state, and a situation of radical uncertainty exists in which basic rights are at risk, groups are justified in attempting to form their own states in order to protect their rights. This addendum coheres with the fundamental idea of a remedial right only theory: that unilateral secession from a rights-respecting state is not permissible and that only the need to protect basic rights can justify something so radical as unilateral secession.

Elaborating this addendum would require articulating an account of the scope and limits of this collective right of self-defense. Presumably, a group's right to form its own state as a means of self-defense is a limited right, just as the individual's right of self-defense is. (For example, generally speaking, I am not permitted to infringe the basic rights of innocent persons in order to defend myself. Similarly, I cannot claim that I acted in self-defense in killing another person if I egregiously provoked him to attack me.) Here I can only issue a promissory note that such elaboration could be successfully achieved. The central point is this: The fact that determining the limits of the right of self-defense is a complex and disputed matter does not show that there is no right of self-defense, either for individuals or for groups. It only shows that the right is qualified.

UTI POSSIDETIS IN THE CONTEXT OF STATE BREAKDOWN

Given the background assumption of a remedial right only theory of the unilateral right to secede and the distinction between secession from a functioning state and *sauve qui peut* or defensive separation in conditions of state breakdown, we can now understand the proper scope and limits of *uti possidetis*. My thesis is that, normatively speaking, *uti possidetis* is of much more limited application than has usually been assumed: It is only applicable to cases of state breakdown, not to cases of secession from a functioning state.

Uti possidetis derives whatever normative weight it has from the instrumental value that following it has in helping to foster the creation of new rights-protecting polities out of the dangerous conditions of state breakdown. The principle is therefore plausible where and only where existing boundaries mark off spaces in which the task of building new political structures capable of securing basic rights is most likely to be successful. When existing state structures are disintegrating – and in consequence basic rights are imperiled – the protection of rights may be better served by building upon whatever economic and political structures remain intact, and *sometimes* internal administrative units will fit this description.

If this is the correct rationale for *uti possidetis*, then it is clear that this principle has no applicability except in situations of state breakdown. It does not apply to cases of secession from a functioning state. Therefore, it is quite misguided for Quebec secessionists to appeal to *uti possidetis* to justify the secession of Quebec from Canada. In particular, the rationale for the principle does not in any way presuppose a right of self-determination for federal units. So once *uti possidetis* is understood as only having instrumental value as a means of helping to construct new rights-respecting polities out of conditions of state breakdown, the second of the two objections to the principle noted above disappears. Properly understood, *uti possidetis* does not support a unilateral right to secede for federal units as such, and therefore a recognition of the principle properly understood does not create incentives that would inhibit federalization of unitary states.

The purely instrumental rationale for *uti possidetis* I am suggesting also avoids the first objection noted earlier: the charge that following it may exacerbate rather than resolve ethno-national conflicts. The instrumental rationale limits the application of the principle. If the goal is to ensure that rights-respecting regimes emerge from conditions of state breakdown, then it will make no sense to try to build new polities from pre-existing units whose internal ethnic conflicts were a primary cause of state breakdown in the first place. Thus, on my reading *uti possidetis* did not in fact provide a sound rationale for constraining attempts to broker peace in the former Yugoslavia by slavish adherence to the sanctity of Republic borders.

In other words, properly understood, *uti possidetis* is not even applicable to all cases of state breakdown – only to those in which there is good reason to believe that existing jurisdictional units provide the most viable political and economic infrastructures for reconstituting political orders that provide secure protections for rights. The key point is that *uti possidetis* is not a basic principle. Whether it has weight and how much weight it has depends entirely upon the extent to which following it would be more conducive to building political orders capable of protecting peoples' rights.

This account of the normative basis of *uti possidetis* both supports and explains what I take to be widespread intuitions about when the principle has been applied appropriately. If the real point behind *uti possidetis* is that existing boundaries should be respected when and only when doing so would contribute to the construction of polities capable of protecting rights, then its application in a number of Latin American and African decolonization contexts has considerable plausibility. For in many cases of decolonization in those regions building new states within the jurisdictions of the former colonial states provided the best prospects for creating rights-respecting orders, because the colonial units provided an administrative infrastructure to build on and other resources were not at hand. But whether in any particular instance building new states on the basis of former administrative structures is in fact most conducive to the goal of creating polities capable of protecting basic rights is an empirical question and can only be decided case by case.

In the case of Yugoslavia, *uti possidetis* looks much less defensible. The process of state breakdown both exhibited and in part was caused by ethno-national conflicts. And for this reason it was much less convincing to argue that the goal of protecting rights under conditions of state breakdown was best served by adhering to federal boundaries that encompassed a plurality of ethno-national groups already in deadly conflict.

Treating *uti possidetis* as an absolute principle is therefore a serious mistake. In some cases, preserving existing boundaries can be counterproductive for the very goal the principle is supposed to promote. The principle should be viewed simply as a kind of rule of thumb, a reminder that in cases of state breakdown, the best mechanism for forming new states capable of protecting basic rights often may be to rely upon pre-existing boundaries.

EFFECTIVITY

If we accept the remedial right only theory of the unilateral right to secede, then the principle of effectivity is ruled out as a principle for recognition of new states in cases in which the seceding entity has no just cause for seceding – that is, when the state from which it is seceding has not failed to protect the rights of the secessionists. In other words, according to the remedial right only theory, mere ability to exercise control over a territory does not confer legitimacy on a secessionist entity; a *bona fide* grievance of serious and persisting injustice is required. So, according to a remedial right only theory, Quebec would not merit recognition as an independent state even if it succeeded in exercising control over the territory of the present province, subsequent to a unilateral declaration of independence. For on the remedial right only theory unilateral secession of Quebec from Canada – that is, secession absent a constitutional amendment allowing it or some other negotiated settlement – would be illegitimate because Quebecois have no valid grievance that their basic rights are being violated. The fact that the secessionists managed to exert control over the territory they had wrongly taken would in no way give them title to it. Canada's right to territorial integrity would remain intact. And other states would be prohibited from intervening to support Quebec secession.

This is not to say that the principle of effectivity has no valid sphere of application. My suggestion is that it has a very limited sphere, namely, in severe cases of state breakdown.

By a severe case of state breakdown I mean a situation of literal anarchy: Not only are massive violations of basic rights either occurring or likely, even worse, no viable political infrastructure remains within the state's boundaries. Neither national institutions nor federal units within the national structure provide the resources for processes of legitimation whereby new structures of political authority might be created. In addition, there is no reasonable prospect of intervention to establish a care-taker government and manage the process of building new institutions. Under such extreme conditions, effectivity may be the only criterion for what might be called *provisional legitimacy*.

If a group manages to secure control over the territory – and if it makes credible pledges to use that control to protect the rights of all persons in that territory – then the best alternative may be to recognize it as provisionally legitimate, that is, as the rightful political authority for the time being. The rationale behind this view is straightforward: Assuming that effective control over territory is a necessary condition for establishing a rights-respecting order out of anarchy, and assuming that order is not to be imposed from the outside, the best we can hope for is to back the strongest contender for political authority.

On this account, the principle of effectivity is not a universal rule for determining when political entities are legitimate. It is of much more limited application, applying only to the most severe cases of state breakdown. As such it cannot be criticized for being a craven submission to the idea that might makes right.

Instead, it makes only this much more limited concession to the reality of force: Where institutional resources for authorizing a legitimate enforcer are lacking, it may be necessary to treat a *de facto* enforcer as provisionally legitimate if there is to be any hope of moving toward a more favorable situation in which a higher standard than mere effective control can be required of those who exercise political power. However, I would emphasize that what I am endorsing, even for this limited sphere of application, is a normatively enriched principle of effectivity: Those exercising effective control must make a credible commitment to protecting the basic right of all within their territory, even in order to warrant provisional recognition.

Given this understanding of the principle of effectivity, the possibility of conflict between it and *uti possidetis* evaporates. Cases where pre-existing boundaries mark political infrastructures capable of protecting basic rights are by definition not cases of *severe* state breakdown, so they are not cases where the principle of effectivity applies.

POSSIBLE CONFLICTS BETWEEN THE RIGHT OF SELF-DEFENSE AND *UTI POSSIDETIS* (PROPERLY UNDERSTOOD)

Earlier I argued that the distinction between secession from a functioning state and efforts to form a new state in conditions of state breakdown is normatively significant. According to the remedial right only theory, unilateral secession from a functioning state is only justified (in the absence of agreement) if secession is a remedy of last resort against serious and persistent violations of basic rights. In an addendum to the remedial right only theory I suggested that in the case of state breakdown, where basic rights are imminently imperiled (though perhaps not yet massively violated), the right of self-defense could credibly be invoked as a justification for efforts to form a new state out of a portion of the territory of the old state. In arguing for a limited and more plausible understanding of *uti possidetis*, I also argued that in some cases the best way to protect basic rights would be to require that new states formed out of the ruins of state breakdown should correspond to existing administrative units within the state.

It should be clear that the principle of justified self-help and *uti possidetis* could in some cases yield mutually incompatible results. It might be best for *most* of the population in a federation that has broken down if existing internal boundaries were preserved as boundaries of new states, but the best prospect for *some particular group* might be to disregard the principle of *uti possidetis* and instead try to carve out its own state, even though its borders would not correspond to those of former federal units. Such may have been the case with Serbs in Croatia in 1991. In these circumstances it appears that there is a conflict of principles, each of which on its own seems quite attractive.

I now wish to suggest that such a conflict is both inevitable and understandable due to the hybrid character of the existing international order. That order is a rather uneasy mixture of a self-help system and a system of global governance properly speaking.

Because there is no world sovereign, no global authority with effective police powers for enforcing human rights everywhere, a sincere commitment to human rights requires international legal institutions that both permit and encourage self-help. Indeed, much of existing international law can best be understood – indeed in some cases can only be understood – as comprising a self-help system. For example, even though current international law does not unambiguously prohibit secession from a rights-respecting, democratic state, it does lend support to the efforts of such a state to oppose secession, in the name of the right of all legitimate states to territorial integrity.[12] Similarly, international law has not yet succeeded in providing all states (whether they supply oil to the West or not) with effective protection against aggression, but it does authorize individual states to help the victims of aggression if they choose to do so. Likewise, international law provides what one international legal expert calls a "legal license" to persecuted religious or racial groups within states to use violence against their governments, even though it does not authorize military intervention in support of them.[13] All of these features of international law become intelligible if we understand that to a large extent the system relies on self-help rather than on centralized enforcement.

From the standpoint of the international legal system as a self-help system, there is much to be said for the self-defense principle. Absent effective international institutions for preventing state breakdown or for managing the rebuilding of rights-respecting regimes when state breakdown occurs, the idea of a right to *sauve qui peut* separation has considerable normative weight.

On the other hand, the international system seems to be making some progress toward evolving away from being almost exclusively a self-help system to one that exhibits some of the characteristics of a complex institution of global governance. The further this evolution proceeds, the more reasonable it is to insist that in situations of state breakdown, *sauve qui peut* separatism is not justified. For example, if the United Nations or the Council of Europe had been willing and able to help negotiate a new federal structure for Yugoslavia – and had provided sufficient economic aid to make it work – secession by Slovenia and Croatia would have been much more morally problematic. The plea of self-defense would look less convincing if there were reasonable prospects for security of basic rights without unilateral secession. The domestic analogy supports this conclusion: the more effective the police are in protecting citizens from violent crime, the more narrowly circumscribed is the individual's right of self-defense.

It appears, then, that so long as the international legal system is an uneasy and shifting balance between self-help elements and global governance elements, there will be a possibility of conflicts between *uti possidetis* and the right to *sauve qui peut* separation in cases of state breakdown. Groups will understandably be more willing to rely on their own efforts to secure their rights in situations of state breakdown than to respect pre-existing boundaries if they are not confident that international legal institutions will play an effective role in protecting their rights within those pre-existing boundaries. Nevertheless, in some cases, there will be no such conflict. And the more capable the international system becomes of intervening effectively for the protection of basic rights in cases of state breakdown, the less scope there will be for the principle of self-defensive separation, and the less possibility of conflict between it and *uti possidetis* or other applicable principles.

CONCLUSIONS

The crisis in Kosovo in 1999 highlighted the inadequacy of existing international law concerning both the right to secede and the right to engage in humanitarian intervention. Many concluded that the NATO intervention was illegal but morally justified. This perceived discrepancy between morality and the law has prompted proposals for changing international law to broaden the domain of legally permissible humanitarian intervention.

It would be a mistake, however, to think that the only change needed is a relaxing of the current strictures on humanitarian intervention. Such an approach overlooks the intimate connection that often obtains between human-rights violations and secession. In the case of secessionist crises, a morally defensible international legal framework must ground the right of intervention in a more adequate account of when a group has the right to secede.

Reforms in the law of secession and of intervention would be mutually enriching. A more permissive legal rule regarding humanitarian intervention – one which did not always require Security Council authorization – might prevent some of the massive human-rights violations that spur secessionist movements. An international legal right to secede for groups that suffer persistent violations of their fundamental rights would authorize intervention in support of secession, prohibit states from aiding efforts to crush secession by groups that have the right, and perhaps deter states from violating the rights of minority groups in the first place. A new international legal right to secede grounded in the remedial right only theory would provide clearer and more morally defensible guidance for intervention without opening the flood-gates to unrestrained state-breaking.

However, two principles of international law that have been invoked in an effort to control the process of state-breaking at first may appear to present a barrier to international legal reform regarding secession and the right to intervene in secession crises: the principle of *uti possidetis* and the principle of effectivity.

Although both principles are traditionally justified by appeal to stability and peace, both have received serious criticisms. I have argued that both the attractions of these principles and the objections to them can be understood if we recognize that they are of much more limited application than is usually assumed. I have shown that they are highly derivative principles that are defensible only when limited to certain kinds of cases in which state breakdown is occurring. Understanding the scope and limits of these principles makes it possible to expose and avoid their misuses and to clear the way for morally progressive changes in the international law of secession and intervention. In addition, the reformist interpretation of the two principles I have proposed sheds light on the peculiar hybrid character of the international system as a mixture of self-help and global governance elements.

I conclude with a cautionary remark: Integration of a remedial right to unilateral secession into international law would be a valuable component of a more enlightened law of intervention, not a substitute for it. Whether intervention in support of secession would be justified in any particular case would depend upon a number of factors in addition to the existence of a right to secede. A fully developed theory of intervention would thus require not only a principled stand on secession but also additional criteria of the sort familiar from just war theory, including the requirements of proportionate force, protection of noncombatants, reasonable prospect of success, exhaustion of reasonable efforts at peaceful settlement of the conflict, and so on.[14]

NOTES

1 See Malcolm Shaw, *International Law* (New York: Cambridge University Press, 1997), pp. 356–57.

2 See Supreme Court of Canada, *Reference re Secession of Quebec* [1998] 2 SCR 217 at section III.B.(2) "Recognition of a Factual/Political Reality: the Effectivity Principle," especially paragraph 146.

3 *Factum of the Amicus Curiae in the Matter of section 53 of the Supreme Court of Canada Act and in the Matter of the reference by the Governor in Council concerning certain questions relating to the secession of Quebec*, File no. 25506 (Supreme Court of Canada), pp. 87–91. See also Allen Buchanan, "Quebec Session: Democracy, Minority Rights, and the Rule of Law," paper prepared for the Department of Intergovernmental Affairs, Office of the Privy Council, Government of Canada, 2000.

4 See *Factum of the Amicus Curiae*, p. 109.

5 See Thomas Frank, "The Emerging Right to Democratic Governance," *American Journal of International Law* 86, no. 46, 46–91.

6 See European Community, *Guidelines on the Recognition of New States in Eastern Europe and in the Soviet Union*, available in *International Legal Materials* 31 (1992), 1485.

7 See Allen Buchanan, "Recognitional Legitimacy and the State System," *Philosophy and Public Affairs* 28, no. 1 (1999), 46–78.

8 See Allen Buchanan, "The International Institutional Dimension of Secession," in *Theories of Secession*, Percy H. Lehning, ed. (New York: Routledge, 1998), pp. 46–91.

9 Allen Buchanan, "Theories of Secession," *Philosophy and Public Affairs* 26, no. 1 (1997), 31–61; Margaret Moore, "Introduction," in *National Self-Determination and Secession* (New York: Oxford University Press, 1998), pp. 1–13.

10 See Allen Buchanan, "Theories of Secession," *Philosophy and Public Affairs* 26, no. 1 (1997), 31–61; "Recognitional Legitimacy and the State System," *Philosophy and Public Affairs* 28, no. 1 (1999), 46–78.

11 See James Gow, *Legitimacy and the Military: The Yugoslav Crisis* (London: Pinter Publishers, 1992); Susan Woodward, *Balkan Tragedy: Chaos and Dissolution After the Cold War* (Washington DC: Brookings Institution, 1995); Misha Glenny, *The Fall of Yugoslavia: The Third Balkan War* (New York: Penguin, 1992).

12 See for example General Assembly Resolution 2625 (xxv), *Declaration on Principles of International Law Concerning Friendly Relations and Cooperation Among States in Accordance with the Charter of the United Nations* (1970), paragraph 7 (also known as the "saving" clause of the UN Resolution on Friendly Relations), UN Doc. A/8028 (1970). International documents confirming these limits on the right of a people to dismember an existing state on grounds of self-determination include: World Conference on Human Rights, *Vienna*

Declaration and Programme of Action (Vienna, 1993), UN Doc. A / CONF.157/24 (Part I), p. 2; and United Nations General Assembly, *Declaration on the Rights of Persons Belonging to National or Ethnic, Religious or Linguistic Minorities,* General Assembly resolution 47/135 (1992), Article 8, paragraph 4.

13 See Antonio Cassese, *Self-Determination of Peoples: A Legal Reappraisal* (Cambridge: Cambridge University Press, 1995), chapter 5, especially pp. 108–25.

14 I am grateful to Don Scheid and Deen Chatterjee for their astute comments on earlier drafts of this paper.

PART IV

The critique of interventionism

Chapter 11

Respectable oppressors, hypocritical liberators: morality, intervention, and reality

RICHARD W. MILLER

One of the few convictions about intervention that is generally shared (perhaps the only one) is that it is only justified as a response to serious injustice. One would expect, then, that the leading accounts of the morality of intervention would be exquisitely sensitive to the moral defects of governments and, more broadly, to their imperfect responsiveness to the kinds of considerations by which people of good will regulate their dealings with other individuals. But in fact, moral theorizing about intervention is frequently disengaged from these morally troubling realities. As a result, influential theories shed little light on live questions of intervention and sometimes introduce much distortion.

I will begin by defending this appraisal of three leading approaches to intervention, namely, John Rawls' attempt to base international justice on a law of well-ordered peoples, Michael Walzer's appeal to the over-riding virtue of communal autonomy, and the arguments, especially influential in recent years, for reducing traditional sovereign prerogatives in ways that expose governments that violate human rights to risks of armed intervention. Then, I will develop an alternative perspective on intervention, more responsive to realities that these theories neglect. In its view of the terms in which governments justify their conduct and criticize the conduct of other governments, this perspective is conservative. Because of, not despite, their vagueness and near-incoherence, the current foundations of the intergovernmental practice of justification and criticism largely provide the right incentives in the world system of flawed governments. In its view of what interventions would be morally justified, this approach is disunified. Rather than basing the judgment of interventions on a single master value or a ranked list of general considerations, it insists on the diversity and variable rank of the relevant considerations and seeks specific constellations of reasons, frequently realized in actual situations, which sustain a case for or against intervention. Finally, in its assessment of episodes of intervention as they have actually unfolded, this approach to intervention in our defective world is frequently subversive. It makes the condemnation of whole, flawed decision-making processes a central aspect of moral assessment, and seeks to improve the practice of intervention by exposing the hypocrisy of world powers, above all, the sole superpower.

In this inquiry, my understanding of "intervention" will be fairly broad. On the broadest understanding, intervention is action by the government of one country intentionally affecting the process of political decision-making in another in some way that is inappropriate in the absence of a relevant injustice. On this construal, the injustice might itself be transnational, so that the Allied powers, in their invasion and military occupation of Germany, could be said to have intervened in German affairs even if the justification was solely German foreign aggression. However, my concern will be the question of when intervention is justifiable as a response to a government's infliction of injustice within its borders. So I will use "intervention" in the narrower sense which is sometimes spelled out as "humanitarian intervention", that is, intervention (in the broadest understanding) in response to domestic injustice in the target. In this usage, the term can refer to both military and nonmilitary intervention, though I will sometimes explicitly single out the most forceful military interventions, namely invasions, for special treatment.

RAWLS AND INDECENT REALITIES

Moral theorizing about intervention plays a large role in Rawls' attempt to base international justice on the norms by which politically well-ordered peoples would express their mutual respect, the first perspective that I will consider. But once his standards of good order are understood, his description of this "law of peoples" turns out to be of severely limited use in resolving questions of intervention in our ill-ordered world.

In Rawls' view, principles of international justice are justified by showing that they are rules governing international relations that all would adopt in a hypothetical negotiation, unaffected by actual differences in bargaining power, among representatives of peoples whose institutions and political culture meet one or the other of his two criteria for being well-ordered: some are liberal and the rest are non-liberal but decent, in his special senses of these terms. In these fair deliberations, each representative would express a well-ordered people's fundamental interest in political independence under its system of basic institutions, a domestic political process in which questions are resolved on the basis of common sympathies, the respect for fellow-members of one's society that well-ordered politics requires and proper patriotic pride. Such deliberations would result in a commitment among well-ordered peoples to "observe a duty of non-intervention" in one another's affairs,[1] a prohibition so stern that it excludes even the use of foreign aid by the governments of liberal peoples to create incentives for decent peoples to become more liberal, a change that would remove defects of injustice (pp. 62, 85.)

If this comprehensive prohibition of all forms of intervention is required by due respect for the political institutions and culture of any well-ordered people, a high standard of good political order must be in play. And both of Rawls' standards for being a well-ordered people, the liberal and the decent standard, are exceptionally demanding. The institutions of a liberal people must provide substantive freedom and equality for all, not just the formal freedom and equality prescribed by the constitutions of parliamentary democracies.[2] This requires universal access to effective, informed participation in a political process untainted by major advantages for the best-off, to means of achieving self-respect on the basis of secure, meaningful work, and to fair opportunities for self-advancement, especially opportunities based on education (p. 50.) According to Rawls' specifications of these "important requirements" for a genuinely liberal regime, the United States is not at present the site of a liberal people. For example, it must be a settled feature of a liberal people's institutions that "society [is] ... employer of last resort" and that there is "public financing of elections" (*ibid.*) And, clearly, these particular measures are no guarantee of the substantive freedom and equality of a liberal people. In western European countries in which electoral campaigns *are* publicly financed, the concentration of wealth gives some citizens important advantages in influencing the outcome of politics; moreover, in most of these countries, limits in the extent to which all are "united by what Mill called 'common sympathies' " (p. 23) preclude equal political responsiveness to legitimate interests of all, regardless of ethnicity, region, religion or culture. It is perfectly possible that there currently are no liberal peoples.

It is even less likely that any people is well ordered in the other, non-liberal way. Although a non-liberal yet decent people lacks democratic political rights and liberal guarantees of state neutrality among faiths and personal ideals, such a people acts through a government genuinely committed to advancing the common good, shared by the politically privileged and the non-privileged, by those within any favored religion or way of life and those outside it. As in the case of liberal peoples, these commitments must be effective, not just verbal, substantive, not just formal. Thus, the one form of decent non-liberal government that Rawls describes takes measures to insure, by adequate consultation, that it will be responsive to the interests constitutive of the common good, whoever's they are, and appreciates the special importance of attending to people's own interpretations of those interests. For example, if women do not vote or hold important offices, the decent nonliberal political elite compensates through regular consultations with women's groups (p. 75.) Of course, mere listening, with no serious tendency to give way when this requires giving up advantages, is the prime example of formal, rather than substantive attention to the common good in a hierarchical process (a lack of substance not unknown in hierarchies that flourish under parliamentary democracies). Rawls has in mind the genuine responsiveness that cedes advantage in the face of cogent appeals to shared moral standards, quite apart from fear of rebellion or disruption (see p. 78). Evidently, the politically privileged elite of such a decent, non-liberal people would willingly give up their power if most subjects could offer good enough reasons to believe that democratic institutions better advance the common good.

Rawls makes a plausible claim about the respect due such a decent people when he says, in effect, that Sweden would fail to show respect for his imaginary decent, non-liberal people of "Kazanistan" if Sweden conditioned some of its aid on Kazanistan's granting more political rights to women, rather than letting Kazanistani consultations with women's groups over women's interests and the common good take their course (pp. 75, 85.) But it is no accident that Rawls has to rely on a made-up example of a society in which a political elite combines political privilege with disinterest in exploiting it to preserve special advantages.

Live questions about the justice of intervention are questions about the just response to serious departures from Rawls' standards of good political order. Someone who tries to extract useful guidance from Rawls' description of mutual respect in a society of well-ordered peoples

confronts a dilemma. On the one hand, the wholesale extrapolation
of the norm forbidding intervention among well-ordered peoples to
a world in which well-ordered peoples are rare or non-existent would
prolifically ignore moral differences which are clearly relevant, for example, the enormous gap between the corruption, rigidity, and intolerance of the Saudi elite (much less the genocidal fury of the extreme
Hutu nationalist regime in Rwanda) and the decent consultative politics
of the hierarchs of Kazanistan. On the other hand, if respect for a people's decency were made the sole basis for a duty of non-intervention,
a capacious license to intervene would emerge, without an adequate
justification. For the characteristic virtue of a well-ordered people, guidance by a political process through which participants work out their
differences, respectfully attending to one another in pursuit of their
common good, is not dishonored in stopping serious abuse of citizens
or subjects by a government with no serious concern for their legitimate interests. This capacious license for intervention would be, at
best, a hasty inference from Rawls' description of the political processes
that are worthy of respect. For intervention that responds to a people's defects of Rawlsian indecency can have serious costs for people
both in the target of intervention and elsewhere, and people, as well
as peoples, are worthy of respect. Charles Maynes, when he was editor of *Foreign Policy*, reported, "CIA officials privately concede that the
US military may have killed from 7,000 to 10,000 Somalis during its
engagement [to end the indecent warlordism of Mohammed Aidid.]
America lost only 34 soldiers."[3] One need not take the Somali people to have attained Rawlsian decency in order to have doubts as to
whether this deadly onslaught respected legitimate interests of people in
Somalia.

Rawls' sole, two-page discussion of justified intervention in regimes
that are not well ordered includes just one specific description of how
intervention might be justified in response to wholly domestic injustice, a brief fiction, in a footnote, of a modern-day version of Aztec
society which "holds its lower class as slaves, keeping the younger
members available for human sacrifices in temples": the advanced industrial Aztecs would appropriately be subject to military intervention
if "tactful" persuasion fails (pp. 93f.) One will not get much further in
guiding the moral assessment of responses to foreign political indecency
without shifting the focus of detailed inquiry to the actual world system in which virtually all peoples are ill-ordered, including potential
interveners as well as plausible targets of intervention.

Richard W. Miller

WALZER: THE ILLUSION OF AUTONOMY

The most detailed and discriminating of current moral accounts of intervention is Michael Walzer's. Although, like Rawls' approach, it is grounded on a political value, this value does not consist of virtue in the protected institutions. Rather, the value ultimately governing decisions as to whether to intervene is the self-determination of political communities, a process to be respected in "all its messiness and uncertainty, its inevitable compromises and its frequent brutality,"[4] even when the outcome is tyranny, so long as the members of the political community "suffer only at one another's hands."[5]

Walzer's underlying moral principle is *"always act so as to recognize and uphold communal autonomy."*[6] However, his attention to the diverse prerequisites for recognizing and upholding this master value leads him to insist on a complex system of precepts as the basis for just choice by foreign governments as to whether to intervene.

On the one hand, there should be a strong presumption, difficult to override, that any government fits the community consisting of its citizens or subjects sufficiently well that intervention would violate the right to self-determination of the political community.[7] Even when a political community is ruled as repressively as Nicaragua was by the Somozas, outsiders should let the domestic political process take its course, for fear of intruding on "self-determination under conditions of political oppression."[8] Since respect for communal autonomy is the basis for the presumption against intervention, it would "rule out any external determination of domestic constitutional arrangements," not just determination by invasion.[9]

On the other hand, this presumption is overidden, creating a right of intervention, if any of three "rules of disregard" apply, rules that are the appropriate basis for a foreign government's judgment that intervention (even, if need be, through invasion) would, for rare and special reasons, be a way of protecting the integrity of a political community. First, since political communities are distinguished by common sympathies, traditions, histories, and a typically shared aspiration to work in common to hand the shared heritage down to future generations, a single government can rule over more than one political community: if one of them is not permitted to opt for political independence and a sufficiently "active revolt . . . has reached certain proportions,"[10] a foreign government may legitimately conclude that respect for communal autonomy would be displayed in supporting the movement toward independence. Second, if a civil war has broken out within a political community and "the insurgents establish control over some substantial portion of the territory and population,"[11] no foreign government should help either side, and if one does, this intervention makes counter-intervention legitimate in order to balance "and no more than balance . . . the prior intervention . . . , making it possible for the local forces to win or lose on their own."[12] Finally, even though " 'ordinary' oppression" is no license for intervention,[13] intervention is permissible in order to end violations of human rights that are so massive that "we must doubt the very existence of a political community to which the idea of self-determination might apply."[14] This third class of reasons consists of the massacre or enslavement of "some substantial number" of citizen/subjects[15] or "the expulsion of very large numbers of people."[16]

I believe that the effort to make communal autonomy the ground for both a presumption against intervention that almost always prevails and the exceptions to the presumption requires illusions about the nature and autonomy of actual political communities. One necessary illusion is a failure to acknowledge how brutal authentic interpretations of shared traditions can be. Walzer does permit intervention to prevent extreme brutality. Yet this permission is not supposed to be a suspension of respect for autonomous political community in the name of something else. It is supposed to reflect the failure of the extreme brutalities to play a role in the self-determination of a community including both perpetrators and victims.

The Taliban routinely inflicted brutal violations of human dignity. This violent repression included such juridical brutalities as executions of men who engaged in homosexual intercourse by crushing them to death, usually by bulldozing a wall over them, and executions of women convicted of adultery by stoning them to death.[17] The interpretation of shared Afghan traditions by which the Taliban justified their violations of human dignity was harsh and extreme, but it was one of the interpretations sincerely and authentically advanced among Afghans mutually engaged in an internal struggle.[18] Foreign material support for a secure anti-Taliban enclave in order to provide refuge and hope for those imperilled by the Taliban's brutality would have violated communal autonomy, but it does not seem (and Walzer has not shown) that such a policy would have been an international injustice. Similarly, the ideal of self-sufficient primitive communism which seems to have motivated the brutalities of the Pol Pot regime was, arguably, one authentic interpretation of Cambodian political traditions; yet the Vietnamese overthrow of the regime certainly seems justifiable, even if it could not be justified solely as a response to Cambodia's very limited incursions into Vietnam itself.

Of course, there are many different defensible understandings of "community". It is far from obvious that, in the most morally important sense, Afghan homosexuals shared a political community with the Taliban or Cambodian intellectuals shared a political community with the Pol Pot regime. But similar doubts about morally important community are appropriate whenever the treatment of citizen/subjects seriously departs from Rawlsian "decency". It is hardly obvious that the Somozas shared a political community with the dissenters tortured by their National Guard. On the more morally robust construal of "political community", the honoring of political community does not require a strong presumption against intervention, since grave domestic injustice destroys political community. In Walzer's less morality-laden construal, political community binds all who contest the future trajectory of a shared history, informed by common cultural sympathies and traditions; but, then, political community by itself is not of sufficient value to exclude intervention to remedy grave injustice.

A self-contained process of struggle can also lack adequate value because of enduring unfair advantages of one side. Perhaps the self-determination of a community in which members struggle in a fair fight, based on the persuasiveness of appeals to rival interpretations of shared traditions, has great value even when unjust interpretations happen to be politically ascendant. But an oppressive regime almost always relies on the enormous unfair advantage of undemocratic control over the armed forces and police. Even if such a regime is the heir of a popular revolution or widely established tradition, it has usually departed from the historical source of its power through corruption, bureaucracy, or rigid adherence to what was always just a part and is now a small part of popular opinion.

The communitarian case against intervention does not just overvalue communal autonomy, it vastly overestimates its prevalence. Autonomous yet internally oppressive political communities are too rare to sustain Walzer's strong general presumption against intervention. An important part of the sustenance of most unjust regimes – certainly the Somozas' – is the use of internationally recognized control over raw materials and land, infrastructure, and foreign policy to obtain resources from abroad for the arming and sustaining of a repressive apparatus and the maintenance of a network of patronage relationships.

So, Cuban support for the Sandinista rebels could be regarded as a form of counter-intervention. Counter-intervention is permitted by Walzer's rules of disregard. But if counter-intervention is stretched to include countering the consequences of foreign reward for sovereign prerogatives, the theory as a whole does not sustain the general thesis that armed invasion (much less milder forms of intervention) is rarely justifiable.[19]

One can imagine a world in which the tyrannical side in a struggle against tyranny normally derives its sustenance from sufficient local popular support for its extremely illiberal interpretation of local traditions, without crucial reliance on resources from abroad or entrenched unfair advantages. One can also imagine a world in which authentic interpretations of local traditions that are implemented by a government never inflict brutal indignities. The argument from communal autonomy to a strong presumption against intervention hedged by Walzer's rules of disregard depends, for its appeal, on ignoring the distance between these worlds and our own.

INTERVENTION AND HUMAN RIGHTS: ILLUSIONS OF SAFETY

The final perspective that I will criticize is very far from ignoring the full extent of domestic injustice that our world displays. A government's serious, widespread, and systematic violations of the human rights of those within its borders are seen as depriving it of the sovereign right to non-intervention, so that intervention, including armed intervention, is permissible beyond the bounds of Walzer's rules of disregard. This expanded license to intervene is offered as an excuse that ought to be available to interveners in the formulas of international law which regulate the global public intergovernmental practice of justification and criticism.

For example, Kofi Annan insists, "The [UN] Charter protects the sovereignty of peoples. It was never meant as a license for governments to trample on human rights and human dignity. Sovereignty implies responsibility, not just power."[20] Offering the military intervention in Kosovo among his examples, he asserts "the overriding right of people in distress to receive help,"[21] declaring, "We will not, and we cannot accept a situation where people are brutalized behind national boundaries."[22] Such proposals to expand the internationally recognized right to intervene have become increasingly common since the end of the Cold War, which made their overt implementation by the United States increasingly feasible.[23]

The world in which a broader license to intervene based on such conditional sovereignty would be justifiable is, I believe, yet another misleading idealization. Because of the actual risks of harm that are posed by armed interventions, risks often reflecting the interests of the specially powerful governments that dominate the worldwide practice of armed intervention, a license for armed intervention that is broader than Walzer's rules of disregard would be too dangerous to be moral. Fear of these dangers by no means requires endorsement of Walzer's communitarian rationale (which will turn out to have its own distinctive liabilities, including excessive constraint on unarmed intervention.)

A risky operation

Armed intervention against a tyranny that engages in widespread violations of human rights but does not defend itself through widespread massacre is a risky operation, which should be rare. Such tyrannies have recourse to loyalties based on dependence, tradition, or profound interests of important social groups. Their resources often make them hard to dislodge without great bloodshed. The social splits creating room for tyranny often would persist after a particular tyranny is overthrown, giving rise to violent instability or a new order not significantly better than the old. If, to create stable basic justice in the wake of armed intervention, a long foreign occupation were imposed, this usually would thwart goals of self-determination which are more important to most victims of a tyranny than the removal of its injustices.

Such risks create special burdens of justification on those who would impose them from abroad. Perhaps, through armed rebellion, people who are themselves victimized by the injustices of a regime can rightly impose grave risks on fellow-victims when there is merely a fighting chance of success in remedying widespread injustice; they can declare, "I could not tolerate this assault on my dignity any longer. Join me. These are your oppressors, too." But this appeal is not available to outsiders who intervene in order to end injustice within the borders. As a condition for imposing the inevitable risks of armed intervention, these outsiders ought to have warranted confidence that the vast majority of the intended beneficiaries of the intervention consent to the risks on the basis of adequate information and that the benefits of the intervention probably outweigh the costs among all whose interests deserve serious concern.

The latter group, all those who have moral standing to complain of risks imposed by intervention, may well include not just intended beneficiaries and innocent bystanders, but also the vast majority of those who would be part of the armed forces defending a tyrannical regime from invasion. After all, most of these defenders may be people who would not otherwise engage in conduct which is rightly stopped through the use of deadly force. Many of them may be unwilling cannon fodder, like the conscripts massed at the Iraqi border when the United States invaded Iraq after Iraqi forces were expelled from Kuwait and Iraq had offered to give up its territorial claims: according to the estimate of the British Ministry of Defense, 30,000 Iraqi troops were killed in the invasion; many conscripts at the border were buried alive in trenches by bulldozers or suffocated and set ablaze by antipersonnel weapons that ignited fuel diffused in the air around them.[24] In between the extremes of conscripts used as cannon fodder and willing participants in the secret police are the usual rank and file of a tyrant's professional armed forces, fleeing poverty for one of the few situations in which the lot of poor young men is improved at public expense, hoping that their job will not include anything more brutal than somewhat rough police work. Such a person's choice was sufficiently constrained and his hope of avoiding gravely unjust conduct was sufficiently reasonable that his death in an invasion to defeat injustice should be counted (though perhaps with some discount) as a relevant cost, a reason not to invade. Both in confronting the conscript and in confronting the rank and file enforcer of a tyrannical order, a rebel in a just cause can rightly say, "I should not be held hostage to the need to avoid harming deadly opponents to my pursuit of my own dignity." But an outsider engaged in humanitarian intervention is not defending his own dignity in making these insiders deadly opponents who must be overcome by deadly means.

(The special nature of risk-assessment in armed intervention – in my "humanitarian" understanding of the term – illuminates, by contrast, special features of transnational military action in response to terrorist attacks, such as the military actions by the United States in Afghanistan after September 11, 2001. Since the United States government was implementing its fundamental duty to defend its own citizens from unjust deadly attack, the justice of the invasion of Afghanistan did not depend on a well-grounded estimate that benefits would probably outweigh costs among those in Afghanistan whose interests deserved serious concern or on a warranted expectation of informed consent of most intended Afghan beneficiaries. In addition, a government defending its citizens against international terrorist groups and governments that aid them may not have to observe the same standards of proof as a government contemplating humanitarian invasion, when it asks whether there is sufficient evidence supporting a hypothesis that costs imposed on foreigners will be adequately contained. But these differences should not obscure important continuities with the ethics of humanitarian intervention. Although a government such as the Taliban, complicit in an international conspiracy to murder large numbers of innocents, is in no position to complain of foreign efforts to depose it in response to consequent deadly brutality, the violent deposing of such a regime inevitably imposes severe costs on victims whose interests and views ought to be of serious moral concern. These costs include the deaths of hundreds, perhaps thousands of Afghan civilians killed in the bombing campaign against the Taliban.[25] Such costs would seem to create a duty to avoid a military response that imposes them when there is no good reason to suppose that it significantly reduces terrorist attacks from abroad as compared with legitimate efforts that do not include it and pose no similar risk to foreigners of moral standing. This burden of proof may be hard to meet given the availability of alternatives which are not as apt to create vengeful outrage that fuels international terrorism, for example, policing and military action limited to terrorist groups of global reach and just foreign policy initiatives reducing the appeal and effectiveness of such groups. Similarly, if, in light of feasible alternatives, impartial concern for all whose fundamental interests are in jeopardy would lead to rejection of a use of organized large-scale violence in response to international terrorism, this is a serious objection to the violence, which is, after all, a means by which a government discharges its local duty to protect the innocent.)

A License and its Dangers

Advocates of the expanded license for humanitarian intervention can certainly acknowledge its liabilities by including a requirement of avoiding excessive imposed risks. But their effort to create a new consensus subscribing to the new norms ought to be judged in light of the difference the new consensus is apt to make in the actual conduct of those implementing the new norms. By way of analogy, consider the rationale for a legal rule excluding improperly obtained evidence from trials. Police

and prosecutors *should* make faithful and discerning observance of prohibitions against unreasonable search and seizure, as specified by courts,
an overriding consideration in their pursuit of criminal convictions. Still,
a criminal justice system in which this norm is affirmed but evidence
obtained in violation of it is admissible is not adequate; the pressures
leading powerful agents to violate the norm are too strong and pervasive. A similar neglect of actual dangers, as opposed to wishes embodied
in norms, is the characteristic utopianism of the interventionists.

For better or worse, militarily powerful governments will be the
leading agents in implementing the risky procedure of humanitarian
military intervention, the more so the more powerful they are. So we
need to consider how the special interests of military powers – above
all, the sole superpower – are apt to affect their use of a new license
to intervene against non-massacring tyrannies. The result would seem
to be serious costs imposed on people with moral standing (not just
tyrants and henchmen) in an intervention process in which beneficent
intervention with adequate informed consent would be rare. The new
license to intervene is like a euthanasia system that outruns doctors'
and family-members' tendencies to act with appropriate restraint and
discrimination.

One interest of any great power engaged in humanitarian military
intervention is the reduction of risks to its troops, even by means that increase morally relevant risks over-all. This special interest is entrenched
in the domestic politics of governments and in standard duties of loyalty
to compatriots. It is part of a generally beneficent inhibition to the use
of deadly force in foreign policy. But in a practice of armed intervention
extending to entrenched tyrannies, it can have disastrous consequences.

Here, Somalia is a troubling warning signal. For the attack on
Mohammed Aidid's forces is the single case in recent history of overt
military intervention by the United States beyond the scope of Walzer's
rules of disregard. During the four months of ultimately unsuccessful
armed intervention against Aidid, the use of overwhelming fire power
to limit United States casualties may have led to thousands of Somali
deaths, while confining US losses to 34.[26] Although the distribution of
food in a famine was supposed to be a major benefit justifying costs of
armed intervention, food deliveries were already taking place, having
begun, in any case, well after the peak of the famine, in time to interfere
with planting by lowering the price of crops.[27]

The over-readiness of the United States to engage in full-fledged
military intervention in Somalia, a highly strategic locale in the Horn

of Africa, reflects a further special interest guiding the interventions of great powers, namely, an interest in securing and extending their geopolitical power. Choices concerning intervention that are strongly determined by this interest are apt to be very different from choices strongly determined by the gravity of the injustices to be remedied. The difference is huge in the intervention decisions of the sole superpower.

In 1999, the United States led the bombing of Serbia in response to a year-long campaign of brutal Serbian repression in Kosovo which had exacted a death toll in the vicinity of 2000, including both civilians and KLA combatants, and had displaced hundreds of thousands of Albanian Kosovars, many intentionally driven from their homes.[28] But when much more death and dispossession has secured control by a government allied with the United States, or a social or military elite whose interests coincide with the strategic and economic interests pursued by the US government, American responses have included vigorous efforts to prevent intervention and outright facilitation of atrocities. Consider the contrast with US responses to injustice in Turkey and Indonesia.

In Turkey, in the fifteen years prior to the bombing of Serbia, the death toll of a conflict over Kurdish autonomy, characterized by widespread government brutality and suppression of minimal expressions of Kurdish identity (including Kurdish names and cassettes with Kurdish songs, much less Kurdish-language schools), was 35,000, according to a Human Rights Watch estimate.[29] At the height of the Turkish government's counter-insurgency, in 1994, the Turkish Minister for Human Rights (who was soon replaced) described the counterinsurgency in one region in that year as "state terrorism": "In Tunceli it is the state that is evacuating and burning villages. In the southeast there are 2 million people left homeless."[30] The previous year, the UN Committee on Torture endorsed an Amnesty International allegation of widespread and systematic use of torture.[31] In 1994, Turkey received $406 million in US military aid in the form of subsidized loans, a $125 million cash grant under the Economic Support Fund program which (as intended) was largely used to offset military purchases, and surplus equipment with an original acquisition value of $109 million (preceded by a value in the previous year of $626 million.)[32] Eighty percent of the armament used by Turkish forces in its offensives against Kurdish villages was American.[33] According to the UN Registry of Conventional Arms, the United States was the only country in 1993 and 1994 to supply Turkey with the most deadly weapons of its offensive in the Kurdish countryside, military helicopters with integrated air-to-surface weapons.[34]

The Carter Administration was notable for its public advocacy of a diplomacy based on the promotion of human rights. In Indonesia's invasion and subjugation of East Timor about 200,000 died, the vast majority civilians, mostly in 1977 and 1978. US-supplied counterinsurgency aircraft used in forcing villagers to leave the highlands were a crucial and very lethal means of conquest, by armed forces deriving 90 percent of their weapons from the United States. The value of the importation of US arms to Indonesia in 1978 was three times that in 1976 (mostly through the government-to-government Foreign Military Sales program.) After 1975, the year of the invasion of East Timor, US military aid increased, totaling $56 million in 1976–78.[35]

In his memoirs of his activities as US Ambassador to the UN, Daniel Patrick Moynihan reports how he was instructed to respond to massacres by Indonesian forces in their initial takeover of East Timor, an invasion that had been reported to have already claimed 60,000 lives: "The Department of State desired that the United Nations prove utterly ineffective in whatever measures it undertook. This task was given to me, and I carried it forward with no inconsiderable success."[36] The regime that invaded East Timor had itself come to power through a military coup followed by massacres which, in Amnesty International's estimate, claimed "many more than one million lives," a campaign of subjugation welcomed, encouraged and aided by the United States.[37]

The molding of the actual intervention process by the interest in geopolitical power further increases the dangers of the expanded license to intervene. To begin with, an interest in geopolitical power makes it likely that a broad norm of intervention will be exploited to consolidate spheres of influence or display impressive firepower, in circumstances in which any injustices that are combatted do not justify the imposed costs. Those who would broaden the license to intervene against foreign oppression may hope to put the thugs governing Myanmar in jeopardy, but if past US practice is an indication, a license to use force in foreign places to defend imperilled human rights is more likely to encourage excessive US military force in rebel-held territories of Colombia or subversion of elected leftist Latin American governments.

The connection between intervention and the pursuit of geopolitical interests also makes more extensive armed humanitarian intervention a threat to peace among non-tyrannized peoples. Military interventions by great powers tend to expand their geopolitical reach in ways that are threatening to other powers, giving rise to tensions that risk further war and produce costly, competitive military build-ups. These were the most important long-term consequences of the interventions by European powers in the Balkans in the late nineteenth and early twentieth centuries, interventions which often responded to unjust violence and ethnic oppression. In recent decades, US-led interventions in Serbia and Iraq have encouraged rearmament in Russia and Russia's pursuit of an alliance with China.

In addition, the broadened license to intervene would expand the global influence over political decision-making of the major intervening powers, and, above all, expand the hegemony of the sole superpower. Unjust regimes with a reasonably firm grip on their subjects, who are secure allies of the United States, faithful to US strategic and economic interests, are not vulnerable to military intervention by the United States. Regimes with defiant leaders who seek independent power in strategic places are vulnerable to such intervention, justified in part by (often accurate) charges of grave injustice. The consequent increase in hegemony would have its own costs for the world's most vulnerable people.

For one thing, the consequent increase in bargaining power in economic negotiations is apt to serve the interests of richer countries at cost to poor ones, for example, the interests of richer countries in IMF austerity regimes, unrestricted flows of capital, favorable terms in world trade agreements, and cheap raw materials. More generally, hegemony increases the extent to which the terms of life in relatively poor countries depend on the decisions of governments of other countries and the impact of global market processes. Most people in virtually every country have an aspiration to work out the local terms of life through local traditions and institutions, on the basis of interactions with those who share them and share a commitment to hand down some distinctive version of what they have inherited. Walzer may have exaggerated the independent value of this goal and the extent to which it is realizable, but it is surely one worthwhile political aim. As the dominance of the United States grows, the capacity of Thais and Malaysians to regulate the impact of global processes on the quality of their lives declines.

The costs of the expanded license to intervene could be justified by a sufficient reduction in tyrannical abuses. But the actual frequency with which tyrannies are deposed through armed intervention would be (and, as we have seen, should be) small. Most tyrannies would be saved from overthrow by the potential interveners' concerns to economize their resources, not to put their troops in jeopardy, and to preserve ties with tyrannical allies – and they would also be saved by potential interveners' fears of the instability produced by frequent resort to armed intrusion. In nearly every case, tyrannical regimes would face, at most, a small increase in the chance of armed intervention; and a small increase may well increase the rigidity and vigor of oppressors' efforts to maintain their rule.

It might seem that all of these risks could be contained through a strict requirement of United Nations approval. But confidence in this restriction would express another, familiar form of utopianism, reliance on an idealized United Nations to cope with real problems. Suppose that Security Council approval were required. Then China would have a veto in discussions of whether a government which is not engaged in widespread massacres may nonetheless be invaded to remedy violations of human rights, and the US veto would determine the outcome of similar discussions of human rights violations by its allies. This is not a prospect calculated to strike an appropriate balance between the ending of violations of human rights and costs of intervention and hegemony. On the other hand, General Assembly approval of intervention in the face of opposition by a major power usually reflects the dominant influence of the most important superpower; it also prompts the destabilizing resentment of major powers that lose the vote, the dangerous phenomenon that led to the provision for veto by permanent members of the Security Council.

In any case, if an invading force is to be effective, it must be reasonably well-integrated, in ways that preclude equal participation by rival powers. The potential remedy, a substantial independent standing army of intervention beyond any nation's control, is not an institution that great powers would permit. If it existed and were genuinely independent of the dominant world power, it would add to world instability.

HELLO, CRUEL WORLD: A REALISTIC MORALITY OF INTERVENTION

The grim realities that I have emphasized in criticizing the leading moral theories of intervention, combined with the grains of truth in all of these theories' overly exclusive foundations, suggest a different, less unified approach. Part of the disunity is the absence of a single normally decisive value, a simplicity that has turned out to be ill-suited to the typical complexities of both intervening powers and perpetrators of domestic injustice in the real world. Part of the disunity consists of very different treatment of different kinds of intervention. In addition, the grim realities of international life separate two questions that might otherwise be combined, "What terms of justification and complaint ought to underlie arguments among governments in the public forum of the global political system?" and "What terms of assessment ought to guide individual morally responsible people assessing governments' decisions to intervene or not to intervene?"

The terms of intergovernmental justification ought to provide appropriate incentives in a world system consisting of governments guided by the actual interests we have encountered. But supporting an institutional standard as the best device for coping with the interests in power of the governments that apply it is not the same as embracing the standard as one's own basis for moral judgment. In Rawls' poignant example, a rule that war captives may be enslaved might be the best means of avoiding their slaughter in a flawed society; this does not make their enslavement just.[38]

Still, the question of how governments should justify and criticize foreign-policy choices is important. Governments have some stake in the international response to their effort to justify what they do to the world at large, otherwise they would not devote quite substantial resources to this effort. I will begin my positive account of the morality of intervention by considering whether the formulas currently underlying this practice of justification should be revised. Then I will consider the different topic, the proper foundations of individuals' moral judgments of whether governments are right or wrong in decisions concerning intervention.

OPTIMAL NORMS FOR A NON-IDEAL WORLD

Should there be a major change in the terms in which governments justify and criticize interventions in the world public forum? There should not, if governments are as far from being guided by justice as they seem to be.

The terms on which governments argue about intervention are codified in the UN Charter and, also, in various international declarations, conventions and major resolutions of the General Assembly and Security Council – some of which have, in effect, amended the Charter. Notoriously, the statements about sovereignty, self-determination, and intervention in these documents approach mutual inconsistency, so that viable interpretations of the whole corpus sharply diverge and are all very strained. Yet because of, not despite, this near exegetic breakdown, these foundations of intergovernmental argument are a nearly optimal source, from the standpoint of humanity, of incentives to actual governments.

The 1970 Declaration on Principles of International Law concerning Friendly Relations and Cooperation among States in accordance with the Charter of the United Nations is the most detailed and synoptic codification. It includes many anti-interventionist statements, some of which, read in isolation, seem to preclude all forms of intervention, most of which, read in isolation, seem to prohibit all armed intervention. Here is a representative passage:

(1) No State or group of States has the right to intervene, directly or indirectly, for any reason whatever, in the internal or external affairs of any other State. Consequently, armed intervention and all other forms of interference or attempted threats against the personality of the State or against its political, economic and cultural elements, are in violation of international law.[39]

On the other hand, there are formulas which, read in isolation, permit intervention, even armed intervention, to remedy certain injustices in the internal affairs of a state. In general, they create special openings to justify intervention against governments whose injustices express contempt for whole groups, defined by nationality, ethnicity or religion. Thus, the second paragraph after passage 1 in the Declaration on Friendly Relations creates such an opening by suggesting that a certain form of domestic oppression has the same status as international aggression:

(2) The use of force to deprive peoples of their national identity constitutes a violation of their inalienable rights and of the principle of non-intervention.

Also, in the Declaration, strong assertions of the duty of states in their international relations to *"refrain...from the threat or use of force against the territorial integrity or political independence of any State"*[40] are eventually followed by a formula which seems to imply that only some governments are strictly protected:

(3) Nothing in the foregoing paragraphs shall be construed as authorizing or encouraging any action which would dismember or impair, totally or in part, the territorial integrity or political unity of sovereign and independent States conducting themselves in compliance with the principle of equal rights and self-determination

of peoples ... and thus possessed of a government representing the whole people belonging to the territory without distinction as to race, creed, or colour.[41]

In the practice of intergovernmental argument, which relies on such texts as its legal resource, an Ambassador from China and an Ambassador from Norway could both declare that there should be no interference in the domestic affairs of a legitimate government. But the Norwegian Ambassador would usually impose a higher threshold of coerciveness in her determination of what constitutes interference, and her criteria of legitimacy would usually involve a more demanding standard of respect for human rights. In these and other disagreements, each could offer an authentic interpretation of international law. Granted, the Ambassador from China ought to admit that vehemently anti-interventionist declarations such as 1 are so extreme that some grain of salt must be intended seasoning. If passage 1 were taken literally, its literal prohibition of intervention in the *external* affairs of another state would prohibit armed responses to outright aggression (a reading ruled out by the last paragraph of the relevant section.) So its use of "intervention" must be understood as subject to interpretations appealing to constraints on the legitimacy of what is interfered with. Still, it is a sound interpretive maxim that any departure from such an emphatic comprehensive declaration should be the minimum required by other passages in fundamental texts, a standard that would protect China's activities in Tibet even from explicit official foreign condemnation. On the other hand, it is also a sound interpretive maxim to seek a unifying interpretation which provides a compelling explanation for the presence of every passage. A corresponding use of passages such as (2) and (3) would sustain the Ambassador from Norway in a claim that intervention in defense of Tibetan rights violates no prerogative under international law, indeed, fullfills an international responsibility to defend a people whose national identity is under attack.

This room for diverse authentic interpretations would make the Declaration a miserably ill-drafted constitution, treaty or domestic law. But the Declaration is almost ideal as a repository of formulas governing intergovernmental justification and criticism. For this formulary does a nearly optimal job of inducing somewhat better conduct from tyrannical members of the world system of suboptimal governments while mitigating tendencies of hypocritical liberators to intervene too much.

In the current normative practice, China has adequate incentives to take part as a full-fledged committed participant in international controversies in the world public forum. Appealing to one viable interpretation of shared formulas, China argues that even official condemnation from abroad of its domestic conduct is inappropriate intrusion. It sometimes succeeds in winning the argument, for example, in removing condemnation from UN human rights reports. But its objection has to be made and is opposed by other parties, who usually are not ruled out of order in an international setting and sometimes carry the day. Moreover, China is aware that if it goes too far (for example, treating Tibetan Buddhism as it treats Falun Gong), it may well be subjected to genuinely annoying penalties, such as trade sanctions. The penalties will be imposed by international bodies which treat them as legitimate intrusions or by governments which do not jeopardize their own status as trustworthy partners, since their intrusion is widely regarded as legitimate.

Why not make these disincentives stronger, by making it explicit that genuinely coercive intervention is a legitimate response to widespread and systematic violations of human rights? For reasons that we have already considered, wide agreement on this determinate limit to sovereignty would give rise to dangers of excessive intervention and heightened hegemony without adequate assurance of a compensating reduction in oppression. Indeed, if the typical regime that engaged in widespread violations of human rights ran a significant risk of coercive intervention, the resulting intergovernmental milieu of distrust might well increase repression over the long run. Governments that envisage a significant risk of hostile treatment by foreign governments have an added incentive to invest in military build-ups, to restrict international communications and to ferret out dissidents who might make common cause with foreign powers. They have a special need for alliances with other governments that share their anxieties. They can often appeal to nationalist sentiment to create popular support that would not otherwise exist.

While it includes vague and contestable bases for intervention which are, to some extent, a disincentive to tyranny, the current practice of international justification and criticism also includes disincentives that to some extent discourage excessive intervention: governments contemplating virtually any intervention can expect some plausible condemnation, which becomes more intense and widely shared as intervention becomes more forceful, overt or frequent. For example, as the forcefulness and frequency of US interventions increases, so, too, does the risk to the United States of being seen as an untrustworthy partner, insufficiently responsive to a consensus based on precepts that it, too, affirms.

The anti-interventionist aspect of current practice could be strengthened by a clearer, more explicit commitment to strict and broad anti-interventionist principles. But this clarification would remove pressure that ought to be exerted on tyrannies. Too much insecurity among non-massacring regimes engaged in widespread violations of human rights may have its costs, but so, too, would too secure an expectation that serious injustice will be cost-free. The current practice of intergovernmental criticism tends to avoid both extremes.

On the whole, then, the current basis for intergovernmental argument functions well as a background for arguments among defective governments, because, not in spite of its straining the limits of coherence. Still, some changes may be in order. For example, if the Declaration on Friendly Relations were written today it ought to include a more explicit statement of what was not quite explicitly stated, that armed intervention is justified if needed to stop genocide, the vast, systematic killing and dispossession of non-combatants that constitutes a deadly attack on a whole people. This threshold, substantially higher than "widespread and systematic violations of human rights," is probably already part of the international consensus. Certainly, there is not the slightest evidence that concerns over sovereign prerogatives were in any way responsible for governments' reluctance to intervene in Rwanda.[42] Still, if consolidation of the sentiment that rescue from widespread massacre justifies intervention increases the disposition to intervene in future Rwandas, this would be to the good.[43]

MORAL JUDGMENT AND THE CONSTELLATIONS OF REASONS

The vagueness of the formulas that should be the basis for arguments among governments does not entail that there are no right answers to questions of whether governments' decisions about intervention are wrong. After all, the arguments in favor of that institutional indeterminacy derived from the impact of morally irrelevant considerations of power on governmental choice. What does make the moral judgment of intervention difficult is the diversity of the morally relevant considerations.

The sources of these diverse and conflicting considerations include grains of truth in the theories that I have criticized, each of which overemphasizes a relevant concern. On the one hand, even if they do not usually provide decisive reasons to intervene, politically imposed harms with no currently adequate internal remedy are considerations favoring intervention to help those victimized or threatened. The graver the harms, the more widespread, and the less likely the eventual occurrence of internal political remedies, the stronger the reason to intervene, provided that the wish for such help is rightly imputed to people who are to be helped.

On the other hand, intervention usually thwarts, to some extent, political processes and aspirations which are, to some extent, worthy of respect. To the extent that a country's political institutions and public culture are a valuable means of working out differences, respect for that value is, as Rawls insists, a reason not to intrude in the process. In addition, a widely shared aspiration to self-determination is an independent source of reasons to complain of intervention, even if communal autonomy is not the central, overriding consideration that Walzer takes it to be. Most people want the political trajectory of their country to reflect collective political activity among their compatriots. Participation in this collective creation of a future by and for those who continue the shared cultural heritage and shared history is a significant life-project for them. If their project is directed at worthwhile goals on the whole (as it usually is, for most participants, even under unjust regimes), then the thwarting of such collective self-reliance by intervention can give rise to morally significant complaints. If, through some miracle of modern technology, China could be successfully invaded without loss of life and if, in a great feat of benevolent imperialism, conquered China was ultimately transformed into a more benign polity, on the model of present-day Taiwan, this intrusion would still impose a morally significant loss on the vast majority of Chinese, given their actual commitments.

In addition, interventions must be judged in the light of their further possible consequences for individuals' wellbeing. While they sometimes lift the yoke of oppression from individuals and prevent future foreign attacks by dangerous regimes, interventions can also worsen individuals through extremely diverse effects and side-effects, both local and international, including deadly conflict, reduced engagement in international commerce, communication and negotiation, increases in international hegemony, increases in regional militarization and instability, and the discouragement of voluntary reconciliation among those engaged in internal strife.

Given the diversity of relevant, competing considerations, none of them generally overriding, it might seem that the moral judgment of whether this or that intervention would be right is, standardly, a hopeless task. But in fact, most political situations instantiate some constellation of reasons that resolves the major questions about intervention in the case at hand. In the absence of a defensible general ranking of relevant considerations, useful guidance in the judgment of interventions can derive from the description of these constellations, a task that might begin with two contrasting arrays, presented by pretty good political situations and utterly appalling ones.

By a "pretty good political situation", I mean a country in which the constitution, as interpreted and enforced, upholds the civil and political liberties characteristic of liberal democracy; the vast majority are committed to these liberties, on some defensible interpretation, and to the political pursuit of fair terms of social cooperation, in a process of principled compromise in which political and economic disadvantage are treated as a source of politically relevant complaints; and virtually everyone strongly opposes the resolution of their political disagreements through pressure from outside. Such a country is rarely if ever the site of a liberal people in Rawls' demanding sense of the phrase. Moreover, the resolution of serious disagreements is always, to some extent, affected by outside pressures, unfair internal advantages, or interpretations of local principles and traditions that are morally flawed. Still, the value of the internal political process, the pervasiveness and legitimacy of the aspiration to collective self-reliance, and the prospects of internal remedies for injustice are great enough to rule out virtually all forms of intervention against injustices compatible with this pretty good situation. A valuable process of self-rule need not fully realize the ideals that serve as measures of its value in order to merit protection. After all, a family need not fully realize the ideals of mutual respect appropriate to family life for most forms of intervention by outsiders to be wrong, to fail to respect what is valuable in the family's working out its own problems. How many families do fully realize those ideals?[44]

Nevertheless, even at this pole, respect for the liberal, democratic, and communitarian values in play would permit official foreign protest of decisions held to violate fundamental human values. A largely liberal people could criminalize abortions, even if this shows insufficient regard for women's control over their own bodies. It could have a death penalty, even if killing convicted murderers in the absence of any compelling case for deterrence shows inadequate respect for human life.

Due respect for the political process giving rise to the injustice would not preclude the mildest forms of intervention, for example, statements against capital punishment in a United Nations resolution. I can, after all, respect the good faith and procedural integrity of the Boy Scouts of America and its genuine concern for the common good and still urge my local United Way to deprive it of funding in response to what I take to be a misguided stance on homosexuality. Indeed, a principled, across-the-board disinclination to intervene even through official disapproval seems disregard for the seriousness of a people's deliberations (like the lofty multi-culturalism that says, "Wifebeating is accepted in your culture? How interesting,") not a sign of respect.

At the other extreme, governments engaged in widespread massacre are the clearest candidates for the severest intervention, humanitarian invasion. In this situation, respect for basic human rights tells strongly in favor of intervention. Less severe measures are virtually certain not to influence brutes engaged in widespread massacre. No morally valuable community binds oppressors and potential victims. The potential victims can be assumed to accept the risks of rescue. Those who are directly or indirectly engaged in the project of massacre have no cause for complaint. The cause for intervention is rare enough, and its discernment sufficiently easy, to reduce dangers of hegemony and international instability. Unless there are specially compelling reasons to believe that rescue will substantially increase subsequent violence, armed intervention is justified, as it was in Rwanda, East Timor, and East Pakistan.

In between these poles, humanitarian invasion would usually be an inappropriate response to widespread, serious injustice. Rather than deriving from respect for internal processes that would preclude all forms of intervention, the case against invasion usually depends on the specially deep opposition between invasion and widely shared aspirations to self-determination and on the distinctive risks imposed by invasion. So other, non-violent forms of intervention, too severe to be appropriate in the pretty good situations, might be appropriate in these worse ones. China is a dramatic illustration. Humanitarian invasion of China would be destructive madness, and would, if successful, profoundly interfere with pervasive aspirations to collective self-reliance. But the suspension of normal diplomatic and commercial relations in response to the brutal suppression of the Tiananmen Square demonstrations posed no such dangers, while affirming important values and expressing international support for their brave proponents inside China.

Also, there are situations in between the pretty good and the utterly appalling in which an atypical context makes the risks imposed by invasion much less serious than usual. In these contexts, invasion to remedy widespread violations of rights may be justified, even in the absence of large-scale atrocities. Suppose, for example, that a great power polices a long-established sphere of dominance by deposing those who seek to continue a regime it created and sustained, tyrants who brutally use control of the armed forces of the client regime in an attempt to cling to power in the face of widespread popular protests. Here, the standard risks that armed intervention will heighten bloodshed, increase hegemony and thwart self-determination are greatly reduced by the background circumstances of subordination. Even in the absence of widespread massacres, the United States would not have done wrong in restoring the Aristide government through military intervention.

The description of determinative, frequently encountered constellations of reasons could, I believe, be extended to nearly all cases in which intervention is a live option. Still, there have certainly been important cases in which it is unclear whether an intervention responding to some people's legitimate pleas for help against injustice was appropriately sensitive to other people's legitimate interests in non-intervention. In some of these cases, the cynicism about great powers that I have defended provides a crucial further resource for deliberation, a principled changing of the subject from the decision to intervene, viewed in isolation, to the whole decisionmaking process that culminated in it. I will conclude by using the NATO intervention over Kosovo to illustrate this final effect of grim reality on moral assessment.

THE LESSON OF KOSOVO: CHANGE THE SUBJECT

Instead of organizing a military offensive against Serbia, the United States could have framed the issue as one of brutal counter-insurgency (which is all that was known to be in play), pursued a solution to the Kosovo crisis in the UN Security Council (where nothing short of widespread massacre would have led China not to veto intervention), encouraged Russia to increase pressures on Milosevic (the tactic that ultimately led him to surrender to NATO), and strengthened UN monitoring in Kosovo (which had led to a reduction in civilian deaths in spite of consistent non-support by the United States).[45] Which course of action would best have served the interests of those at risk?

Either answer was and is a speculation. The NATO bombing triggered a vast expansion of violence against Kosovars (more properly, "Albanian Kosovars." I will usually employ the shorter term, instead.) This vengeful sequel should have been no surprise, given Milosevic's special dependence on aggressively anti-Kosovar themes in his exploitation of Serbian nationalism. Anti-Kosovar repression in the year before the bombing seems to have resulted in a death toll in the vicinity of 2000, including Kosovo Liberation Army combatants, with declining civilian casualties in the previous six months.[46] During the 78 days of the bombings about 10,000 Kosovars were killed.[47] There was no non-speculative basis to suppose that terror and dispossession on the scale that started with the bombing was imminent in any case, regardless of military intervention.[48] But there may have been this preestablished commitment. The growing opposition to Milosevic, which was temporarily utterly quelled by the bombing, might, in the absence of military intervention, have produced an eventual viable compromise concerning autonomy, with protection for the Serbian and Roma minorities. This, too, is a speculation. So, too, is the hypothesis that the combination of US threats and Russian diplomatic pressures might have led to adequate UN monitored protection of Kosovar civilians.

Despite the widespread, systematic terror triggered by the bombings, the intervention was welcomed by virtually all Kosovars as their best chance of liberation from Serbian domination. But consequent harm to non-Kosovars was significant and predictable. Through reverse ethnic cleansing in the wake of the NATO victory about 100,000 Serbs have been driven out of Kosovo by vengeful persecution, which has also brutalized the Roma minority.[49] 600 Serbian Army soldiers and about 500 Serbian civilians were killed by the bombing.[50] Because ground cover, bad weather and the decision to fly above the range of Serbian anti-aircraft made the bombing of traditional military targets largely ineffective, the main target was the Serbian infrastructure outside of Kosovo. Seventy percent of electrical capacity, 80 percent of oil refinery capacity, 59 bridges and 9 major highways were destroyed.[51] (Lower-altitude bombing would have reduced the risk of civilian casualties from a given sorty, but the consequent losses of NATO aircraft might have prolonged the war, or have led to its pointless termination, with no positive outcome. Ground invasion was not politically feasible, and risked a vast expansion of killing among combatants without guaranteeing a corresponding reduction of civilian deaths.) Outside of Serbia, the intervention actually and foreseeably increased ethnic violence in Macedonia by encouraging initiatives on the model of the KLA, increased Russian concerns over US intentions in Eastern Europe, and increased US dominance worldwide.

Just on the basis of foreseeable costs and uncertainties, it might be claimed that there was insufficient reason to believe that military intervention would probably be beneficial. This argument is certainly worth pursuing, but I will not pursue it, because I find the relevant standard of sufficiency unclear. When the vast majority of those whose lives are at stake are pleading for rescue from violent injustice, it is not clear, in general, how solid a case for net benefit is needed to justify an intervention which does, admittedly, put others at risk.

Such unclarity would be a discouraging conclusion to moral inquiry. But a further factor has been left out, which revives the prospects for determinate moral judgment: the nature of the whole decisionmaking process that ended with the decision to intervene militarily.

The final negotiations before the bombing took place at the Rambouillet conference, in February 1999, in which the United States and other members of a Contact Group that had been active in the Bosnia crisis (Britain, France, Italy, Germany and Russia) participated along with Serbia and the KLA. The eventual ultimatum, on which the United States government insisted, while resisting arguments for compromise by other members of the Contact Group,[52] had two parts, basic principles, which Serbia accepted, and an agreement on implementation, which Serbia did not accept. Rather than leaving open the option of a multinational force of more neutral composition, for example, one including a significant Russian component, the implementation agreement had "the Parties invite NATO to deploy a military force (KFOR), which will be authorized to use necessary force to ensure compliance with the Accords..."[53] The scope of the NATO force's authority, as prescribed in the ultimatum, involved a surrender of Serbian sovereignty going far beyond the requirements of protection of the Albanian Kosovars. "NATO personnel shall enjoy, together with their vehicles, vessels, aircraft, and equipment, free and unrestricted access throughout the FRY [Federal Republic of Yugoslavia, that is, Serbia and Montenegro], including associated airspace and territorial waters. This shall include, but not be limited to, the right of bivouac, maneuver, billet, and utilization of any areas or facilities as required for support, training, and operations" (chapter 7, Appendix B, p. 8); "NATO shall be immune from all legal process, whether civil, administrative or criminal" (chapter 7, Appendix B, p. 6a); "[In matters concerning KFOR activities] the KFOR Commander is the final authority in theater regarding interpretation of this Chapter [the chapter concerning military implementation] and his determinations are binding on all Parties and Persons" (chapter 7, xv, p. 2.)[54]

On February 20, after a meeting with the Serbian President, Milan Milutinovic, who accepted the political terms of the settlement while rejecting the role provided for NATO, Albright explained, "The Serb refusal to even consider the presence of a NATO-led military implementation force...is largely responsible for the failure to reach agreement."[55] By the same token, US insistence on this presence, in an extremely provocative form, made Serbian refusal inevitable, and rapid surrender highly unlikely, virtually guaranteeing that severe costs would have to be imposed on many people in order to make Milosevic back down. An ultimatum putting US power at center stage was in keeping with earlier phases of the Kosovo crisis, in which the United States regularly marginalized relatively independent agents and processes, such as the non-violent Kosovar movement, the LDK, and the unarmed observer teams monitoring the compromise over Kosovo endorsed in a March 1998 Security Council resolution.[56]

Was the decision to launch the NATO bombing campaign justifiable? Given the level of uncertainty as to whether a Serbian plan of terror was already unfolding on a scale that would justify the risks of the intervention, the most plausible judgment of the decision to bomb would respond to the whole decision-making process and condemn it: severe costs were imposed on many unwilling subjects without a strong basis for confidence in net benefit, in a process that culpably neglected opportunities worth pursuing to avoid these costs. In general, moral inquiry into a decision that imposed grave dangers on innocent people properly takes as its subject the whole decision-making process. Suppose a police chief issues a bold ultimatum to an evil hostage-taker and, when the ultimatum fails, dispatches a rescue squad to storm the hostage-taker's lair, killing innocent people. At the final stage, the failure of the ultimatum might have made the dangerous rescue the only reasonable option (as, perhaps, the Rambouillet ultimatum would have made subsequent nonintervention evidence of empty bluff or utter confusion.) Still, inquiry into the final decision would properly extend to the whole process leading up to it, and should result in condemnation if the chief, in his boldness, did not take sufficient account of the legitimate interests of all those whose lives were in jeopardy.

It might seem that moral focus on flaws in the Rambouillet process abdicates precisely the moral responsibility that I have been emphasizing, namely, the responsibility to take seriously the enduring limitations of the actual world system of governments. But in fact, for people with some chance to have some impact on public opinion in the United States and its allies in intervention, exposing the moral flaws in a whole process of response to injustice is the sort of project most apt to improve the practice of intervention. More precisely, this is the best deliberative strategy if my general view of the interests and dangers involved in US foreign policy is right. On this view, in the absence of strenuous public criticism, the process culminating in the bombing campaign against Serbia will be typical of US-led processes of intervention directed at regimes that are guilty of grave violations of human rights, but not of widespread massacres on the scale of Rwanda or, for that matter, of Kosovo after the bombings began. Grave risks will be imposed. They will respond to real abuses, described in rich and vivid detail. They will be part of a process in which the United States enhances the geopolitical importance of its military power, devaluing strategies that primarily rely on face-saving compromises with defiant tyrants, negotiations steered by independent parties, or supervision by multi-lateral agencies beyond US control. Given the dangers posed by this pursuit of power, criticism of this way of arriving at decisions to intervene is the most effective way to improve the practice of intervention.

More generally, in a world of hypocritical liberators and respectable oppressors, those who seek to reduce harms of interventions by the most powerful hypocrite should be concerned to combat the self-righteousness to which spokespersons for US foreign policy appeal, the demonization of intervention targets that makes imposed risks seem morally irrelevant and the smug assertions of American purity that make fears of intervention seem virtual endorsements of tyranny. Exposure of the flaws of US foreign policy, including the arming of tyrannies and the neglect of help in rescues that are fully justified, may contribute to a state of public opinion in which a Rambouillet process is harder to sell, while the shame of Rwanda is not repeated.[57]

One could even hope for the day when self-righteousness would so subside that at most a few extremists on the far right would welcome declarations such as this: "...we are at war with the Serbian nation...Every week you ravage Kosovo is another decade we will set your country back by pulverizing you. You want 1950? We can do 1950. You want 1389? We can do 1389, too." In a world in which this was the declaration of the foreign policy columnist of the *New York Times*,[58] this hope is probably utopian. But unlike some other utopian wishes, it will do no harm. If more people in the United States viewed the effective goals of US foreign policy with appropriate cynicism and anxiety, they might more often tip the balance against dangerous and hegemonic intervention processes, while favoring rescues that genuinely serve human interests worldwide. Through moral arguments connected at once with global realities and broad moral principles, political philosophers can advance this project. By the same token, through moral arguments presupposing a world that is not and, for the foreseeable future, will not be, political philosophers may help to thwart what realistic hope there is for improving the practice of intervention.

NOTES

1 John Rawls, *The Law of Peoples* (Cambridge: Harvard University Press, 1999), p. 25. Parenthetic page numbers in this section refer to this book.
2 Rawls says that a political outlook that solely affirms formal freedom and equality is "indeed not liberalism at all but libertarianism" (p. 49).
3 Charles W. Maynes, "Relearning Intervention," *Foreign Policy* 98 (1995), 98.
4 Michael Walzer, "The Moral Standing of States: A Response to Four Critics," *Philosophy and Public Affairs* 9 (1980), 229.
5 Michael Walzer, *Just and Unjust Wars* (New York: Basic Books, 1977), p. 86.
6 *Just and Unjust Wars*, p. 90. Emphasis in the original. Walzer presents this as the implicit underlying principle in Mill's essay, "A Few Words on Non-Intervention" (1859), but his own endorsement of this stance is clear.
7 See, for example, "The Moral Standing of States," p. 212.
8 *Ibid.*, p. 219.
9 *Ibid.*, p. 223. Walzer adds, "I don't mean, however, to rule out every effort by one state to influence another or every use of diplomatic and economic pressure. Drawing the line is sure to be difficult." And he does think that outsiders should try to set things right by making arguments on at least some occasions in which armed intrusion is inappropriate (p. 229). I do not mean to suggest that total passivity must be his prescription even when his standard presumption is in play. One can honor and recognize the autonomy of, say, a couple's struggle to come to terms with the problems in their marriage while offering unsolicited advice. Each is free to ignore it. And one can, without intervening, refuse to provide aid that one otherwise would, because of what the aid would facilitate. I don't intervene if I decide not to invite a party to marital turmoil to join my gun club. But by the same commonsensical standards, many measures short of invasion fail to recognize and honor the autonomy of a process of struggle, for example: material aid to nonviolent dissidents, the organization of explicit condemnation in international governmental organizations, economic discrimination meant to interfere with the prosperity of an

oppressive elite or its capacity to recruit support, military aid to hard-pressed rebels. After all, if I give the wife of a wrongly enraged husband an interest-free loan to hire a first-rate divorce lawyer, try to get all of the husband's friends to join in a public statement condemning his misbehavior, or give him a long-term out-of-town work assignment in the hope that absence will make his heart grow fonder, I have intervened.

10 *Ibid.*, p. 217.

11 *Just and Unjust Wars*, p. 96.

12 *Ibid.*, p. 101.

13 "The Moral Standing of States," p. 218.

14 *Just and Unjust Wars*, p. 101.

15 *Ibid.* In "The Moral Standing of States," p. 217, Walzer notes that he means strict and literal enslavement: "by 'enslavement' I mean enslavement: the dictionary definition will do well enough."

16 "The Moral Standing of States," p. 218.

17 See Amnesty International, "Afghanistan: Cruel, Inhuman or Degrading Treatment or Punishment," www.web.amnesty.org./ai.nsf/index/ASA11051999, p. 3; Amnesty International, "Women in Afghanistan: The Violations Continue," www.web.amnesty.org.ai.nsf/index/ASA11051997, p. 2.

18 The similarities accompanying the real and important differences between Taliban and post-Taliban Afghanistan are one mark of this authenticity. On resuming his position after the defeat of the Taliban, Ullah Zarif, chief judge of the High Court of Kabul, noted, in an interview with Agence France Presse: " 'There will be some changes from the era of the Taliban'... those guilty of adultery... will still be stoned, 'but we will use smaller rocks.' In this way, those convicted will have a chance: 'If they can escape, they are free'... With a proviso: the chance will be reserved for those who confess their crime. 'Those who refuse to confess will be bound hand and foot, so tightly that they will not be able to escape.' A stoning can last between three and four hours..." See "Les talibans passent, la justice reste," *Dernières Nouvelles d'Alsace*, December 19, 2001, www.afhga.net//article.php?sid=2613 [my translation]. See also Christian Colombani, "En vue," *Le Monde*, December 20, 2001, www.lemonde.fr/archives. A year after the defeat of the Taliban, Human Rights Watch reported extensive Taliban-like abuses, including the persecution of women for not wearing the burqua, the arrest, sometimes accompanied by prolonged and vicious beatings, of musicians violating prohibitions against music at weddings, and arson and rocket attacks on girls' schools in five provinces. See Human Rights Watch, "*We want to live as humans*," www.hrw.org/reports/2002/afghwm 1202, pp. 5f.

19 Charles Beitz, also, casts doubt on the availability of communal autonomy in "Nonintervention and Communal Integrity," *Philosophy and Public Affairs* 9 (1980), 385–7. Beitz's thoughtful appeals to a diverse array of reasons for and against intervention provide the best framework in the literature for the views

that I will advance. See, in particular, Beitz, *Political Theory and International Relations* (Princeton: Princeton University Press, 1999), pp. 69–92 (also in the original, 1979 edition) and pp. 191–98.

20 Kofi Annan, *The Question of Intervention* (New York: United Nations, 1999), p. 6.

21 *Ibid.*, p. 13.

22 *Ibid.*, pp. 13, 20.

23 See, for example, Michael Glennon, "The New Interventionism," *Foreign Affairs* v. 78, n. 3 (May 1999), 2–7; Antonio Cassese, *Human Rights in a Changing World* (Philadelphia: Temple University Press, 1990); and the Independent International Commission on Kosovo, *The Kosovo Report* (New York: 2000), pp. 190, 293. David Luban, "Just War and Human Rights," *Philosophy and Public Affairs* 9 (1980), 161–81 is a a resourceful argument in an earlier era of world politics for analogous interventionist changes in the traditional doctrine of just war.

24 See John Laffin, *The World in Conflict: War Annual 6* (London: Brassey's, 1994), pp. 99–101. For similar estimates (and some substantially higher ones) see "Experts Put Iraqi Deaths in War at 25,000 to 50,000," *New York Times*, March 21, 1991, p. 1.

25 In a detailed assessment of reported bombing casualties in the first two months of the United States bombing campaign, largely relying on news dispatches from reporters in Afghanistan to British, French, Canadian, and American newspapers, Marc Herold estimates a civilian death toll over three thousand. See Herold, "A Dossier on Civilian Victims of United States' Aerial Bombing of Afghanistan," www.zmag.org/herold.htm. Carl Conetta bases a lower estimate, of 1,000 to 1,300 killed, on an interpretation of news dispatches such as Herold's which applies much more conservative standards; for example, refugees' reports of "some deaths" in a bombing incident are treated as indicating one, "a dozen or more," three to four, "dozens," eight to ten, "hundreds," 40 to 60. See Conetta, "Operation Enduring Freedom: Why a Higher Rate of Civilian Bombing Casualties," Project on Defense Alternatives, www.comw.org/pda/0210ef.html#appendix2. Ian Traynor reports estimates of civilian deaths from the bombing campaign, by Western medical or demining workers in post-Taliban Kabul that range from "between 2000 to 3000" to "up to 8000." See Ian Traynor, "Afghans Still Dying," *Guardian* (London), February 12, 2002, www.guardian.co.uk/archive.

26 In addition to the previously cited report of a CIA estimate of 7,000 to 10,000 Somali deaths, there is a more conservative estimate of 1,500 Somalis killed, 6,000 wounded in Thomas G. Weiss, *Military-Civilian Interactions* (Lanham, Md.: Rowman and Littlefield, 1999), p. 93.

27 See *ibid.*, pp. 86f.; Alex de Waal and Rakiya Omaar, "Doing Harm by Doing Good? The International Relief Effort in Somalia," *Current History* (May 1993), 198–202.

28 See Independent International Commission on Kosovo, *Kosovo Report*, p. 83.

29 Cited in Seth Ackerman, "Fairness and Accuracy in Reporting," in Peter Goff, ed., *The Kosovo News and Propaganda War* (Vienna: International Press Institute, 1999), p. 89. "Kurdish first names have been banned since the first decades of the republic, with just one receiving official blessing in the 1990s ... The lifting in 1991 of the official ban on Kurdish resulted in a brief spurt in sales of Kurdish music cassettes," Nicole Pope and Hugh Pope, *Turkey Unveiled* (London: John Murray, 1997), pp. 256, 258. "Kurdish-language television remains illegal. Schools and universities are still forbidden to offer instruction in Kurdish, and academies where people may freely learn English, French, German, and even Japanese may not teach Kurdish," Stephen Kinzer, *Crescent and Star* (New York: Farrar, Straus and Giroux, 2001), p. 132. Nicole Pope and Kinzer are recent Istanbul correspondents for *Le Monde* and *The New York Times*, respectively.

30 See Jonathon Randal, *After Such Knowledge, What Forgiveness?* (New York: Farrar, Strais and Giroux, 1997), p. 259.

31 Amnesty International, "Turkey: No Security without Human Rights," www.amnesty.org/ailib/intcam.turkey.turk5.htm [1996], p. 3.

32 *United States Statistical Abstract 1995* (Washington, DC: US Census Bureau, 1995), table 1305 and, on the basis of further government figures, Tamar Gabelnick, William Hartung and Jennifer Washburn, *Arming Repression: US Arms Sales to Turkey during the Clinton Administration* (World Policy Institute and Federation of American Scientists, 1999), www.fas.org/asmp/library/reports/turkeyrep.htm, pp. 10–12.

33 See Randal, *After Such Knowledge*, p. 269; see also Gabelnick et al., *Arming Repression*, passim.

34 Amnesty International, "Turkey: No Security without Human Rights," p. 8. Thirty-one attack helicopters were supplied. In 1992 and 1993, the US was the leading supplier of armored combat vehicles to Turkey, supplying 250 (*ibid.*, p. 9.)

35 See William Hartung, "US Arms Transfers to Indonesia 1975–1997" (New York: World Policy Institute, n.d.) http://www.worldpolicy.org/projects/arms/reports/indoarms.html, pp. 5f. Hartung's military aid total does not include such indirect help as grants of Economic Support Funds.

36 Patrick Moynihan, *A Dangerous Place* (Boston: Little, Brown, 1978), p. 247.

37 For the Amnesty International estimate and references to evidence of US involvement, see Noam Chomsky, *Year 501: The Conquest Continues* (Boston: South End Press, 1993), p. 123.

38 See John Rawls, *A Theory of Justice* (Cambridge: Harvard University Press, 1971), p. 248.

39 See Hurst Hannum, ed., *Documents on Autonomy and Minority Rights* (Dordrecht: Martinus Nijhoff, 1993), p. 41.

40 *Ibid.*, p. 39; emphasis in original.

41 *Ibid.*, p. 43.
42 In the non-public UN Security Council deliberations over Rwanda, whose records were subsequently leaked by Secretariat staff, the permanent members were simply concerned, in spite of the UN Commander's vigorous arguments to the contrary, that they would have to invest large resources in a successful rescue. As the genocide took shape and then engulfed half a million victims, the American delegation, with ample intelligence concerning the situation in Rwanda, successfully argued for doing less than nothing, that is, first for reducing the already small UN peacekeeping mission and then for evacuating it, with no provision to resupply the 470 volunteer peacekeepers who remained. See Linda Melvern, "The Security Council: Behind the Scenes," *International Affairs* 77 (2001), 101–10 and Nicholas Wheeler, *Saving Strangers* (Oxford: Oxford University Press, 2000), p. 241.
43 A realistic assessment of incentives and disincentives should, similarly, govern the judgment of proposed international norms for military responses to terrorism. For example, even if all forms of terrorism are profoundly wrong, an international norm that all governments ought to join in making war on terrorism everywhere, whether it is of global reach or essentially domestic, would be dangerous. It would make military powers even more ready than they are to contribute to the violent suppression of insurrections against governments whose continued rule suits their interests, often supporting these governments in their own terroristic intimidation of civilian populations by violent attack and dispossession.
44 A parallel description of a close-enough approach to Rawls' ideal of non-liberal decency could, no doubt, be devised. For reasons already given, I doubt that it would be useful in the project of describing constellations of intervention-relevant factors encountered in the real world.
45 Independent Commission on Kosovo, *Kosovo Report*, pp. 83, 141. For reasons of space, I will usually base factual claims on the findings of this widely respected investigation of the NATO intervention and the crisis that led to it. The Commission had the official support of the United Nations, but pursued its inquiry as an independent body, deriving most of its financial support from the Swedish government. Richard Goldstone, former Chief Prosecutor of the International Criminal Tribunal for the former Yugoslavia, was co-chair.
46 *Ibid.*, p. 83.
47 *Ibid.*, p. 97.
48 *Ibid.*, p. 201. Shortly before the bombings began, George Tenet, Director of the Central Intelligence Agency, testified to the House Intelligence Committee that NATO military action "could include the chance of ethnic cleansing"; the Committee Chair offered this summary of Tenet's testimony, "If we stuck a stick in this nest, we would stir it up more" (Thomas Lippman, "Albright Misjudged Milosevic on Kosovo," *Washington Post*, April 7, 1999, p. A1.)

49 *Ibid.*, pp. 108, 261f.

50 *Ibid.*, p. 94.

51 *Ibid.*, p. 93.

52 *Ibid.*, pp. 152–7.

53 US State Department, "Fact Sheet on Rambouillet Accords," www.state.gov/ www.regions/eur/fs_990301_rambouillet.html.

54 *Le Monde Diplomatique*, text of "Interim Agreement for Peace and Self-Government in Kosovo," www.monde-diplomatique.fr/dossiers/kosovo/ rambouillet/html, pp. 73, 72, 78.

55 *Kosovo Report*, p. 156.

56 Although the United States voted for the resolution and anti-Kosovar violence significantly declined during the UN monitoring, "the Euro-American coalition that was the core of the later NATO undertaking was not seriously mobilized behind the effort to rely on an international unarmed presence under UN auspices," *ibid.*, p. 141.

57 It might also help to reduce the use of excessive deadly force in response to international terrorism.

58 Thomas Friedman, *New York Times*, April 23, 1999, Op-Ed page.

Chapter 12

Violence against power: critical thoughts on military intervention

IRIS MARION YOUNG

In *Virtual War*, Michael Ignatieff reproduces a debate between himself and Robert Skidelsky concerning the moral acceptability of the NATO intervention in Yugoslavia in response to repression of Kosovar Albanians. Skidelsky insists that a principle of sovereignty must have priority in international relations as the best way of preserving international peace and stability. An appeal to human rights as a basis for military intervention within the jurisdiction of a sovereign state cannot work because there exists no international agreement about precisely what human rights require and just what violations could authorize outside intervention. This NATO action, furthermore, has taken place without the assent of the only organization that might be said to represent the world community, the United Nations. In by-passing the UN, NATO sends a message to all the countries of the world that force, not law, governs international affairs.

For his part, Ignatieff agrees that there should be a general presumption in favor of sovereignty. States are not justified in intervening with military force in the jurisdiction of another state whenever they believe they see a violation of human rights. Such intervention is justified only if abuses are systematic and involve large numbers of relatively defenseless people, and only if less violent means of pressuring the offending state are not available. While the war over Kosovo did indeed not receive UN authorization, NATO approval may be almost as good, because NATO has deliberative procedures by which its nineteen member nations must approve a NATO-led military action.

This debate plays out the most common definition of the moral issues involved in so-called humanitarian intervention. Either the sovereignty principle is absolute or it can be overridden by a higher principle of response to threats to masses of people. If such threats exist, outside agents can legitimately intervene militarily especially if they obtain authorization by means of legal or quasi-legal procedures.

In this essay I challenge the terms of this debate, which reflects most of the range of opinion expressed at the time about the NATO war, and which seems to me to reflect the major positions on the question of humanitarian intervention in general in the world today. The terms of this debate are too stark and dichotomous: either sovereignty is absolute or it can be overridden; either human-rights violations legitimate the use of military force or they do not. I think that expressing the debate so starkly allows moral reflection to avoid considering many issues that arise about the use of violence for supposedly humanitarian ends, whether and how international action can and should be legitimated through legal principles, and what counts as exercising power to protect human lives and resist domination.

In what follows I assume agreement with Ignatieff that a principle of state sovereignty has prima facie moral validity, but that it can be overridden by interest in protecting basic human rights, particularly protecting lives. Respecting sovereignty is the best way to respect the self-determination of peoples and helps make international relations more predictable and stable than they would otherwise be. Principles of human rights have no meaning at all, however, unless moral agents outside of states can rightfully take an interest in harms and threats people within a given state's jurisdiction suffer either at the hands of their state or others within the state's jurisdiction. Especially where such harms and threats are severe and widespread, it is wrong for outsiders to ignore them and accept a state's claim that these events are none of their business. So outsiders have a moral right to do what they can to prevent or halt egregious violations of human rights, and this right in principle overrides sovereignty rights.

Many assume that such a principled right of intervention itself justifies the use of military force in response to violations of human rights. It by no means follows, however, that a right of intervention entails a right to use violence. Many actions other than military actions can and have been considered as means of pressuring states to change behavior and policies that violate human rights. Too often international relations theorists and politicians speak as though once we have established a right of intervention, then this is sufficient to sanction any form of intervention, including bombing and invasion. Once we open the intervention/non-intervention dichotomy, however, the need arises for justifying particular means employed under particular circumstances.

Drawing on Hannah Arendt's distinction between violence and power, I argue that the use of violence in public affairs is always questionable, even when its aims are well intentioned. I elaborate a distinction that Arendt only gestures at, between justifying violence and claiming that it is legitimate. My reading of Arendt's distinction implies that violence can never be *legitimate*, in the sense that its use can be thought to follow from principles and procedures of law. Violence can nevertheless sometimes be justified. The justification of violence must involve consequentialist reasoning demonstrating that in the longer as well as the shorter term, the violent acts have prevented more harm than they have caused. Such justification is difficult, though not impossible.

DISTINCTION BETWEEN POWER AND VIOLENCE[1]

In her essay, "On Violence,"[2] Hannah Arendt notes that political theorists have rarely reflected on violence as such. While there is a long tradition of theoretical writing on warfare, most of it theorizes strategy, balance of power, or the meaning of sovereignty violation, rather than specifically considering the meaning of use of violence per se. She speculates that one explanation for this neglect of a subject which is so important to public affairs is that political theorists think they have theorized violence when they discuss political power. Theorists and political actors typically confuse violence with power. They either take power to be based on the capacity for violence, or they conceptualize violence as an extreme manifestation of power. In the essay Arendt argues, to the contrary, that power and violence are distinct phenomena that should be clearly distinguished conceptually as well. I shall elaborate the meaning of her distinction, and argue that it has important normative implications.

Curiously, Arendt does not define the term violence. For the purposes of this essay I shall define violence as acts by human beings that aim physically to give pain to, wound, or kill other human beings, and/or to damage or destroy animals and things that hold a significant place in the lives of people.[3] A key characteristic of violence, says Arendt, is instrumentality, in at least two senses. First, violence in public affairs is usually a means to an end. Violence is rarely wanton, indiscriminate, or pursued as a desired end in itself. Especially in a political context, use of violence is most often calculated, deliberate, and carefully planned to further specific objectives. Second, violence relies on instruments. Violent acts are more or less fierce in proportion to the ability of their instruments to inflict damage and destruction on people and things. Technological developments magnify the destructive effects of instruments, at the same time that they distance the perpetrators from the victims.

Arendt insists that power is conceptually and practically entirely different from violence. Power consists in collective action. Power is the ability of persons jointly to constitute their manner of living together, the way they organize their rules and institutions through reciprocal self-understanding of what the rules are and how they foster cooperation. Thus power relies not only bodies and instruments that exert force, but primarily on speech – the interpretation of meaning, the articulation of new ideas, the dynamics of persuasion, the linking of understanding and action. Power establishes and maintains institutions, that is, regulated and settled means of cooperating to bring about collective ends. It has its basis and continuance in the consent and support of those who abide by, live according to, and interpret rules and institutions to bring about new collective ends. Those who engage in collective action must communicate and cooperate, discuss their problems and jointly make plans. Insofar as successful institutions mobilize the cooperation of a large number of people in their operations, who understand the meaning and goals of the institutions, know the rules, and in general endorse their operations, they embody power.

Power is distinct from strength in that it exists *between* people rather than in them. Power is a feature of action and interaction insofar as people understand one another's words and deeds and coordinate with one another to achieve mutually understood ends. Thus power involves some kind of agreement, whether in word or action. Those who participate in the collective action that founds and maintains institutions and the enactment of their ends must know what they are doing and engage with one another to coordinate their actions.[4]

With these distinctions, Arendt stands opposed to a major tendency in modern political theory. She holds that the confusion of violence with power stems from a common understanding of state power as the exercise of sovereign domination. Political power, on this view, is nothing other than the rule of some over others, the exercise of command and successful obedience. While Max Weber is hardly alone in this view, his theory of the state may have exerted the most influence over contemporary thinking. For Weber the state is the monopoly over the legitimate use of violence. In this paradigm, state and law are founded on the capacity for violence: the state and its legal system is simply the vehicle that a hegemonic group creates for itself to further its purposes, maintain itself in power, and rule over the rest.[5]

Arendt agrees that if in fact political power, government, means simply that state officials of whatever sort – kings, lords, presidents, cabinet ministers, generals – exercise dominion over the territory and actions of others, then power and violence are sensibly associated. There is no doubt that many rulers have relied on killing or torture and their threats to induce compliance with their wills and goals from subjects, and that they often succeed. "If the essence of power is the effectiveness of command, then there is no greater power than that which grows out of the barrel of a gun" (p. 37).

Arendt argues, however, that the success and stability of even despotic regimes over a long term depends on eliciting the cooperation of at least a large mass of subjects with rulers and institutions in enacting their living together and their common projects, that is, on power understood as collective action. Even government understood as sovereign dominion depends for its success on a regularity of mutually understood, cooperative activities, and in this respect on the consent of those ruled. This fact becomes most apparent if and when people withdraw their consent, when people begin to act collectively toward different ends than those the rulers intend or desire. Rulers are often nearly helpless before such a shift in power. If they have the means of violence at their disposal – which usually means depending on the power of organized armies – they can attempt to impose their will on a disobedient public through force. The ruler can bomb neighborhoods, eliminate opponents, and keep a threatening watch over people to limit their ability to communicate and cooperate. Although violence and the threat of violence can in this way undermine power, they cannot create or sustain it. Since power depends on collective action, it rests on the freedom of a plurality of distinct individuals aiming to foster their institutions. The tyrant who rules through violence may be able to prevent action and resistance, and enforce service of his needs and desires. The rule of terror, however, tends to destroy the capacity of a people to cooperate in ways that will produce goods, bring about new inventions, or make public works.

Of course history bristles with regimes structured by relations of ruler and subject, and these often rely on the threat of violence to compel obedience to the ruler's will when actions threaten to undermine or resist that will. But such regimes of domination are weak just insofar as they must depend on compulsion in this way. They are powerful only if the people they govern cooperate through consent and collective will sustaining the institutions in which they live together, express their meanings, and enact their collective goals.

Thus Arendt contrasts power and violence. "Power and violence are opposites; where one rules absolutely, the other is absent. Violence appears where power is in jeopardy, but left to its own course it ends in power's disappearance. This implies that it is not correct to think of the opposite of violence as nonviolence; to speak of nonviolent power is already redundant. Violence can destroy power; it is ultimately incapable of creating it" (p. 56).[6]

Though violence and power are opposites in this conceptual and phenomenological sense, Arendt says that they often occur together. Although governments often rely on the use and threat of violence, systems of government that rest on command and obedience must also rely on the collective action of subjects – power – for their effectiveness. While movements to resist or overturn such regimes must mobilize mass power of collective organization to succeed, they often also use means of violence to aid their objectives. That epitome of violence, war, is also an example of power. A disciplined army depends on the solidarity of its soldiers, their willingness to work together and protect each other under stress.

Arendt proposes her distinction between violence and power as descriptive only. In her work generally she refuses to take explicit normative positions which she justifies with moral arguments. Yet her writing expresses affective commitments and judgments, of anger, indignation, disdain, and a desire for human excellence. She eschews normative theorizing, yet she makes strong normative sounding judgments. In this respect she is much like another important theorist of power, Foucault, who also writes as morally engaged in politics but rejects a project of normative theory for politics. The stance is not sustainable, I think. Judgments that carry normative force are most honest and persuasive when their statement relies on arguments that explicitly invoke norms and values whose meanings are clearly delineated on which critical scrutiny can be trained.

In appropriating Arendt's distinction between power and violence, then, I interpret it as normative as well as descriptive.[7] While violence and power *in fact* often occur together, they need not, and they *ought not*, at least not often and not very much. The interpretation of governance that identifies it with sovereign dominion is problematic because it conceives political power as necessarily oppressive, and living under government as necessarily a denial of freedom. There is another interpretation of government, however, that does not assume the inevitability of a relation of command and obedience, and the necessary connection with violence these seem to entail. Arendt uses a Greek word for this alternative: *isonomy*. Jeffrey Isaac describes *isonomy* as "a concept of power and law whose essence did not rely on the command-obedience relation and which did not identify power and rule or law and command."[8] *Isonomy* names a process of governance as self-government, where the citizens have equal status and must rely on one another equally for developing collective goals and carrying them out. Just insofar as government depends on speech and persuasion, it precludes violence and violence is its opposite. Government ought to be the exercise of power as the expression and result of people coming together, assessing their problems and collective goals, discussing together how to deal with them, and persuading one another to adopt rules and policies, and then each self-consciously acting to effect them. This is a normative ideal, of course, a limit concept that is important to have in view when acting politically, designing institutions, and evaluating political action and institutions.

Power, and the political, then, I interpret as an aspect of any social institution or collective activity, including some of those that enact sovereign dominion or repressive domination. Institutions cannot be effective for long unless they have occasions when at least some of their participants set their collective goals, discuss what institutions rules and practices would best coordinate their actions to achieve those goals, and make commitments to one another to carry out their responsibilities in the system of cooperation.

Power is thus necessary for collective action to achieve social objectives, but it is also fragile. People easily and often lose the sense of public promise *isonomy* offers, and disperse into the impotent privacy of a concern for their own survival or pleasure. To the extent that governing institutions remain, they freeze into routinized bureaucracies, become cronyist semi-private operations, or elicit conformity through terror. The use of violence in public affairs is normatively questionable not only because killing and maiming are prima facie wrong. Violence is also morally problematic because its use, especially if routine and widespread, endangers power. "Violence appears where power is in jeopardy, but left to its own course it ends in power's disappearance" (p. 56). When rulers or those who most benefit from a given order of things find that they or their goals lose popular support, they often try to restore their power through the use of violence. Such actions may well reduce resistance but they do not restore power. Violence not only harms individuals, but it makes their lives difficult to carry on as before. When either rulers or resisters adopt the use of violence as a regular means of trying to induce the cooperation of others, they tend to produce the opposite effect: flight, retreat into privacy, preemptive strikes, distrust of all by all. The use of violence in politics is problematic, moreover, because its consequences so easily and often escalate beyond the specific intentions its uses have. Violent acts tend to produce violent responses in an escalating spiral. Too often generals and politicians arrogantly assume that they can control the violent consequences of their own violent actions.

My reason for invoking Arendt's distinction between power and violence is to address the question: is military intervention morally obligatory or permissible in response to grave violations of human rights? The interpretation of power and violence as normative opposites already suggests an answer that puts the use of military force into question. If those who call for making war on human-rights violators think thereby that they are bringing power to bear on the situation that will positively change relationships, produce new institutions of cooperation, restore routines in which people can safely carry out collective activities of production, distribution, administration, regulation, and play, they are almost certainly mistaken. The use of violence only destroys, creates a rupture, and always endangers the cooperative relationships on which institutions are based. This fact does not imply that the use of military force is never morally appropriate, as I will discuss in the next section. The important point for now is that in this context as in others we should not confuse the use of violence with the exercise of power.

LEGITIMACY AND JUSTIFICATION

In her essay Arendt makes another distinction that she correlates with the distinction between power and violence, between *legitimating* power and *justifying* violence.

Power needs no justification, being inherent in the very existence of political communities; what it does need is legitimacy ... Power springs up whenever people get together to act in concert, but it derives its legitimacy from the initial getting together rather than from any action that then may follow. Legitimacy, when challenged, bases itself on appeal to the past, while justification relates to an end that lies in the future. Violence can be justifiable, but it never will be legitimate. Its justification loses in plausibility the farther its intended end recedes into the future. (p. 52)

Like so much else in Arendt's corpus, her claims here are provocative and suggestive, but she does not elaborate them further. In this section I puzzle through this distinction between legitimation and justification, as applied to power and violence respectively. This is important for the issue of humanitarian invention, just because many proponents of a cosmopolitan view of human rights and the right of outsiders to intervene under circumstances where human rights are under threat are looking for legal legitimations of such actions. Much of the discussion surrounding the NATO war over Kosovo concerns whether the action can be considered legitimately *authorized* by the international community, and if not, what sort of institutions and procedures it would take for an interventionist war that claims humanitarian ends to be legitimately authorized. If Arendt's distinction holds, however, then even war for humanitarian purposes cannot be made legitimate, though it may sometimes be justified. This is the claim I will try to support by explicating the above passage.

I interpret legitimation and justification as two forms of moral reasoning. They are two different ways of arguing that an action or policy is morally appropriate, permissible, or obligatory. In the passage quoted, Arendt offers only one hint about the difference in these forms of giving an account: legitimation appeals to the past, while justification appeals to the future in relation to the act.

To find more texts that will help unlock this mystery one can turn to *On Revolution*. There Arendt draws a connection between power, in the sense of original collective action, and the activity of founding new institutions which can preserve that power and give it embodiment in law.

Power comes into being only if and when men join themselves together for the purpose of action, and it will disappear when, for whatever reason, they disperse and desert one another. Hence, binding and promising, combining and covenanting are the means by which power is kept in existence...Just as promises and agreements deal with the future and provide stability in the ocean of future uncertainty where the unpredictable may break in from all sides, so the constituting, founding, and world-building capacities of men concern always not so much ourselves and our own time on earth as our "successor" and "posteriorities."[9]

Power consists in collective action, people coming together and supporting one another to do deeds and accomplish goals the likes of which "would never enter his mind, let alone the desires of his heart, had he not been given this gift." (OV, p. 82) Power is often fleeting, however; it springs out of relations between people who accomplish something, and then dissipates. For power to be a force in politics, it needs to be institutionalized, and this is what foundings accomplish. In founding a constitution the empowered collective gives itself relative permanence, a permanence guaranteed through covenants. In the moment of founding participants in a public mutually promise to abide by principles that guide institutions, to organize and give their energy to the implementation of the institutions, and to be loyal to the institutions and to one another through them. The mutuality of promise making is important for Arendt. She cites the spirit of American revolutionaries who, she says, found legitimate power only in the reciprocity and mutuality of promises made between equals, as distinct from the spurious power of kings and aristocrats, which was not founded on mutual promising.

Arguments that government actions, policies, laws, or representatives are legitimate, then, are backward looking because they refer to founding promises. To say that these leaders or policies are legitimate is to make the argument that they are in conformity with, a present embodiment of, the principles and promises that institutionalize the public's power. Making such an argument, I suggest, requires more than the recital of a history of the citation of founding documents. An argument for the legitimacy of present officials, actions, or laws, I suggest, involves reinvoking the power that came into play in the original process, which often involves reestablishing it by means of new commitments. It appeals to the principles of what we as a collective stand for, the principles and purposes of the institutions that enable us to act together. To argue that a government or policy or action is legitimate in these ways does not itself imply that they are just, right, or good. Interpreting this notion of legitimation means, however, that in their promising and commitment those who appeal to their founding institutions aim at the good or the just, and that their institutions and actions are accountable to claims that they do wrong or perpetrate injustice.

In the passage I quoted from *On Revolution*, Arendt distinguishes mutual promise and covenant that gives power legitimacy from simple consent. I take it that consent is only the absence of opposition and resistance, a willingness on the part of subjects to go along with the rules and decrees, and such consent usually has some basis in belief. Each subject consents alone, however, in relation to the state. Covenants to which accounts of the legitimacy of political officials and actions appeal, on the other hand, are public; indeed they are the effects and institutionalizations of publics that emerge from collective action.

As I understand Arendt's distinction, justification is a less complex affair than legitimation. First, only an action whose moral value is *in question* requires justification. This is why Arendt says that power needs no justification. The default judgment about power is that it is valuable; acting in concert enables a unique and wonderful kind of freedom that human beings experience in no other way. The default judgment about violence, on the other hand, is that it is a disvalue. Violence destroys, and it is not very violent unless it destroys valuable things – human lives or things meaningful to human lives and action. Both power and violence are instrumental, of course. Power can be used to bring about great injustice. Violence may be used to prevent one. In suggesting that power is valuable and violence disvaluable by default, we acknowledge that violence brings risks and harmful costs that exercise of non-violent power usually does not, and that these must be calculated in the judgment that its use is good.

Thus any act of violence calls for justification, an account of why it is morally acceptable. When Arendt claims that such an account is always forward looking, she refers to the instrumental character of violence. A justification of violence can only appeal to the good it brings about, its consequences. Justification of violence cannot be retrospective in the ways that are arguments about legitimacy, because violence is always a rupture that breaks through the continuity of the present with the past.

As with the distinction between power and violence, I interpret both the concepts of legitimation and justification as normative, and the distinction between them as relevant for moral argument. Arguing that a policy or action is legitimate has the form of a *legal* argument in the following way. It shows that the policy or action follows from or conforms to the legally established public institutions, and contributes to their collective ends. For example, a zoning plan for the city has been drawn up by legitimately authorized officials, in accordance with regulations established by the city council; it fulfills the purposes of collectively regulated planning, namely to ease the conduct of a plurality of activities in a limited space.

For such a notion of legitimacy to have a morally normative meaning, however, its arguments must also implicitly and sometimes explicitly make the claim that the laws and institutional principles to which they appeal are right, just, or good. Without such implicit moral force one might well be able to claim legitimacy for evil acts; removal of Blacks from urban townships in apartheid South Africa was legally authorized. To the extent that arguments about legitimacy must have this double meaning – as expressing the power of collective action established in institutions and as doing so justly – they are always contestable. The extent to which existing law and institutions do in fact express the power and will of the people whose consent and cooperation keep them going, promote their well being and maintain fair relations between them, is always contestable. Every claim to legitimacy, I suggest, is an invitation to such a question, because existing institutions are always imperfect from the point of view of justice, and sometimes are very bad.

Because violence necessarily destroys, it cannot be taken as follow-ing from the rules and practices that facilitate collective action toward productive and creative ends. Even if perpetrated by legitimately autho-rized public officials, the use of violence is always a rupture in the estab-lished fabric of institutions and always endangers their fragile power. On this view of the meaning of the role of violence, it is incoherent to have a general rule according to which established institutions may rou-tinely engage in violent acts, which can make acts of violence morally acceptable. In this sense violence can never be legitimate.

Instead, every act of violence must be separately justified, case by case. General rules may delimit circumstances under which specific agents may consider whether they are justified in behaving violently. Each case must be justified on its own terms, however, and this justifi-cation is necessarily consequentialist. Most often the use of violence – that is, the bringing about of a harm – must be justified on the grounds of responding to or preventing greater harms that will occur or con-tinue without the violent acts. On this analysis, for example, police are authorized to keep the peace, try to prevent crime, pursue and appre-hend suspected lawbreakers. The legal system gives general rules for what counts as crime and the legitimate limits of pursuit and investi-gation. Police may also sometimes be justified in using violent means to protect innocent people or themselves from harm. Their legitimate role as police, however, does not itself authorize them to use violence at their discretion. Independent justifications are required in each case, and these will appeal to the consequences of the action. Moral validation of violence to enforce international law, I will now argue, has a similar form.

MILITARY INTERVENTION FOR HUMANITARIAN PURPOSES

Are states or alliances of states morally obliged or permitted to use military force in response to egregious wrongs committed by another state or army against some of those in its jurisdiction? If so, must such warfare for alleged humanitarian ends be authorized through a legal or proto-legal procedure? Assuming such authorization is attained, is this sufficient morally to validate military intervention?

In the last decade we have seen the evolution of a set of institutional norms which tend to require that non-defensive military actions be multi-lateral and legally authorized. There is a tendency within international opinion to think that such authorization morally vindicates interventionist military action. Many regard the 1990 war against Iraq as a turning point in international relations because the military alliance that waged the war sought and received authorization from the United Nations security council. A major aspect of the debate between Sidelsky and Ignatieff which I referred to above concerns whether the NATO war against Yugoslavia had something like legal authorization, or could have had it. In his much discussed commentary on the NATO war, to take another example, Jurgen Habermas holds up the ideal of a cosmopolitan legal order in which legal compulsion of some global actors by others would be legitimated through a framework of a democratic society of world citizens. He argues that the NATO action goes some way toward this level of legitimacy because its European members, unlike the United States "understand by 'a politics of human rights' a project for the creation of a comprehensive legal framework for international relations that has changed the present parameters of power politics already."[10] Because such a framework of cosmopolitan legal authorization of interventionist war is still more aspiration than reality, however, according to Habermas, NATO was acting paternalistically, for good moral reasons, but without the force of law that is necessary truly to validate this enforcement action.

In light of the distinction between the legitimation of power and the justification of violence that I have elaborated from Arendt's suggestion, this hope of an international legal framework that will legitimate the use of military force against human rights violators appears flawed. A right of intervention is indeed most valid if it can be legitimated through legal mechanisms that are public, regular, and in whose formation and renewal in principle all the world's peoples have a role. In principle such a cosmopolitan legal assembly and procedure could authorize particular agents, whether states, alliances of states, or non-governmental organizations, to exert power with the aim of preventing abuse or promoting institutions to secure recognition of human rights. Today the United Nations is the only body that can claim to fulfill this role, and for many reasons it falls far short of constituting a legal cosmopolitan authority.

Such authorization of the potential exercise of power to intervene to affect the policies and actions of a state over affairs internal to its jurisdiction should not be confused, however, with morally validating the use of violence allegedly for humanitarian ends. While a general right of intervention may require authorization to be morally acceptable, military action requires justification, not legitimation. Such justification has a situation-specific and consequentialist form.

It is useful to compare this issue to the use of violence by police. Through specific procedures, police have authorization to order people to move away from buildings, question people, serve warrants, search homes, arrest people, and many other activities that interfere with people's actions. Although many people, including not a few police officers, seem to assume that this legitimate role itself gives police authority to use violence at their discretion, this is not so. Even police are morally permitted to resort to violence only to defend themselves or to protect third parties; that is, the use of violence is not legitimated in advance, but must be justified in each case as a last resort which prevents a greater harm. On the other hand, it is morally permissible and perhaps sometimes required for ordinary citizens to use violence under similar circumstances, even though ordinary citizens do not have legitimated authority to enforce the law. If a person or group of people is able to prevent a rape by restraining and hurting the would-be rapist, for example, they are justified in doing so. A similar distinction obtains between the legitimation of acts of intervention with sovereignty, on the one hand, and the need additionally to justify bombing and killing people in the process. The legitimacy of interfering with sovereignty in a particular case does not itself condone violence; additional consequentialist arguments are required.

More completely, I suggest that military action with the aim of saving human lives and creating conditions for the future security of people can be justified only under the following conditions:

(1) use of military force is a last resort;
(2) there is good reason to think that the military action will be effective in achieving its humanitarian ends;
(3) there is a high level of confidence that the military action will not result in more harm than they prevent, including unintended collateral harm;
(4) the use of military force will not undermine the social infrastructure and cohesion necessary to a well functioning post-war society
(5) the material, social and political consequences of the military action will be immediate and constrained in time and place, and not ripple out with longer term or more spatially extended destructive or destabilizing effects.

Can military intervention be justified, according to these conditions? In her 1969 text Hannah Arendt doubts that warfare can be justified today, and this is solely because of its instrumental character. The means of violence, and of military violence in particular, in the twentieth century have become more horrible and destructive than previous eras of history could have imagined. Such hugely destructive instruments make more likely than ever before that with the use of violence in public affairs "the end is in danger of being overwhelmed by the means which it justifies and which are needed to reach it" (p. 4).

Arendt has the proliferation of nuclear weapons in mind, of course, but she was also writing at a moment when the United States military was carpet bombing Southeast Asia, planting land and sea mines, destroying forests and poisoning people with napalm. "The technical development of the implements of violence has now reached the point where no political goal could conceivably correspond to their destructive potential or justify their actual use in armed conflict. Hence, warfare – from time immemorial the final merciless arbiter of international disputes – has lost much of its effectiveness and nearly all its glamour" (p. 3).

The instruments of war that Arendt found apocalyptic have become largely antiquated, of course. The cleverly destructive power of weaponry has increased many times and some of the most horrible sorts of weapons have piled up in more arsenals around the world. Although the character of contemporary war that relies on such weapons brings into question moral justifiability of almost any war today, this issue rarely arises in discussions of the morality of military intervention for humanitarian ends. To make matters worse, military and political leaders deceive themselves and their citizens that a new generation of "smart" weapons make warfare more justifiable because they are allegedly more accurate. These more precise bombs allow pilots to protect themselves from being shot down while flying their missions. They still often miss, or cause collateral damage.

Ignatieff remarks that such technologies of warfare make it possible to conduct "virtual" war: a war that is "unreal" from the point of view of those waging it, who witness it largely on computer monitors and televisions, but at the same time whose effects are devastating on those against whom these instruments are used. He considers the NATO war against Yugoslavia was such a "virtual" war for both the military personnel, political leaders and citizens of the NATO countries, and that this capability raises new moral questions about waging war.[11]

The use of military means in the attempt to protect the lives of masses of people and set up conditions of future security can possibly be justified, and should not be ruled out. In practice, however, both the instruments of contemporary war, and the complex conditions of contemporary social relations and politics make it very difficult to justify any particular military intervention.

THE WAR AGAINST YUGOSLAVIA

After 1989 the Republic of Yugoslavia removed the policies that had allowed Albanians in Kosovo considerable political and cultural autonomy in the context of the Serbian Republic. While some Serbs claim that they suffered disadvantage and discrimination in semi-autonomous Kosovo, there is no question that after the reassertion of Serbian authority, Albanians, who composed at least 80 percent of the population of Kosovo, lost many freedoms: self-government, work in civil service, right to education in their own language, to name a few.

Beginning in the early 1990s Albanian movement of peaceful resistance developed. Albanians withdrew their cooperation from Serbian dominated public institutions, such as courts, social service agencies, and schools, and created a large network of alternative institutions of their own, using their homes, places of worship, and other sites, and sharing their relatively meager resources to keep these institutions operating. While it is unlikely that threats of violence were absent from the operation of this alternative society, it was founded on and kept going largely on the active commitment and detailed coordination of masses of Albanians. The success of this shadow society operating under very strained conditions illustrates the possibilities of power in Arendt's sense. By 1994 the society was strong and organized enough to mount an election for an alternative government. The Western powers who later so concerned themselves with the plight of Albanians in Kosovo, however, all but ignored this peaceful resistance movement. For example, Kosovar Albanians' pleas that the issue of autonomy for Kosovo be placed on the agenda of the Dayton meetings to negotiate a settlement for Bosnia-Herzegovina, went unheeded. The Independent International Commission on Kosovo suggests in its report that this failure to support the peaceful resistance movement is a likely cause of Kosovar Albanians joining or supporting the Kosovo Liberation Army in the years following Dayton.[12]

By 1998 serious warfare between the KLA and the Serbian army was underway. Serbian forces not only attacked the KLA, but also killed several thousand civilians and drove tens of thousands more from their homes. Even though the Republic of Yugoslavia saw itself fighting a legitimate war of counterinsurgency within their own sovereign territory, its actions, especially attacks on non-combatants, were grave violations of human rights. Outside agents such as Russia, the United States, the United Nations and NATO not only had a right but a duty to try to prevent further killing displacement by putting pressure on Yugoslavia to reach an agreement on the protection of Albanians in Kosovo and respect for their rights. Agents outside Yugoslavia helped broker such an agreement in 1998 and tried again in early 1999.

Was the war that NATO waged against Yugoslavia from March to June of 1999 justified? By the criteria I have stated above, I claim not. First, there is some reason to think that all other possibilities for changing the situation of the Albanians in Kosovo had not been exhausted. It is arguable that the NATO countries gave Yugoslavia an unreasonable ultimatum when they insisted that Kosovo come under the protection of NATO forces which would have also had a right to move in the whole territory of Serbia. The Rambouillet process wrongly sidelined Russia, furthermore, as a mediator with Yugoslavia. The agreement negotiated after the three-month war called for a UN force instead of a NATO force, and Russia's role was crucial in making the agreement. The fact that in June 1999 the United States and its allies yielded on certain points about which they had been uncompromising in March 1999 (even though they reneged on some of these points after the agreement was signed) would seem to point to the conclusion that not all diplomatic alternatives had been exhausted in March.

We cannot know what might have happened, however. So we should turn to the second and major point: it is very difficult to claim that the war did more good or prevented more harm than it caused. If the war's justification consisted in its saving lives, and promoting the well being of the Albanian Kosovars, it failed miserably. Before March 1999 Serbian forces had terrorized many Albanians in Kosovo away from their homes, but after European protection monitors were pulled out in advance of the NATO bombing campaign, the forced removal and killing of civilians by Serb forces hugely increased. Between March 24 and June 19, 1999, at least 10,000 people died in Kosovo, most of these Albanians killed by Serb forces. About 863,000 civilians sought or were forced into refuge outside Kosovo and another 590,000 were internally displaced. The NATO campaign not only failed to prevent ethnic cleansing, it made these horrors more likely and more possible. The report of the Independent Commission lays first responsibility for the death and suffering in this mission of "ethnic cleansing" at the feet of the leaders of the Republic of Yugoslavia. The Commission nevertheless finds that the NATO campaign aided and abetted the operation.

It is certainly not true that NATO *provoked* the attacks on the civilian population – the responsibility for that campaign rests entirely on the Belgrade government. It is nonetheless likely that the bombing campaign and the removal of the unarmed monitors created an internal environment that made such an operation feasible. The FRY forces could not hit NATO, but they could hit the Albanians who had asked for NATO support and intervention.[13]

Not only did the Western "humanitarian" war enable suffering on such a mass scale, but neither the NATO states nor the United Nations were at all prepared to respond to the masses of people flooding over border states with few resources and serious political problems of their own. To be humanitarian, warriors must have a plan for helping people who suffer as a consequence of their actions.

After the war most of the refugees returned to Kosovo, but it is hard to say that they went home. The bombing virtually destroyed the country. Approximately 120,000 houses in Kosovo were destroyed or damaged by the war, and 250 schools needed repair. Roads were in ruins, bridges destroyed, telephone lines down and there was no electricity. Thousands of unexploded cluster bombs lay in fields and alley ways, which are still killing people. Both the uranium dioxide released into the atmosphere by some of the shells and the toxic leaks caused by some of the bombs made Kosovo an environmental disaster.

The war not only destroyed economic and environmental infrastructure, but institutions as well. At war's end, there was no functioning health care system, judiciary, or banking system. To the extent that any local governments remained, most were unable to police the streets or perform even the most basic municipal services. Some argue that the war and its aftermath undermined an emerging human-rights culture in Kosovo.[14]

The moral evaluation of war must count the consequences to the lives of all parties equally.[15] Thus a calculation of whether the NATO war did more good than harm must count in harm to Serbs, both in Kosovo and in the north. Because NATO was unable seriously to weaken the Serbian military with its air war, it took the war to the cities of the north, where endangering civilians was unavoidable. About 500 civilians were killed and at least 820 wounded by NATO sorties in 90 separate incidents, the majority of these Serbs. Fifty-nine bridges, nine major highways and seven airports were destroyed in Serbia. Most of the main telecommunications transmitters were damaged, and two thirds of the main industrial plants were nearly destroyed. Seventy percent of the electricity production capacity and percent of oil refinery capacity was knocked out. The disruption of health and social services and commercial activity the bombing cased doubtless led to more suffering.

Nothing can justify this kind of ruin both to the society an alliance attacks nor to the society it claims to be saving. The immediate and longer term consequences of the war add fuel to the judgment. The forces occupying Kosovo under the official mandate of the United Nations could not prevent the ethnic cleansing of at least 100,000 Serbs from Kosovo, or hundreds of revenge killings. Since June 1999 Albanian Kosovars have not exercised the self-government they desired, but have effectively been ruled by an international organization. Ethnic conflict and distrust in the region has not abated and it is probably worse as a consequence of the war and its aftermath.

The only "good" that might be attributed to this war is that Melosevic is no longer president of Serbia and is now standing trial for war crimes. A cynic might say that the war has also done the good of creating business opportunities for Western corporations contracted in the effort to rebuild infrastructure in Serbia and Kosovo.[16]

In concluding that the NATO war against Yugoslavia did more harm than good, and was for this reason not morally justified, I am mindful that many believe that the conduct of this war showed it better than many. Despite the fact that some terrible mistakes occurred, such as bombing the Chinese embassy or a caravan of Albanian refugees, there seems to be a consensus that the NATO commanders tried to avoid hitting civilians and did well at keeping down the number of casualties. Especially if one accepts the suggestion that the NATO war was *as good as an air war can be*,[17] this evaluation calls into question the assumption that the international community can properly think of military action as a routine form of humanitarian intervention.

My argument that NATO's war against Yugoslavia was not morally justified is not an argument that the world should have respected Yugoslav sovereignty and stood by while the Serbian army fought the KLA and sowed terror in Albanian non-combatants. There were alternatives that many observers think were not exhausted when NATO began bombing. Some of these might have involved a justified use of violence on a much smaller and less destructive scale, such as giving troops of the OSCE more authority to use force to protect civilians. My concern is that arguments for the right to override the claims of state sovereignty for the sake of defending human rights often move too quickly to the position that the means of intervention should be war.

The war against Yugoslavia seems to me to illustrate and support Arendt's claim that violence cannot create power and only destroys it. Kosovo is the story of spiraling violence to which actors respond with more violence wrecking great destruction. The power that Albania Kosovars may have had in their civic institutions is completely shattered, and it will not reappear soon. Serbian people of the north too have lost social power.

This war also validates Arendt's claim that a state's resort to open violence is often a sign of powerlessness rather than power. If those who wish to protect human lives and well-being from repression and domination were to put the use of violence aside, they would find that they have paltry other tools available for the task. The world should face up to this stark fact: at the moment, we are nearly powerless to enforce respect for human rights against organized forces determined to violate them. There may be rare instances when the use of military forces can prevent a harm without causing greater harm, but we must also face up to the truth that war frequently hurts a great deal more than it helps. Effective protection of human rights, then, requires the creation of new institutions through which the world's peoples and governments can act collectively to adjudicate disputes, make clear rules, and apply sanctions and punishment to those who violate them.

What does this mean? A number of international relations theorists in recent years have called for the exercise of the political imagination to "unbundle" sovereignty in order to, among other things, protect endangered groups through regional and global cooperation and regulatory agreements.[18] While the level of governance that we now refer to as the nation-state should stay in place for many powers and policies, the dangers and opportunities of increased global interdependence call for the creation of stronger global regulatory and enforcement powers. The peoples of the world have democratic procedures through which to promulgate such regulations and multilateral means of backing them with incentives, sanctions and coercion. Some of the most exciting work in international relations theory today aims to imagine some such institutions and theorize the actions and policies that might move the world toward them.[19]

NOTES

This essay benefited from conversations with Robert Pape and Neta Crowford.

1 The arguments of this section and the next are based on the corresponding sections in another paper, "Power, Violence and Legitimacy: A Reading of Hannah Arendt in a Age of Police Brutality and Humanitarian Intervention," in Nancy Rosenblum, ed., *Cycles of Hatred* (Princeton University Press, 2002).

2 Hannah Arendt, *On Violence* (New York: Harcourt Brace and Company, 1969).

3 For the purposes of this essay, I am limiting discussion to physical forms of violence; their incidence is frequent and horrible enough to call urgently for inquiry. I recognize that there may well be phenomena of psychological violence, various ways that people are able to destroy the spirit of other persons without doing them bodily damage. Indeed, some of Arendt's other writings have rich veins to mine for such a concept of psychological violence. Because non-physical forms of violence present additional conceptual problems, I limit my discussion here to physical violence.

4 Arendt, *The Human Condition*, especially ch. 28.

5 Max Weber, "Politics as a Vocation," in H. H. Gerth and C. Wright Mills, *From Max Weber* (New York: Oxford University Press, 1946), pp. 77–78.

6 Compare Leah Bradshaw, "Political Authority and Violence," paper presented at the Canadian Political Science Association meetings, Quebec City, August 2000.

7 Jurgen Habermas also gives Arendt's theory of power an explicitly normative interpretation. See "Hannah Arendt on the Concept of Power," in *Philosophical-Political Profiles* (Cambridge, MA: MIT Press, 1983), pp. 171–88; see also *Between Facts and Norms* (Cambridge, MA: MIT Press, 1996), ch. 4.

8 Jeffrey Isaac, *Arendt, Camus and Modern Rebellion* (New Haven: Yale University Press, 1992), p. 149.

9 Arendt, *On Revolution* (New York: Viking Press, 1965), p. 175.

10 Habermas, "Bestiality and Humanity: A War on the Border between Law and Humanity," in William Joseph Buckley, ed., *Kosovo: Contending Voices on Balkan Interventions* (Grand Rapids, MI: William B. Eerdmans Publishing Company, 2000), p. 313. Martin Matustik critically evaluates Habermas's argument. See Matustik, *Jurgen Habermas: A Philosophical-Political Profile* (Laham, MD: Rowman and Littlefield, 2001), pp. 271–73.

11 Michael Ignatieff, *Virtual War: Kosovo and Beyond* (New York: Henry Hart and Co., 2000), especially pp. 161–215.

12 Independent International Commission on Kosovo, *Kosovo Report: Conflict, International Response, Lessons Learned* (Oxford: Oxford University Press, 2000), p. 64.

13 *Kosovo Report*, pp. 88–89.

14 Julie Mertus, "The Impact of Intervention on Local Human Rights Culture: A Kosovo Case Study," paper presented at the American Political Science Association, San Francisco, 2001.

15 William McBride criticizes the NATO war partly on such consequentialist grounds, and argues that this consequentialism is important however valuable the principles allegedly humanitarian intervention claims to defend. See McBride, *From Yugoslav Praxis to Global Pathos: Anti-Hegemonic Post-Post-Marxist Essay* (Lagham, MD: Roman and Littlefield, 2001), ch. 14.

16 Noam Chomsky suggests that this is one of the purposes of US wars; see Chomsky, *The New Military Humanism: Lessons from Kosovo* (Monroe, ME: Common Courage Press, 1999), pp. 138–39.

17 There are many who question the rejection of ground war by NATO. They argue that putting NATO troops on the ground in Kosovo would have better protects the Albanians and done more to damage the Yugoslav army, thus perhaps making it less necessary to resort to bombing infrastructure in the northern cities. See Michael Walzer, "Kosovo," and Jean Bethke Elshtain, "Kosovo and the Just-War Tradition," both in William Joseph Buckley ed., *Kosovo: Contending Voices on Balkan Interventions* (Cambridge: William B. Eerdmans Publishing Co., 2000), pp. 333–35 and pp. 363–67 respectively. I find this argument plausible, but do not take it up here because I am primarily concerned to evaluate the war as it happened. Even if a ground war might have reduced refugee flight and reduced reliance on bombing in the north, it is not at all certain that fewer lives would have been lost or the consequences cleaner.

18 See Robert O. Keohane, "Political Authority after Intervention: The International Transformation of Sovereignty," paper prepared for a conference sponsored by the Carr Center for Human Rights Policy, Harvard University, September 2001.

19 For some more discussion of these issues see, Iris Marion Young, *Inclusion and Democracy* (Oxford: Oxford University Press, 2000), ch. 7; Daniele Archibugi, David Held, and Martin Koehler, *Re-Imagining Political Community* (Cambridge: Polity Press, 1998); for an analysis of responses to terrorism after September 11, 2001, with such imagining in view, see Daniele Archibugi and Iris Young, "Envisioning a Global Rule of Law," *Dissent*, June 2002.

Chapter 13

War for humanity: a critique

C. A. J. COADY

When we debate the contemporary problem of humanitarian intervention, it is useful to recall history. It teaches some of the pitfalls of high-minded motivation. Consider President McKinley, at the end of the nineteenth century, facing the problem of annexation of the Philippines:

It came to me one night that we could not turn the island over to France or Germany, our commercial rivals; that would be bad business and discreditable. We would not give them back to Spain; that would be cowardly and dishonorable. We could not leave them to themselves; they were unfit for self-government. There was therefore nothing left for us to do but to take care of them and educate them and Christianize them.[1]

I shall want to say more about the relation of these underlying attitudes to interventionist proposals, but, for the moment, let me just emphasize that Filipinos had been Christians for four centuries at the time McKinley spoke of his mission to Christianize them. They had also sought political independence for years, with martyrs, exiles, and widespread support. The United States' humanitarian takeover was unsuccessfully resisted with arms for two years and the "taking care" lasted for fifty years.

It is clear from this that the desire to use political and military muscle to "take care," benefit, and prevent harm to others is not a novel phenomenon created by the end of the Cold War. It is also fraught with ambiguities both moral and political. One ambiguity is the fluctuating enthusiasm for it. Indeed, in the aftermath of September 11, 2001, the urge for humanitarian rather than punitive or retributive intervention may appear extinguished for some time to come. But prediction of this sort is hazardous. Adam Roberts claimed in the mid-1990s that the thrust for humanitarian intervention was on the decline,[2] but the

NATO military response to the Kosovo crisis proved him wrong, and, as he himself subsequently pointed out, this response was partly a reaction of shame after inertia in the face of earlier horrors.[3]

THE MEANING OF "INTERVENTION"

My central focus is armed intervention, though I will have something to say later about various forms of coercive intervention short of the use of armed force. I define intervention as an intentional act of one state or group of states or an international agency aimed at exercising overriding authority upon what are normally the "internal" policies or practices of another state or group of states. Absent the intervention, that is, the behavior being interfered with would be under the authority of the state against which the intervention is made. It is crucial here that the target state (as I will call it) does not consent to the intervention. So the bombing of Serbia as a means of protecting Kosovo Albanians clearly counts as intervention where actions of the coalition that went into East Timor with the consent of the Indonesian Government do not. The Gulf War wasn't an intervention because it was not essentially an intrusion into the internal politics of Iraq but an effort to aid Kuwait (with their consent) against an invasion by Iraq. The subsequent persistent bombing of Iraq, ostensibly to protect minority groups, is another matter.

Some find this definition too restrictive. Stanley Hoffmann, for instance, rejects the consent requirement, mainly because consent is not always voluntary or genuine. But if it isn't genuine then it isn't consent. The definition should speak of genuine consent, but the standards for genuine consent should not be set too high. When people agree to some proposal, especially a political proposal, there are often background pressures and conditions at work, appreciation of which constitute reasons for their agreement. Often some or all of the parties don't much like these conditions, and they constrain choices to some degree without being strong enough to vitiate consent. Compromise agreements are nonetheless genuine agreements. And it is true, as Hoffmann says, that consent can turn sour, but this hardly counts against requiring it in the first place. It merely reminds us that something that begins as one thing may turn into another.[4] Hoffmann also worries that even where formal consent has been obtained the outside military involvement may still be morally problematic: indeed so, but this just shows that military intervention is not the only morally and politically problematic use of violence.

THE MEANING OF "HUMANITARIAN"

What is "humanitarian" about humanitarian armed intervention? Such interventions are aimed at rescuing foreign people from harm that is being done, or might be about to be done, to them by the state authorities who are responsible for their protection. This is the primary motive for the intervention. I say "primary" because we must allow for mixed motives (as in McKinley's justifications) for these are never absent from international affairs or any other area of human agency. It may indeed be too much to require that the humanitarian reasons should constitute sufficient conditions for the intervention, but they should at least be necessary and prominent.

I have defined "humanitarian" in terms of a conspicuous motive, but some participants in the debate show a tendency to define the expression in terms of beneficial outcome, giving it what philosophers have called "success grammar." Tesón seems inclined this way when he discusses the objection that interventions are very likely to involve partiality and ultimate abuse by the interveners. He says, "If part of the definition of the class of actions 'humanitarian intervention' is that states do not abuse, then it is difficult to resist the conclusion that the adoption of the rule allowing for humanitarian interventions will have beneficial consequences."[5] And he adds, "An intervention in which foreign troops abuse their power is not an instance of humanitarian intervention."[6] But this suggestion is disastrous for serious discussion of the merits or pitfalls of embarking upon such interventions as are proposed as humanitarian, since we need a vocabulary for debating them which doesn't assume success in advance.

It is of course a hotly contested question whether humanitarian motives should, or can, be encompassed by the term "national interest." Several theorists have argued that the term "national interest" has been understood far too narrowly, and that, at least in the case of democratic nations, the national interest should include a concern that genocide and egregious human-rights violations should not occur anywhere in the world. This is a very interesting debate, and one problem in resolving it is the opacity of the phrase "national interest" which is used extensively in realist and neo-realist writings and is widespread in political discourse, but seldom used with precision. One realist, for instance, explicitly restricts it to material interests, claiming that a state's national interest relates only to "its territorial integrity (or political sovereignty), its military security, and its economic well-being."[7] Other writers include broader value elements of a nation's political system, but the shiftiness of the concept is inherent in the fact that it is derived by extension from the idea of an individual's interest, and this concept itself is enmeshed in an ethical and theoretical quagmire centered on the word "egoism." The history of debates about ethical and psychological egoism, that is, discussions of the significance of self-interest as a justificatory and motivational factor in individual behavior, is bedevilled by a picture of morality and motivation that initially puts far too stark an opposition between the individual and the community and then, understandably, has great difficulty getting them back together. In reaction, it is tempting to make too much of their integration.

The truth is that individual and group interests are profoundly linked, but can also come into opposition. Normally, morality and prudent self-concern are self-supporting; indeed much traditional ethical thought treats prudence as a crucial part of morality, and doesn't always link it to self-interest. But it is possible for the individual's interest to conflict with the group's – otherwise the idea of self-sacrifice would have no point. Unravelling these matters is difficult enough at the individual level; at the elusive level of collective national identity the difficulty is even greater. Hence it is really quite surprising that politicians and theorists operate so casually with the idea of the national interest, and invest it with such normative power. But if there is any weight to the analogy between individual interest and national interest, then it will not do to understand the national interest too narrowly, and, in particular, the idea should not exclude *ab initio* any concerns for the well-being of humans other than one's own nationals. It is a further question whether such concern can require or license armed intervention.

HUMANITARIAN VIOLENCE: A PARADOX?

The question of the morality of military intervention seems part of the broader question of the morality of war; it therefore inherits much that is morally problematic about war and other uses of political violence. Bryan Hehir apparently disagrees since he wants to "distinguish... sharply" between war and intervention, treating the morality of war as governed by the anti-aggression paradigm whereas intervention is not.[8] I am not impressed by this proposal, but it is not clear how much turns on it. Hehir, in fact, thinks that "in many ways, the character of intervention makes it more difficult to justify than war"[9] and he treats the task of moral justification as essentially provided by the framework of just war thinking with suitable adaptation. One reason for not sharply distinguishing the two is that intervention frequently has all or most of the behavioral features of war, as in the intervention against Serbia over Kosovo or the Vietnamese intervention in Cambodia.

So the air of paradox is connected with the morally problematic nature of resort to war, and this explains, to a large degree, the strong bias in international law and the UN Charter against military intervention. The idea that one can initiate for humanitarian purposes such horrors as war invariably involves must retain an air of paradox. *Can* aggressive war be "humanitarian"?

THE JUST WAR TRADITION

The primary ethical machinery for considering this must at least begin with the "just war tradition." This tradition has been criticized in various ways, but, suitably understood, it provides a reasonable apparatus for tackling the questions of war and intervention. Indeed, if you are not a pacifist about war, then there is a minimal sense in which you have to be a just war theorist, that is, you have to give reasons why going to war can be justified and under what circumstances. No matter how common war has been as an instrument of state power and policy, the fact that it involves deliberate killing and maiming and great destruction of property, and of the natural and cultural environment, means that resort to it demands the discharge of a heavy burden of justification. Further, there are convincing reasons (connected with the power of the concept of "atrocity") why your mode of justifying war will have to include considerations about what ways of conducting war are off-limits morally.[10] The former issues are often discussed under the rubric of what is called the Jus ad Bellum (JAB) and the latter under the heading of the Jus in Bello (JIB). All this is largely independent of the precise form a just war theory will take, and it is also, incidentally, relatively independent of culture. The idea that a just war theory is merely "Western" or "European" is somewhat like the idea that the science of physics is merely "Western" or "European." Both claims are rough approximations to the truth in terms of the origin of these explicit intellectual practices, but this says nothing of their validity nor of their relations to parallel theories from other cultures. In fact, there is a great deal of writing in the Chinese philosophical tradition that addresses precisely the questions that a moral theory about resort to war and the conduct of war must address. The writings of Mo Tzu and Hsun Tzu are just two significant examples.[11] As critics often point out, just war theory has undoubtedly been abused by militarists and politicians as a license for easy and destructive resort to war. As I understand it, however, and as it has been increasingly interpreted by philosophers, theologians and lawyers in the twentieth century, the ethic of the just war is restrictive. Not only does it insist on the justice of the cause for which war is conducted, but also upon certain other restrictive conditions, chief amongst which are:

The proportionality of resort to war for such a cause (that is, is the move to war, fully considering its effects, out of proportion to the offense occasioning it?);

The requirement of "last resort" which emphasizes the value of the peace that war breaks and cautions against too hasty a recourse to violence;

The criterion of right intention. This orients the military action towards justice rather than revenge, blood-lust or mere expansionism;

The test of appropriate authority. This is aimed at keeping the resort to violence under the control that authority, at least in principle, can give it;

The consideration of the realistic prospects for success which is an attempt to rein in the passions of war by the desiderata of rationality in practical reasoning;

Various moral criteria for the means used in waging the war, such as non-combatant immunity.

Many of these conditions might be justified in utilitarian terms alone, since it is plausible to think that the outcomes of observing them are likely to be optimal for all concerned. Others are more persuasively addressed from a non-utilitarian perspective, especially the requirement of non-combatant immunity. In broad terms, then, the just war tradition treats war as a sometimes necessary evil, rather than an heroic romp, and in terms of just cause, the idea has been that war can only or principally be justified as a defensive measure, a defense against aggression. This has in modern times become the center-piece of the JAB and the international law of war that reflects it to a large degree. One of the most instructive features of the debate about humanitarian intervention that emerged in the 1990s was its challenge to this paradigm.

CHALLENGING THE PARADIGM: THE CASE
FOR INTERVENTION

The contemporary debate about intervention, where it is not simply a debate about what great powers can get away with in pursuit of various geopolitical strategies, raises the question whether there can be legitimate aggressive wars to prevent or correct great wrongs. In some respects, as Bryan Hehir has pointed out, answering this question in the affirmative represents a return to a much earlier just war model that the current paradigm displaced.[12] The reigning paradigm, it is true, had always recognized certain extensions of the anti-aggression model, such as wars to help others defend themselves against aggression, wars against a clear threat to world peace, and interventions in civil wars to balance prior unjust interventions. But these all had a recognizable, if sometimes stretched, connection with defense against aggression. In recent years, the permissibility of interventions to prevent genocide within state boundaries has been suggested, and some have thought this could be seen as aiding or creating a defense against a sort of aggression. Now, however, we see increasing resort to arguments that advocate interventions to prevent egregious human-rights abuses or other grave internal moral crimes. The crucial question thereby raised is whether the prominence given to defense against aggression, upon which much legal regulation rests, needs radical revision in the light of the problems created by tyrannical regimes, or failed or profoundly unstable states.

There is a powerful moral intuition at work in the thinking of those who advocate interventions that apparently go beyond current international law and depart from the self-defense model. It is the intuition captured by the word "rescue." Humanitarian interventions are seen as attempts at rescuing the innocent and helpless from persecution and extreme distress.[13] We can dramatize its appeal by resort to a simple analogy. You are on your way home from work and you see a very strong man involved in an argument with his own child. It's noisy and unpleasant, but (you reason) it's their family and none of your business. But the dispute rapidly heats up and the man begins beating the child with a heavy stick. You protest and remonstrate with the man, but he tells you to get lost. He continues beating the child viciously, and indeed draws a knife and begins to brandish it at him. You fear for the child's life and as it happens you are (legitimately) carrying a gun. Surely you should threaten the father, and if the threats don't work, you are morally entitled to shoot. Similarly, the argument goes, at the level of states where the amount of power exercised repressively and even murderously is so much greater. It is perhaps significant in this connection to note that the strong objections to "offensive war" made by Mo Tzu fall short of condemning the initiation of altruistic wars, and indeed favor some righteous wars of punishment.[14] There is no denying the power of this intuition, and the images of death and displacement from Cambodia, Rwanda, Bosnia, East Timor, and Kosovo reinforce it.

THE SOVEREIGNTY DEBATE AND THE THEORY OF AGGRESSION

It is often argued that the opposition to military intervention or war for any purpose other than defense against aggression (or causes closely related to it) is based upon the modern concept of sovereignty arising from the Peace of Westphalia which put an end to the European wars of religion.[15] Simplifying somewhat, we may say that the concept limited states from intervening militarily in matters that were the concern of other sovereign states, and gave the sovereign states themselves the right to govern and decide upon the use of force internally for control and externally for defense. This constituted the recognition of a form of "absolute sovereignty." It is then argued that this concept is dangerously outmoded, since the idea of sovereign power has been eroded by the economic and informational processes known as "globalization," and by the development of cosmopolitan political processes, such as the UN and the various global NGOs. Moreover, the concept was always flawed insofar as it left citizens at the mercy of their governments with frequently alarming consequences. The nation-state must now be regarded therefore as having "conditional sovereignty," that is, sovereignty which is conditional upon some minimal level of discharge of obligations to respect the human rights of its citizens. The critique and rejection of aggressive resort to war needs to be viewed against this background, and therefore amended appropriately.

There is undoubtedly something in this line of critique. The modern nation-state and its pretensions are by no means sacrosanct. Nonetheless, the reigning paradigm is not so easily dismissed. The opposition to intervention, even for the purposes of doing good, is based on deeper insights than the needs of a seventeenth-century political settlement, even though these insights had relevance to that settlement. There are two sorts of insight involved. The first concerns *the need to limit resort to war*. This puts an emphasis upon restricting the impulses to violent solutions to political problems and does so by allowing such resort only in the most palpable circumstances of justification – for example, self-defense. If you are actually under attack you may be presumed to have a right to the means needed to repel the attack. And much the same point seems to apply at the communal level. On the other hand, making the world safe for God, Democracy or Free Markets may be presumed to yield a much less secure right to unleash large-scale killing and maiming. This is especially so when we consider the ambiguities inherent in that trinity of concepts.

The second concerns *the right to national self-determination*. Here, it is not Westphalia that is significant, but a combination of the much earlier insight that jurisdiction should have a strong local and popular element (which need not be the same as democracy) and the much later developments associated with de-colonization which gave prominence to the ethical-political value of national self-determination.

These insights are in danger of being forgotten in the renewed enthusiasm (amongst those who are enthusiastic!) for humanitarian intervention. Both insights are moral though they have prudential components. The first needs no further explanation here, except to note that the concern to limit war extends beyond the non-aggression paradigm to the other just war restraints. The second insight needs some expansion under both elements of the combination. Colonialism got its bad name, not merely from the explicitly repressive policies of the colonial powers, grim as they commonly were, but also from the inherent difficulties foreigners face in understanding their subject peoples, in properly comprehending their religious, cultural, and historical circumstances. Colonialism is also intrinsically committed to certain attitudes of inequality built into the idea of imperial rule and encapsulated in McKinley's patronizing remarks about Filipinos. The theme about "unfitness" is found even in so enlightened and profound a thinker as J. S. Mill whose famous essay on non-intervention made an exception against the prohibition on intervention for the case of "uncivilized" peoples.[16] It was a theme of the far less noble-minded Spanish conquistadores in South America: paganism allegedly deprived the Indian peoples of rights to self-government. This proposition was decisively undermined by a number of courageous Spanish theologians, notably Vitoria, Las Casas, and Montesinos who argued for a natural right of self-government possessed by peoples whatever their religion. The American Indians, said Vitoria, "undoubtedly possessed as true dominion, both public and private, as any Christians."[17]

The self-government argument needs supplementation by some account of what is meant by a "people" and "self-government". For the
first, the idea of "a nation" when cashed in ethnic terms is surely too narrow, and when cashed in terms of state-identity it tends to beg the question. For the second, the requirement of democracy seems too strong,
though it indicates the ideal, and absence of rebellion seems too weak.
This is not the place to explore fully the contours of the difficult ideal
of self-government, but it is important to stress that this norm is not
identical with the value of "absolute sovereignty" and hence the critique of the latter is in danger of ignoring or demeaning the value of the
former. The critique of sovereignty has some merit, but it surely suffers
from the remarkable fact that enthusiasm for conditional or qualified
sovereignty is often asymmetrical. Many of those who are keenest on
the conditional sovereignty of others commonly resist strenuously the
slightest diminution of their own sovereign rights. This indicates that the
value of self-government is connected to some form of sovereignty and
this in turn should caution against any revived enthusiasm for benign
imperialism.

JUST WAR, HUMANITARIAN INTERVENTION
AND JUST CAUSE

One thing that emerges from the previous section is that any argument
for humanitarian intervention has to overcome the presumptive case
against aggressive war, and has to discharge the other requirements of
just war theory. For the purposes of our discussion I am going to assume
that the criterion of "right intention" is met, at least for the stark cases of
severe oppression that provoke calls for humanitarian intervention. By
making this assumption, I do not mean to deny that nations will often be
tempted to use the cloak of humanitarian intent for military adventures
that have predominantly quite different motives. No less a figure than
General Wesley Clark, Supreme Commander of NATO's forces during
the Kosovo intervention, seems now to have conceded that the primary
motive for the NATO bombing of Serbia was to preserve the credibility
of the NATO Alliance.[18] But the more interesting moral and political
issues arise when we concede humanitarian motivation and address
the other conditions of just-war theory.

It is plausible to assume that the condition of just cause is also readily met for the situations of extreme oppression that raise the cry for
humanitarian intervention, but there is one commonly voiced objection

that can be viewed as a rejection of the claim to just cause (though in some forms it is perhaps meant as a criticism of right intention). This is the objection from lack of universality of response.

The objection is one of inconsistency: if humanitarianism is the issue why intervene here and not there? It is notorious that there are civil wars, persecutions, widespread torture, forced refugees, and tyrannies in most parts of the globe. Intervention here and failure to intervene there surely show a flawed moral response, since what is right to do in one place must also be right to do in another exhibiting the same morally relevant features. There is an implicit appeal here to a form of the universalization principle beloved of many moral philosophers, especially those influenced by Immanuel Kant.

There are several things wrong with this response in the present case and one thing right with it. The first point is that we should distinguish between a right and a duty to intervene: we may have both a right and a duty to intervene, but we may have a right without a duty. In the latter case, it is permissible for us to intervene but not obligatory. Many of the discussions of the ethics of intervention are concerned with the permissibility of intervention; this is understandable given the prevailing legal and moral presumptions against intervention. Were the question merely one of a right (but no duty) we could choose to exercise that right wherever we may do good, and it is no objection that we have not exercised it elsewhere. But in cases of extreme disaster, it may be thought that there is a duty to intervene (Henry Shue speaks of a "default duty" activated by the failure of the domestic state to act protectively[19]), and several commentators write as if that were so.

Does this give universality of response more bite as a criticism of just cause? Not very much more. For one thing, questions of capacity to respond and likely outcomes must condition where one chooses to relieve suffering. The idea of "triage" has been plausibly invoked in this connection by Thomas Weiss and others, since considerations of effectiveness and available resources will often determine who gets what help where not everyone can be assisted.[20] So, the risks to world peace involved in intervening on behalf of the Tibetans or the Chechnyans make non-intervention there morally sane rather than a dereliction of duty, even though this means tolerating great sufferings. For another thing, it may be argued that certain relationships can legitimately dictate the choice when a choice must be made.

There is something of a divide in moral theory here between those who give a special weight to the demands of certain relationships and those who do not (or do so only reluctantly and indirectly). Classical act utilitarianism claims that, in calculating the greatest happiness of the greatest number, we must be totally impartial between all those affected. But the normal conscience is plainly not so indifferent to the claims of kinship, friendship, and love. It is a further complex question what restrictions should be put upon filial and other partialities, and a further question again how far the partiality of bonds should extend. Can it be a relevant factor in deciding where to intervene that this state is European, that state is Asian, the other state is African? I raise this question, not because I have a clear-cut answer, but because it highlights questions of race, ethnicity, and culture in a disturbing way. It also points to something right lurking in the mostly misguided demand for universality: disparate responses to exterminations need close examination lest they do contain elements of mere prejudice, illegitimate partiality, or sheer blindness to need elsewhere. Many believe that the failure to intervene in Rwanda poses this question very sharply in terms of race. More generally, we may ask why the humanitarian impulse is so relatively silent about the ravages of AIDS in Africa, where military interventions are irrelevant, but medical and social measures might prove invaluable. The consistency challenge is worth raising even if it is not always decisive.

RIGHT AUTHORITY—WHO IS TO INTERVENE?

There is an ethical dimension to this question that can be seen by imagining that we had in place some legitimate form of world government, presumably in the shape of a federation. When a potentially violent police action was required to restore seriously violated human rights in one of the component states, the action taken would have to be centrally authorized. It would be quite wrong for a powerful neighbor state simply to take the (international) law into its own hands. Even in the absence of a world state, there is a similar, if weaker, presumption against unilateral action. This is partly because the UN, with all its faults, has some shadow of the international authority that a world state, as envisaged, would possess. It is also related to the broad requirements of impartiality in the exercise of justice that any humanitarian intervention purports to serve. The more an intervention is removed from the partial interests of particular states, especially powerful ones, the more likely it is to approximate to justice, and the more likely it is to be perceived as legitimate by the parties in conflict and by the international community.

On the other hand, this requirement raises serious practical questions about implementation since a single state is often likely to be more decisive and act with greater unity of purpose. The UN Security Council is also a cumbersome mechanism for achieving justice since the existence of the veto means that powerful states are in a position to block humanitarian interventions that do not serve their interests. There is no simple way to resolve this dilemma, but what is suggested by the legitimating role of the UN is that any unilateral intervention should be presumed illegitimate unless it is in some significant way authorized by the UN. The condition of UN authorisation, of course, should also apply to multi-lateral interventions, since without UN authorization they will invariably wear the appearance of sectional bias. All interventions that bypass the UN at least need a very strong case to rebut the presumption that they are ethically dubious.

PROPORTIONALITY AND ITS AMBIGUITIES

The first thing to be said about proportionality is that a response to humanitarian need should itself be humanitarian. Altruistic military interventions need as much, if not more, than other military activities to ensure they do not do more harm to human rights than the harms they aim to correct or prevent. If one ethnic group is engaged in genocidal activities against another, then the wrong way to respond is to visit genocide on them in return. Proportionality is not a matter of imitating the enemy but of giving a morally appropriate response. (It is worth noting that the same point, of course, applies to defensive responses to terrorist attacks.)

The second thing to consider is the scale of likely outcomes of a military intervention. The prevention of Russian atrocities in Chechnya by military means would have been too dangerous for world peace and involved disproportionate risks. A response proportionate to one situation may be disproportionate to another situation that is similar in terms of oppression but dissimilar in context and in the likely consequences of intervention.

A third issue, overlapping to some extent with the just cause condition, concerns whether the violations are grave enough to require intervention. There is a high degree of moral and political consensus that human-rights violations have to reach a certain plateau of "outrage" before such intervention even seems morally feasible.[21] Persistent rigging of elections, state torture of small numbers of dissidents, drastic restrictions of free speech are all plausibly viewed as grave denials of human rights, but they seem inadequate to create the demand for intervention. Why is this? Part of the answer may reside in the residual power of the idea of state sovereignty and related ideas of the good of self-government, and part of it concerns the grossness of the oppression and the way it is perceived within the target state. Part no doubt is the recognition that various deplorable injustices disfigure the workings of all political communities so that intervention would become unmanageable if required to deal with that scale of wrong. The interveners would also have less authority to act where they could so readily be subject to a "tu quoque" retort. Amnesty International, for instance, lists 142 countries and territories, many of them democratic, where governments and oppositions committed serious human-rights abuses in 1998. Some of these violations are controversial: they include, for instance, the practice of capital punishment, so notable a feature of public life in the United States. Yet this only highlights the problem of taking systematic violations of human rights (or "basic, civil and political rights" as Teson has it[22]) as criterial for humanitarian war. Those of us who regard capital punishment as such a violation would not think of initiating humanitarian war to eradicate its practice, even were it feasible to do so.[23]

A fourth problem that has emerged in recent years and deserves treatment here (though it is partly a matter that relates to the criterion of prospect for success) is that of "cost-free intervention." It is a significant element in the current debate about humanitarian intervention that the various guidelines laid down by Western governments considering the problem insist upon conditions for intervention that are profoundly self-regarding. In some respects this is merely prudent, but there is reason to believe that the emphasis on interventions that will be cost-free to the interveners in terms of risk to their own forces has become excessive because it leads to a disproportionate response to the problem. It is very understandable that interveners want to minimize risks to their own forces: the concern for one's own troops represents a moral advance over many military policies of the past, for example, the treatment of one's own soldiers as cannon fodder in the trenches of World War I. In democracies, there is also a question of the political costs of acting in defiance of widespread public fears.[24] Nonetheless, if the saving of foreigners from massacre or mass expulsion from their homelands is a worthy cause for war then governments and commanders must be prepared to put troops in harm's way.

The refusal to do so inevitably leads to the reliance upon remote forms of air power and technological wizardry that tend to shift damage on to largely blameless civilian populations, as in the bombing of Serbia. The damage in terms of immediate killing of civilians, estimated by the London *Times* to be in the order of 1500,[25] is significant enough, and Amnesty International considered that such NATO killings "may have violated international humanitarian law."[26] But in addition to this, the bombing of what are called "dual-purpose" targets (especially power, water, and transport facilities) clearly creates a serious humanitarian problem for civilian populations.

LAST RESORT: EXPLORING THE ALTERNATIVES

The just war provision of "last resort" contains many puzzles and ambiguities, especially those that raise semantic and logical problems to do with what it can mean to call something a last resort. There will always be *something* that might be tried as an alternative to violence, but if there is a great evil to be prevented we cannot be expected to wait upon every possibility other than effective violence. Clearly, some principle of feasibility is required to screen the realistic availability of alternatives to violence. And it needs to be remembered that waiting to try numerous such options may actually reduce the likely effectiveness of the military option when it is tried.

Nonetheless, bearing these difficulties in mind, the criterion of last resort has a common sense interpretation in which it functions as a reminder that the resort to violence must be, to a significant degree, reluctant. It enjoins us to make serious efforts at peaceful resolutions of our political problems before resorting to the sword. The term "peaceful" is itself open to varied interpretations, depending on how rich or thin a notion of peace is in play.[27] Here I mean to include a comprehensive range of non-violent methods that may certainly involve pressure and coercion. In the case of intervention, the emphasis needs to be put upon such non-violent efforts, including coercive interventions of an economic and political nature.

These include what has been called "coercive diplomacy" or "forceful persuasion" by Alexander George.[28] George's definitions of this phenomenon are a little loose, but they are meant to cover threats of violence and lesser forms of deprivation, as well as the combination of these with concessions, promises and other "carrots" or positive inducements. Threats to withdraw existing support, such as aid, trade status, or diplomatic recognition, or threats not to proceed with economic or political aid that has been anticipated, are coercive interventions in domestic affairs in that they exercise power in seeking to constrain the choices of national agents. The imposition of economic sanctions constitutes an extreme form of such coercion, and this can shade into violent measures, as when a sanction regime is enforced by military means. Clearly, there are more problems with some of these than with others. Sanctions, in particular, were once viewed as a clean alternative to violent intervention, but can now be seen often to have very harmful effects upon the least guilty, and only minimal impact upon the primary agents of the evil they were intended to prevent or restrict. Of course, there are sanctions and sanctions. One of the most successful forms of sanction, only partially economic, was the sporting sanction imposed on South Africa which had a great imaginative impact on a fanatically sports-loving society and politically hurt the predominantly oppressive white community more than the black, though it did not cause starvation and death. The other problem with sanctions is that they are sometimes difficult to operate and they frequently take time to have an effect, but in many cases military intervention and other military enterprises are also protracted (witness the miscalculations about how long the bombing of Serbia would need to go on, and, more dramatically, the US misjudgment about the scope and duration of its involvement in Vietnam). Both persuasion and certain non-violent coercive measures should be employed in the early stages of a crisis, or as a crisis looms, when opportunities for prevention or mitigation of humanitarian disasters may present themselves, or can be constructed. This sort of prevention is likely to be less costly and less damaging than the military response to the headline-grabbing disaster though it is a curious quirk of human psychology that it is easier to create support for very expensive, dramatic military efforts, especially where the risks to the interveners are low, than for cheaper non-violent activities aimed at prevention.

Another form of sanction that is in the process of development and needs further encouragement is the criminal sanction of law. War crimes tribunals, the proposed international criminal court, and even foreign domestic courts have deterrence potential as well as retributive power. Even though their processes are slow, they target only individuals and have difficulty getting those they indict to appear, their political impact is significant and likely to increase. Indicted political and military leaders may be secure for a time in their own countries, but (as the Pinochet case showed) they will be at risk traveling abroad, and can have no confidence in immunity if the leadership in their own nation changes, as eventually it is likely to do.

Of course, these non-violent approaches are not guaranteed to work and they need imagination and political savvy in their implementation if they are to be successful, but both these points apply to the use of violence as well.

THE PROSPECTS FOR SUCCESS

It is particularly important here that enthusiasm for rescue does not swamp a prudent assessment of what armed intervention can and cannot achieve. What counts as success is to some extent determined by the aims of a campaign, and limited aims make success more likely. On the other hand, if aims are too limited then what success is achieved may fall short of the success demanded by the humanitarian crisis. The point about limitations is a difficult one, since it was observed strictly in the Gulf War with the result that Saddam Hussein remained in power. Even so, it is not at all clear what the internal political consequences of external military overthrow of Hussein would have been, given the divided opposition forces, the ethnic hostilities, and the religious oppositions in Iraq. This point has continued relevance today.

There is a conflict here between different understandings of success. Should we think of success in a short-term way as saving these lives now, or restoring these people to their homeland, or should the criterion of success embrace longer-term objectives such as ensuring political stability and enduring safety for any in the area threatened with the same kind of persecution? Clearly, both accounts of success have their attractions, but equally clearly they are in tension. In particular, the shorter-term objective is compatible with, and, in some respects, suited to military procedures, whereas armed forces alone are unlikely to deliver the longer-term objectives.

My earlier discussion of the simplified example of responses to child-beating brings out some of the tension involved between the two interpretations of success. You kill the father thus preventing death or severe damage to the child, but then who is to look after the child? Within the structures of a stable state, there will be trained personnel to deal with this question and to relocate the child, but in the international realm the parallel question is much harder to address, a lesson that is still being painfully learned in Kosovo and Afghanistan. The metaphor of rescue needs completion not only with the phrase "from what" but also with the phrase "for what." We need to understand both the complexities of the background to the crimes and disasters and the best way forward in the light of that.[29] For many international situations, the appropriate domestic analogy would be a father visiting dangerous violence upon some of his children while other family members stand by and others again actually help with the beating. After the father is killed or removed, what do you do with the rest of them?[30] There is also the question of the adequacy of your response in the first place. I have imagined you with a gun, but suppose all you have is a heavy cane. Maybe you can prevent the violence with counter-violence, but maybe you will gravely endanger your own life or, by blundering in, escalate the antagonism against the victims.

Advocates of the short term will say that at least we saved this child's life here (or these people's lives now), but the long termers will say that this is small comfort if our intervention merely delays the death for a day and makes it likely that others die with him in response to the intervention. Furthermore, if you are going for the longer term, you will need more than mere violent intervention. Some longer-term solution is ideally preferable in both the domestic and the international spheres, since most short-term solutions risk futility. But "longer term" cannot be too long. An intervention must avoid escalating into a colonial saga or even an enduring protectorate.

But even sensible longer-term solutions that avoid these perils require many things that are not readily available. First, they require non-military techniques and personnel, second they require a commitment of will over a relatively long time, and third, they require the dedication of financial and other resources for a non-glamorous long haul. They necessitate, in short, what Thomas M. Frank has called an "holistic approach" to humanitarian rescue.[31]

CONCLUSION

I have been arguing that the moral presumption against unsought military intervention in the affairs of other nations is broadly defensible in just-war terms, and should still carry considerable weight even when the primary motive for intervention is humanitarian. But when peaceful alternatives fail, the cries of the victims will still carry an urgent appeal to conscience. Sometimes, even here, there will be nothing that a resort to violence can, or should, achieve. We cannot solve every problem, we cannot answer every cry, and it is a particularly dangerous illusion to think that we can solve every problem with military might – a lesson that the "war against terrorism" also needs to learn. Nonetheless, outsiders may be able to solve, or help solve, some. I think that this is true and that the presumption against armed humanitarian intervention is sometimes, though more rarely than often supposed, rebuttable.

Despite all its paradoxes, the cry for destruction and killing in defence of human rights and for prevention of human suffering makes a certain appeal to the John Wayne lurking within us all. And sometimes, rarely, this appeal will be legitimate. But it is bedevilled by the problems discussed above. In addition, the attractions of decisive violence frequently tend to distract from the more fundamental, though less glamorous, task of reconsidering and reconstructing our domestic and international politics so that our world will be a less dangerous and exploitative place for all its inhabitants. We can admit the grain of truth in the cynical slogan, "If you want peace, prepare for war," but the surer path to a more tranquil world is to prepare for peace directly.

NOTES

1 Quoted by Henry Steel Commager, "Ethics, Virtue, and Foreign Policy," in *Ethics and International Relations* ed. Kenneth W. Thompson, vol. 2 (New Brunswick: Transaction Books, 1985), pp. 127–37.

2 See Adam Roberts, *Humanitarian Action in War*, Adelphi paper 305, IISS (Oxford: Oxford University Press, 1996), p. 7.

3 Adam Roberts, "NATO's 'Humanitarian War' over Kosovo," *Survival* 41, no. 3 (1999). Roberts says that the striking unanimity of the NATO members in taking action was "a sense of shame" at failures to act during the Yugoslav wars of 1991–95, p. 104.

4 Stanley Hoffmann, "The Politics and Ethics of Military Intervention," in his *World Disorders: Troubled Peace in the Post-Cold War Era* (Rowman and Littlefield, 1998). As Hoffmann says, his approach "does not distinguish between cases in which intervention occurs with the formal consent of a government and those in which it does not, mainly because consent is not always voluntary or genuine. Initial consent may turn into resentment and hostility later on. Nor does it fully separate the political from the ethical aspects of intervention, because political actions, even when they are not preceded by

any explicit discussion of moral concerns, always raise such issues. Even actions that seem to aim only at the establishment or restoration of order have implications for justice" (p. 153).

5 Fernando R. Tesón, *Humanitarian Intervention: An Inquiry into Law and Morality* (New York: Transnational Publishers, 1988), p. 104.

6 *Ibid.*, p. 105.

7 Felix Oppenheim, *The Place of Morality in Foreign Policy* (Lexington, Mass: Lexington Bks, 1991), p. 11.

8 J. Bryan Hehir, "Intervention: from Theories to Cases," *Ethics and International Affairs*, 9 (1995), 7.

9 *Ibid.*

10 For a good recent account of just war thinking see Coates, A. J., *The Ethics of War* (Manchester: Manchester University Press, 1997).

11 Mo Tzu, "Against Offensive Warfare," in *Basic Writings of Mo Tzu, Hsun Tzu and Han Fei Tzu*, ed. and trans. Burton Watson (Columbia University Press, 1967), pp. 60–61.

12 J. Bryan Hehir, "Intervention: From Theories to Cases," *Ethics and International Affairs* 9 (1995), 5 ff.

13 Michael Walzer, a somewhat reluctant convert to the cause of intervention-ism, explicitly invokes this idea. See Michael Walzer, "The Politics of Rescue," *Social Research* 62, no. 1 (1995).

14 Mo-Tzu "Against Offensive War," p. 56. This is also allowed to some degree by the sixteenth-century European just-war theorists.

15 See, for an influential argument related to this, Hehir, "Intervention," p. 6. Also Henry Shue, "Conditional Sovereignty," *Res Publica* 8, no. 1 (1999), 1–7.

16 See J. S. Mill, "A Few Words on Non-Intervention," in *Collected Works, Vol. XXI, Essays on Equality, Law and Education,* ed. John M. Robson (Toronto and Buffalo: University of Toronto Press, 1984), pp. 118–20. Mill's whole-hearted defense of British imperialism and the civilizing mission of the English also invokes what might well be called "English exceptionalism." By comparison with other civilized nations, England is "a novelty in the world" (p. 111).

17 Vitoria, *On the American Indians*, 1.6.conclusion. Vitoria thinks that if it could be shown that the barbaric state of the Indians was such that they could be regarded as virtually mad, then they might have to be governed by others for their own good (though certainly not for the profit of those others), but he considers this prospect merely "for the sake of argument" and palpably does not believe the madness premise.

18 As reported by Michael Ignatieff in a review of Clark's book, *Waging Modern War: Bosnia, Kosovo, and the Future of Combat*, Public Affairs (2001), in *The Age* (October 8, 2001), p. 11.

19 Shue, "Conditional Sovereignty," pp. 8–9.

20 Thomas G. Weiss, "Triage: Humanitarian Interventions in a New Era," *World Policy Journal* 11 (1994).

21 Hannah Arendt has explored a connection between violence and rage in her *On Violence* (New York: Harcourt Brace Jovanovich, 1969), see especially p. 63.

22 Tesón, *Humanitarian Intervention*, p. 117.

23 It is notable that David Luban, who eloquently supported intervention for human-rights violations against Michael Walzer's more cautious position in the late 1970s, and whose work is often cited in this connection, has recently modified his position, and argues that intervention is only justified for acts of barbarism. David Luban, "Intervention and Civilization: Some Unhappy Lessons of the Kosovo War," in *Global Justice and International Politics*, eds. Pablo De Greiff and Ciaron Cronin (Cambridge, Mass.: MIT Press, 2002).

24 As several commentators have pointed out, it is not clear that there is quite as much public opposition to humanitarian military operations (including interventions) that involve genuine risks to the lives of troops as is commonly believed. At least this seems so prior to intervention and in its early stages. But what worries politicians is public opinion when the body bags start arriving.

25 "The War So Far," *The Times* (London), World Wide Web edition (May 23, 1999).

26 Amnesty International Annual Report 2000. AI gives a figure of 500 civilians killed by NATO though it is somewhat unclear from the report whether this is meant to be civilians in Kosovo alone, as the context seems to indicate. Estimates vary dramatically about the number of civilians killed by Serb forces in Kosovo, though the US State Department claims that "probably around 10,000" Kosovar Albanians were killed in the Serbian purge. See US Department of State report "Ethnic Cleansing in Kosovo: an Accounting," Archive Site, January 20, 2001. This is at the high end of estimates and does not distinguish civilians from Kosovo Liberation Army combatants. Moreover, the vast majority of these killings occurred, during the dreadful expulsion of Kosovar Alabanians by Serb forces, *after* the NATO bombing campaign began.

27 Jeff Ross and I sketch some of the relevant distinctions in C. A. J. Coady and Jeff Ross, "St. Augustine and the Ideal of Peace," in *The American Catholic Philosophical Quarterly*, LXXIV (2000).

28 Alexander L. George, *Forceful Persuasion: Coercive Diplomacy as an Alternative to War*, United States Institute of Peace Press, Washington DC, 1991.

29 Similar doubts about the idea of rescue have been raised by Amir Pasic and Thomas G. Weiss, "The Politics of Rescue: Yugoslavia's Wars and the Humanitarian Impulse," *Ethics and International Affairs* 11 (1997). The authors comment, "Rescue is misleading in that it fails to acknowledge the possibly irreparable disorder which preceded the crisis that motivated the rescue" (p. 129).

30 The comparison with family violence is only an illustrative analogy for certain purposes. I do not mean to endorse the view that state–citizen relations closely mirror parent–child relationships.
31 Thomas M. Frank, "A Holistic Approach to Building Peace," in Olara A. Otunnu and Michael W. Doyle, eds., *Peacemaking and Peacekeeping for the New Century* (Lanham, Maryland: Rowman and Littlefield, 1998), pp. 275–96.

Index

Index

Rwanda, 5, 32, 47, 81, 162, 236, 239, 244, 285
  Tutsi minority, 5, 162
  Hutu, 5, 162, 219

Said, Edward, 32
Saudi elite, 219
Schroeder, Chancellor Gerhard, 37
secession, 11–13, 149–50, 157–64
  compared with foreign intervention, 168
  concept of, 168–69
  from functioning states, 196–209
  in cases of state breakdown, 196–209
  international law, 189–209
    inadequacy of, 189–91, 208
    need for reform, 189–209
  international responses to, 196–97
  normative theory of, 195
  of Norway from Sweden, 197
  of Quebec from Canada, 192–93, 197, 200, 203, 204
  of Slovenia and Croatia from Yugoslavia, 200, 207
  principle of effectivity, 13, 191–209
  right to secede, 161–64, 168–78, 180–87, 193, 197
    consensual, 197–202
    unilateral, 197–209; remedial right only, 197–209; primary right, 197–200; ascriptive-group theories, 198–200; associative-group, or plebiscitary, theories, 198–200, 197–209
  sauve qui peut separatism, 201, 207–08
  uti possidetis, 13, 191–209
self-determination, 11–13, 146–51, 161–64, 170–71, 174, 179–86, 222
  right of, 193, 194
September 11, 2001, 32, 69, 72, 161, 274
Short, Lieutenant General Michael, 110, 112, 113
Shue, Henry, 9–10, 284
Skidelsky, Robert, 251, 263
social contract theory, see: reciprocity
Somalia, 2, 219, 227
  Aidid, Mohammed, 219, 227
  Somali people, 215–16, 219
  Somalis killed by the US military, 219, 227

South Africa
  South African blacks, 148
sovereignty, 169–70, 251–52, 281–83
  absolute, 281, 283
  concept of, 168, 169
  conditional, 224, 281, 283
  sovereign people, 184
  value of, 179–81
Soviet Union, 148
  dissolution of, 146, 191–92, 194
  former Soviet Constitution, 197
Spain, 167
  militant Basque nationalists, 12, 149, 167
Sri Lanka
  Tamil rebellion, 149
State Department, US, 294
state sovereignty, 5, 11, 22, 85–86, 132, 153
strict liability, 120
Sudan, 149, 193

Taliban, 2, 32, 82, 215, 221, 222, 226, 246
  brutality of, 221
  post-Taliban governance, 246
Tamir, Yael, 151
Taylor, Charles, 65, 174–75
Ten Commandments, 40
terrorism, 21, 92
  terrorist attacks, 225
  international terrorist groups, 226
  military responses to, 249, 292
Tesón, Fernando, 276, 287
Thucydides, 143
Tibet, 234
  in defense of Tibetan rights, 234
  Tibetans, 284
  Tibetan Buddhism, 235
Toulmin, Stephen, 42–44
triage of world trouble spots, 35
truth commissions, 28
Turkey, 228
  Kurdish autonomy, 228
  Kurdish identity, 228
  Kurdish villages, 228
  Minister for Human Rights, 228
  US military aid, 228

United Nations (UN), 11, 13, 147, 165, 179–84, 207, 231, 239, 264, 268, 269, 281, 285–86
  not a holy congregation of moral saints, 188

300